A Midwinter's Tail

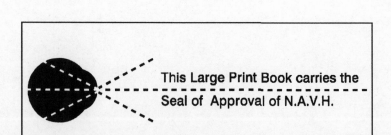

This Large Print Book carries the
Seal of Approval of N.A.V.H.

A MIDWINTER'S TAIL

BETHANY BLAKE

WHEELER PUBLISHING

A part of Gale, a Cengage Company

GALE
A Cengage Company

Copyright © 2018 by Beth Kaszuba.
A Lucky Paws Petsitting Mystery.
Wheeler Publishing, a part of Gale, a Cengage Company.

LIBRARY OF CONGRESS CIP DATA ON FILE.
CATALOGUING IN PUBLICATION FOR THIS BOOK
IS AVAILABLE FROM THE LIBRARY OF CONGRESS

ISBN-13: 978-1-4328-7290-8 (softcover alk. paper)

Published in 2020 by arrangement with Kensington Books, an imprint of Kensington Publishing Corp.

Printed in Mexico
Print Number: 01   Print Year: 2020

To my parents,
Donald and Marjorie Fantaskey

CHAPTER 1

The weather outside was beyond frightful, with near-blizzard conditions pummeling the quaint, pet-friendly town of Sylvan Creek, Pennsylvania, and burying the surrounding Pocono Mountains under a thick blanket of fine, icy snow.

But inside my snug little home, Plum Cottage, conditions were truly delightful as my sister Piper Templeton, my best friend Moxie Bloom and I prepared for Christmas and two of our hometown's favorite traditions: a free showing of *It's a Wonderful Life* at the old Bijoux theater and the local chamber of commerce's Bark the Halls Ball for people and pets. A fire crackled in the arched stone fireplace, bayberry-scented candles burned on the mantel, and mulled wine simmered in a Crock-Pot, the warm drink the perfect complement to a savory blue cheese and pecan strudel that waited on my kitchen counter. Soft, staticky Christmas music, which played on an ancient Bakelite radio left behind by my home's former tenant, added to the cozy, jolly ambiance.

Not that there weren't a few glitches as we jingled all the way toward the holidays.

"Um, can someone please help me?" Moxie asked from my tiny living room, where she was stringing big, colorful, old-fashioned lights onto the pint-sized, crooked, needle-challenged Christmas tree I'd found discarded behind the lot at Pinkney's Pines tree farm, just outside of town. Moxie's voice sounded a bit panicked when she requested, a second time, "A little help here, please!"

I was busy mixing dough to make several dozen dog-friendly Pupper-Mint Candy Cane Twists for the ball, which would be attended by most of Sylvan Creek's many canines, but I glanced over to see that Moxie had not only managed to wrap herself in the lights, but also plug herself in.

"Oh, good grief," Piper said, in suitable Charlie Brown fashion. My sensible sibling, who was sitting on the living room floor assembling goody bags for the dance, untwisted her crossed legs, rose, and went to unravel poor Moxie, who actually looked quite festive, in my opinion.

8

Vintage-loving Moxie wore a 1950s Nordic-patterned sweater with knitted reindeer prancing across the chest, and her short, spiky hair — dyed Santa-suit red — fairly glowed like the lights that were inexplicably looped around her body.

"How did this even happen?" Piper asked, unplugging my best friend and slowly spinning her, as a particularly strong gust of wind slammed into the cottage, causing the fire to nearly gutter out before it crackled merrily to life again. Outside in the darkness, the plum tree that lent my home its name rapped against one window, a sure sign that the weather was bad. Then Piper nodded at the indoor tree, which was surrounded by a dusting of newly fallen needles. "Moxie, why are *you* decorated, while the latest 'fir-ry' stray Daphne's brought home is still bare?"

Although she was a veterinarian and loved animals, Piper was sometimes frustrated by the fact that — as proprietor of Daphne Templeton's Lucky Paws Pet Sitting service — I was supposed to earn money by caring for pets, but often ended up taking in fosters for free. That wouldn't have been any of her business if Plum Cottage hadn't been located on her property, gorgeous Winding Hill Farm, making her my landlord. Not that I was *too* far behind on my rent any-more, since my other business, a mod-themed bakery for pets called Flour Power, was kind of booming.

"Seriously," Piper said, when Moxie was finally free. My sister stepped back and planted her hands on her hips. "What went wrong?"

"I have no idea," Moxie admitted, giving the lights, which lay tangled on the floor, a wary look, as if they were poisonous snakes. Or, worse yet, rabid turtles. She had a very bad case of chelonaphobia. "It just seems to happen every year!"

Piper clearly didn't know how to respond. But over by the fireplace, where he lay on his favorite Turkish rug, my taciturn basset hound sidekick, Socrates, rolled his eyes and *thunked* over sideways.

Socrates was often exasperated by Moxie Bloom. And he sometimes seemed disap-proving of me, too. Especially when I got caught up in murder investigations — which would not happen again, after my last at-tempt to solve a homicide ended with my facing my own worst fear of getting locked in Flour Power's unpredictable walk-in re-frigerator.

As I shaped plain and pink-tinted dough into cute candy-cane-shaped cookies, I thought back to that horrible evening, when Detective Jonathan Black had practically torn off the walk-in's heavy, metal door, and I'd tumbled into his arms, close to hyperventilating.

I hadn't run into the handsome, enigmatic former Navy SEAL since that fateful, somewhat embarrassing night, although I sometimes wondered how he was doing. In particular, I hoped that an illness he'd once battled remained at bay. And I kept my fingers crossed that he'd continued to bond with the dogs I'd sort of foisted upon him. I knew that, as a former handler in the Navy, he got along with Axis, a chocolate Lab with agility experience, but even I had to admit that reserved, thoughtful Jonathan was a strange match for one-eared, drooling, exuberant Artie the Chihuahua.

"So, do you think Detective Black will attend the ball?" Moxie asked, as if reading my mind, which I believed she could do. She seemed to have shaken off the light incident and had joined me in the kitchen, where she ladled wine into three waiting earthenware mugs. Apparently, she was done decorating for the evening. And I was almost finished with the cookies, too. Opening the door to my old gas oven, I slid a tray inside, then dusted flour off my hands

11

before accepting one of the drinks from Moxie, whose green eyes were twinkling. "I would love to see Jonathan Black in a tux!"

"I have no idea if Jonathan will show up at the dance," I told her, setting the mug on the counter again, just for a minute, so I could put two of the already baked and cooled candy canes onto a plate, which I set on the floor in case Socrates got hungry. Spying a pair of orange eyes blinking at me from behind the herbs I grew on my windowsill, I also found a treat for my surly, black Persian boarder, Tinkleston, who was being his usual Scrooge self — although he didn't bite my hand when I offered him a Holly Jolly Chicken Muncher. We'd made a lot of progress since the days when he used to ambush everyone who came within a few feet of his deceptive puffball paws.

Daring to pat Tinks's head — and earning a halfhearted hiss — I again picked up my wine and the wooden tray that held the strudel. Leading the way to the living room, I set my mug and the log of crispy phyllo, stuffed with cream cheese, Roquefort, and candied pecans, onto a steamer trunk that served as my coffee table.

Moxie put Piper's wine on the trunk, too, before curling up on my loveseat, while my sister, who in two minutes had managed to artfully arrange the lights on the tree, stuck the plug back in the socket.

Suddenly, ringed with softly glowing red, orange, yellow, and blue lights, the little tree seemed more adorable than pathetic.

"I haven't seen Jonathan in months," I noted, taking a seat on a Moroccan floor pillow and cutting a few pieces of strudel. "But I guarantee you that, if he does attend, Axis and Artie, at least, will *not* be in formal wear."

Piper joined me on the floor, but she didn't take a break. She resumed assembling the goody bags, using scissors to curl red ribbons she'd tied to the handles of green paper sacks that were filled with local products and coupons for Sylvan Creek businesses. I'd contributed cat treats and a voucher for a dog walk, while Moxie, who owned a unique salon for people and pets, called Spa and Paw, had offered one free shampoo and blowout. The little card she'd created didn't make it clear if the treatments were for human or animal clients. Maybe both.

"I love this dance, but I have to agree with Detective Black about the wisdom of putting bow ties and ball gowns on dogs," Piper said, swiping at a ribbon and making a perfect spiral. The springy coils were like better versions of my long, curly, dirty-blond hair. Then she jerked the scissors toward Socrates. "I bet he's not wearing a suit!"

Socrates, who'd righted himself, hung his head and averted his gaze.

"Actually, he will wear a tie," I told Piper, whose brown eyes, very different from my grayish-green ones, widened with disbelief. "While he doesn't believe in tacky sweaters or costumes, he has a sense of decorum," I added. "He wouldn't show up at a black-tie affair naked!"

Socrates whined softly, as if he still felt uncomfortable about the prospect of wearing the very understated neckwear I'd purchased for him at my friend Tessie Flinchbaugh's pet emporium, Fetch!

"So, what are you wearing, Daphne?" Moxie asked, breaking off a tiny piece of phyllo and offering the treat to her white rat, Sebastian, who'd popped out of his mobile den — a furry white muff Moxie had left by the door — then trotted fearlessly across the floor and climbed onto the love-seat. I used to worry that Tinks would make a snack of Sebastian, but the two animals seemed to have reached a peace accord. That was probably Sebastian's doing. He was a very sweet rat. Moxie settled back, absently stroking Sebastian while he nibbled on the pastry. "More important, who are you going with? Gabriel?"

I occasionally dated the devilishly handsome owner of and sole reporter at the Sylvan Creek *Weekly Gazette,* but we kept things casual. In part, because Gabriel, while always funny and often charming, had a complicated past that had left him somewhat scarred and jaded.

Piper, who was getting serious with incredibly nice, uncomplicated Professor Roger Berendt, didn't hide the fact that she was wary of my sometime suitor.

"Yes, Daphne," my sister said, looking up from her task. The lenses of her eyeglasses glinted in the firelight. "Will you be attending the ball with your dashing, witty journalist friend?"

She made those compliments sound like insults. But I was more forgiving of Gabriel's sometimes acerbic, morbid sense of humor, because I knew its roots.

"Gabriel hasn't even mentioned the dance," I told Moxie and Piper, as I licked some cheese off my fingers. "He's swamped at the *Gazette,* and I've been busy, too, between pet-sitting gigs for holiday travelers and baking for Flour Power. Gabriel and I had a difficult enough time scheduling a quick cup of coffee tomorrow, at Oh, Beans." I shrugged. "Plus, I get the sense that he's not a big fan of yuletide traditions."

"Hmmm . . ." Moxie had a funny gleam in her eyes again. The kind she got when she was thinking of a certain detective, upon whom she had an unabashed crush. "Daphne, since you probably aren't attending Bark the Halls with Gabriel, and we all know that poor little Artie would love to dress up, why don't you call Jonathan Black and offer to be in charge of Artie's attire? And if Detective Black wanted to tag along with you and the dogs —"

"No!" I protested, speaking over Moxie and Socrates, who was whining softly again, urging me not to meddle, although Artie was his best . . . only . . . canine buddy. "Jonathan allowed me to dress up Artie for Halloween and the Winterfest sled parade," I reminded Moxie, sort of cringing, myself, at the memories of the Chihuahua in a clown costume and an old-timey velvet dress. "I don't think I can offer again. And I'm not asking Jonathan to the dance!"

"Why not?" Piper asked, finally abandoning the goody bags and edging closer to the trunk. Although I felt like we were back in the 1950s, between Moxie's outfit and the soft, crackly version of "White Christmas" playing in the kitchen, she reminded me, "It *is* the twenty-first century. Women ask men out!"

That was true, and I was all for equality. But I still didn't plan to call Jonathan, who might very well have another date already. I looked to Moxie. "I was thinking maybe we could go together. Make it a girls' night out."

"Oh, I don't know. . . ." The glimmer in Moxie's eyes suddenly faded. "While I'm definitely going to *It's a Wonderful Life* with you, Daph, I'm not sure about the ball this year."

Piper and I both reared back, because *everyone* went to Bark the Halls, and Moxie, in particular, loved the event, which gave her the opportunity to wear one of the many vintage gowns that were stored some-where — I could never figure out the spot — in her tiny garret apartment above the Philosopher's Tome used bookstore.

Socrates also seemed baffled by Moxie's comment. His wrinkly brow was more fur-rowed than usual.

"Why in the world are you even *thinking* about skipping Bark the Halls?" I finally asked. "Did you accidentally schedule something else for that date? Because I'm

17

sure you could get out of it. . . ."

I gave up trying to persuade her, because Moxie was shaking her head. And she seemed a little confused, too.

"Haven't you heard the talk around town?" she asked me and Piper, although we were usually out of the loop when it came to local gossip, all of which passed through Spa and Paw. Seeing that we obviously didn't know what she was referring to, Moxie proceeded to fill us in, telling us, in dramatic fashion, "There's no way that I, of all people, can attend a holiday dance when *Celeste French* is going, too!"

CHAPTER 2

"So, who in the world is Celeste French, and why does she inspire so much fear and loathing?" Gabriel Graham inquired, when we finally secured a free table at Oh, Beans, the morning after Moxie's surprising announcement about the ball. The tiny Market Street coffee shop was crowded — and, to my dismay, currently staffed by one of my former high school teachers, Bitsy Bickelheim.

For the last few weeks, I'd been trying to avoid Ms. Bickelheim, who was not only a barista, and slightly erratic since quitting Sylvan Creek High years ago, but also heavily involved in the Sylvan Creek Players community theater league. I'd heard she was desperate to cast the Ghost of Christmas Future for the Players' rapidly looming production of *A Christmas Carol,* and I did not want to be approached about taking on the role. I had a bad habit of agreeing to things without thinking them through.

Catching my eye, Ms. Bickelheim waved, and I waved back, then quickly averted my gaze, looking around at the café's honey-colored, shiplap walls, which were hung with pine wreaths. Hundreds of white twinkle lights glowed like stars in the rafters, and candles burned in the old wooden-framed windows, warding off the gloomy, gray weather outside.

Gabriel certainly seemed oblivious to the dismal day. Rubbing his goatee, he sat back in his chair and grinned at me. "It's not like you to hate anyone," he noted. "Yet you've mentioned this Celeste woman three times since we got here, and you don't seem happy that she's coming to Sylvan Creek."

" 'Hate' and 'loathing' are strong words," I told him, breathing a sigh of relief, because Ms. Bickelheim apparently wasn't going to come over and ask me about the part. She likely recalled that I'd played a small, spectral role in a previous local production of that same play, with disastrous results. Shaking off the memory of myself swinging from the high school auditorium's rafters, I wrapped my hands around my red enamel mug, which contained a gingerbread house-blend latte, and focused on Gabriel, who was watching me intently with his dark, intelligent eyes. "And I don't feel either hatred or loathing toward Celeste," I assured him. "Those are not productive emotions."

The corners of Gabriel's mouth twitched. "I suppose you have a dozen philosophical quotes on the dangers of succumbing to even intense dislike."

He was mocking my PhD in philosophy. "I could give you fifty quotes from Socrates alone," I told him, referencing the ancient Greek, not the dog who'd wisely stayed home by the hearth. "Plus, I haven't seen Celeste in years. She might be perfectly nice these days."

"Then why are you so worried about her coming here?" Gabriel asked. He sipped his drink, a plain Colombian roast, one cream, two sugars. Then he leaned forward, studying me more closely. "What's the story?"

"There's no story," I told him, my gaze flicking again to Ms. Bickelheim, to make sure she couldn't overhear us talking about one of her former students. Fortunately, she was distracted, struggling to fill carafes with milk and cream, her progress hampered by an unwieldy, amorphous, somewhat "artsy" fringed poncho. I turned back to Gabriel, warning him, "At least, there's nothing you can print in the *Gazette.*"

While frequently kind and considerate, Gabriel Graham was also a hard-nosed journalist in a town that wasn't used to reporters who dug for — and printed — whatever they unearthed, if that news would sell papers. That was one of the reasons Piper didn't completely trust him.

"Okay, fine," he promised me, crossing his arms over a chunky, cream-colored fisherman's sweater that made his eyes appear even darker than usual. "Everything's off-the-record."

"You'll probably think it's silly, anyway," I told him, pausing to sip my drink before the whipped cream all melted down the side of the mug. Then I confided, quietly, "Years ago, back in high school, Celeste French — head cheerleader, then-future valedictorian, and frequent bully — stole away Moxie's boyfriend, Mike Cavanaugh, at the Sylvan Creek High Rockin' Around the Christmas Tree formal, causing Moxie to have the only meltdown of her entire life and spill a punch bowl all over the gymnasium floor before running off crying."

Gabriel tried not to laugh, but his lips twitched.

"It honestly wasn't funny," I assured him, although, in his place, I might've chuckled, too. But I'd been there, and I'd seen how

22

upset my best friend had been when Mike had disappeared from the gym for nearly a half hour, only to return with Celeste, both of them looking a little rumpled. "It was horrible, really. Moxie and Mike had been serious since junior year. He was her first, and, to this day only, love."

Gabriel got his mirth under control. "Sorry. But I have to say, it sounds like this Mike guy was to blame, too."

"Yes," I agreed. "But the funny thing was, he never even defended himself. And the day after we graduated, he gave up a full scholarship to Wynton University and joined the Army, shipping out to heaven knows where, to punish himself."

"Lots of people — including your friend Jonathan Black — choose life in the military," Gabriel reminded me. "Not everyone's running from heartbreak."

I ignored the edge in his voice when he spoke Jonathan's name. Gabriel was very competitive, used to fighting for scoops in a big city during his days as a reporter with the *Philadelphia Inquirer,* and I got the sense that he considered Jonathan a rival when it came to solving crimes.

"Mike came from a blue-collar family, and he worked hard for that scholarship," I said. "Plus, he sent Moxie a letter, telling her how

23

sorry he was that things had been ruined between them." I suddenly felt as deflated as my whipped cream. "That was the last contact she ever had with him."

"So, what happened to Celeste?" Gabriel asked. "Where has she been in the past few years?"

"Harvard Business School, at first," I informed him. "Then she went on to become incredibly rich."

"By doing what?" I saw a glimmer of interest in Gabriel's eyes, and I knew I'd have to remind him that our chat was off-the-record. "What's her line of work?"

"Pet care — but in a big way," I said, glancing outside at the street, where my old VW advertised my own little business. Thanks to Moxie, who'd overestimated her talent for auto-body painting, the pink bus featured a misshapen dog that was often mistaken for a misshapen pony. I'd never bothered to have the van repainted, and I never considered expanding beyond my comfortable, steady list of regular clients. Celeste, meanwhile, had followed a different path. I returned my attention to Gabriel. "Celeste French is the founder of the big pet-care chain, French's Poodles & More. The franchises are everywhere."

Gabriel's eyes widened. "Celeste, is

'CeeCee' French?"

I drew back, surprised that he knew my high school classmate's nickname, which I didn't think I'd used. "You know her?"

"I know *of* her," he said. "She *is* the CEO of a Fortune 500 company that recently suffered a major scandal about a shoddy product line. It was all over the *Wall Street Journal*!"

"Which I'm afraid I don't read," I said, with another glance out the window. My poor van had developed a rust spot near one of the rear fenders, so it looked like the misshapen dog had had an accident. "I'm not exactly obsessed with money — but I am worried about unsafe products being sold for pets. So what happened?"

"Typical box-store issues," Gabriel said. I wasn't sure if he'd forgotten details, or if he was distracted, already considering how he might use CeeCee's impending arrival to boost the *Gazette*'s circulation. I knew that, while he wouldn't bother printing Moxie's story of heartache, he'd cover CeeCee's visit from some angle. "Cheap dog food, cheap products," he added vaguely. "Some animals got sick from eating the store-brand chow, or something like that. Or maybe it was something about the products she used at her in-store grooming 'salons.' "

"I guess it escaped me because pretty much everyone here buys pet food from Tessie Flinchbaugh at Fetch!" I said, sipping the last of my latte. I needed to get going soon. "And Moxie's the go-to groomer."

Gabriel laughed. "Yes, you, Tessie, Moxie, and a handful of other entrepreneurs pretty much have the lock on business in this pet-centric paradise."

That was true. But we certainly hadn't engaged in any price gouging. Moxie and I, especially, practically gave our services away. Which was fine by me, although my lack of profit motive irked my mother, realtor Maeve Templeton, who ran a mini-empire of her own.

"Speaking of business," I said, digging into my pockets and glancing at Ms. Bickelheim, who was weaving her way toward our table, carrying a pot of coffee, as if she planned to refill Gabriel's mug. But I saw a gleam in her eyes, like she might have other intentions, too.

"Yoo-hoo, Daphne!" she said, waving to me with her free hand, so the fringe on her poncho swung.

I smiled weakly at her, then turned back to Gabriel, rising from my seat. "I *really* need to get to Flour Power before I end up being a ghost!" He seemed confused, but I didn't have time to explain. I pulled a few dollars from my pocket. Thankfully, Ms. Bickelheim had been detained by another customer, but I knew I didn't have long to make my exit. "We'll catch up later, okay?" I promised Gabriel, placing the money on the table. "I'll text you."

"Daphne . . ." Before I could withdraw my hand, he clasped my wrist, trapping me. And when I met his gaze, I was surprised to see that he appeared uncharacteristically uncertain. Almost . . . nervous.

"What's wrong?" I asked.

Gabriel released me, but it was too late to beat a hasty retreat. Ms. Bickelheim had arrived at our table and was refilling Gabriel's mug, whether he wanted that or not. I again smiled warily at her, while Gabriel appeared slightly annoyed by the interruption. Then he turned back to me. "I wanted to meet you here for a reason. And I didn't mean to waste all our time talking about CeeCee French's visit home —"

"CeeCee?" Ms. Bickelheim's voice was sharp enough to cut through the chatter in the crowded café, and her hand locked in place, so coffee overflowed the mug. But she didn't seem to notice the sudden silence or the mess as she repeated in disbelief, "CeeCee French is coming *here*?"

CHAPTER 3

"Nobody seems happy about CeeCee's return to Sylvan Creek," I muttered, only to realize that Socrates wasn't by my side, as usual, and I was strolling down Market Street alone under a sky that had grown even darker while I'd been inside Oh, Beans.

When I'd left the café, Gabriel had still been trying to assure Bitsy Bickelheim that his pants were machine washable, and that the coffee she'd spilled all over his lap probably wouldn't leave a stain.

"I take it my former English teacher didn't know CeeCee was coming to Sylvan Creek, and for some reason, she's not exactly thrilled," I added, only to catch myself again.

Glancing around, I was happy to discover that the street was empty, maybe because the Poconos were definitely destined for another blast of snow. Sylvan Creek's iconic, three-globed streetlamps, which usually flickered out at dawn, were glowing, as were the thousands of white lights that were strung in the bare branches of the many trees that lined the road.

Looking down the street, I saw that the Bijoux's marquee, which jutted out over the sidewalk, was also lit and advertising the upcoming free showing of *It's a Wonderful Life,* which would be attended by practically everyone in town.

Well, the movie wasn't exactly free, but anyone who brought a canned good or bag of food for the local food bank or one of Sylvan Creek's pet rescues was welcome to attend the screening.

In fact, it appeared that fundraising had already started. Crossing the street and stepping under the marquee, I discovered a small kettle hanging from a tripod, next to a sign that said monetary donations would be added to the goods collected the next day.

Rooting around in the deep pockets of my oversized barn jacket, I located a few crumpled dollars, just as something moved in the shadows near the Bijoux's ticket booth.

"Oh, hey there," I said, greeting the cutest pug I'd ever seen. He waddled toward me on stiff, stubby legs that didn't look up to the task of carrying his squat body, made bigger by his bulky red sweater, which had the phrase BAH, HUM-PUG knitted across the chest. Stopping at my feet, the dog looked up at me with big, round, brown eyes, and his pink tongue darted in and out of his pushed-in mouth each time he took a breath of the frosty air. "Are you guarding the money?" I asked, smiling at him as I crammed my wad of bills into the pot's narrow slot. "Because you look pretty fierce."

Apparently, that was the wrong thing to say, because, all at once, that adorable pup leaped up and banged the kettle with his tiny, tawny-and-black paws, tipping the whole tripod, as if on purpose.

To my dismay, the kettle's lid popped off, and all the change that had been collected scattered around the sidewalk, while my money flew off on a gust of air — just like the canine troublemaker, who'd already disappeared on surprisingly quick little legs.

"Oh, no!" I cried, first running after the bills, which were rolling down the sidewalk, tumbleweed-style, in the wind that was rising before the storm. "Stop!" I called, although I knew I had no power over the breeze or the cash.

And yet, all at once the wind did die down, and the wad of bills came to a stop right in front of a tiny storefront that had long been unoccupied.

Grabbing my donation, I started to turn back, so I could clean up the change, too. Then I stopped in my tracks when I noticed someone inside the previously abandoned storefront. A young woman who was bustling around several racks of garments. And a small, hand-lettered sign had been propped in the narrow glass window, announcing IVY DUNLEAVY — CUSTOM CREATIONS (AND TAILORING, TOO).

Catching sight of me, the woman smiled and waved, urging me to come inside.

Waving back, I shook my head, indicating that I wasn't in the market for a "custom creation," and that I didn't need anything hemmed or repaired, either.

Yet the pretty young woman smiled and waved once more, still beckoning me.

I was again replying silently in the negative when I spied a reflection in the glass near the sign. Someone stood behind me, across the street. And I was pretty sure he was watching me.

Turning, I sucked in a sharp breath, because I could've sworn I'd just seen a *real* ghost from my own Christmas past darting — *limping* — into Cherry Alley.

Forgetting that I was trying hard not to

talk to myself, I whispered uncertainly, *"Mike Cavanaugh?"*

CHAPTER 4

"So, tell me about this new seamstress," Moxie urged, as she, Socrates, and I stood in front of the Bijoux the next day, waiting in a long line with our donations cradled in our arms. Or, more accurately, I was lugging a practically human-sized bag of premium dog food for one of my favorite charities, Fur-Ever Friends rescue, while Moxie had wisely focused on a smaller species. Her three packages of rat food couldn't have weighed more than a few pounds. Not that Sylvan Creek had a rodent rescue that I knew of.

Socrates also seemed doubtful about Moxie's contribution. He kept shooting the rat snacks skeptical glances.

Then the line moved, and we all advanced a few steps, so we were under the marquee and practically on the spot where the little bah, hum-pug had knocked over the kettle — right before I'd mistaken some stranger for Moxie's ex-boyfriend.

Having decided the night before that my identification had been wrong, I hadn't mentioned the sighting to Moxie, who continued to press me for details about a business that intrigued her, given her own love of sewing — a topic I couldn't discuss with her. "It would be nice to have someone to talk about darts, beading, and notions with," she said, immediately shooting me a guilty glance. "No offense."

"None taken," I assured her, hoisting the bag and shuffling a few more feet forward. I pictured the young woman's smile and almost desperate wave. "And, while she looked a little younger than us, she did seem friendly. She kept trying to get me into the shop, in spite of the fact that I don't exactly look like someone who wears custom-tailored anything!"

"You *will* need a dress for Bark the Halls," Moxie reminded me. Then her green eyes clouded over. "Are you sure I can't help you this year?"

"Honestly, I'm just going to wear the gown I wore last year," I promised Moxie, who usually accompanied me to Thrifty Threads consignment, helped me sift through the rack of recycled prom and bridesmaids' gowns, then made any neces-

34

sary alterations. But I couldn't ask her to help me get ready when she didn't plan to attend the ball herself. "I'm pretty sure I got most of last year's marinara stain out," I added, although I was not sure about that at all. In fact, I was nearly certain that I'd stuffed the dress into my closet without washing, let alone pretreating, the mark.

Moxie opened her mouth, and I knew she was about to insist that we follow our usual tradition, so I cut her off, asking, "Are you sure you don't want to attend the ball, Moxie? *You* have a whole wardrobe, ready and waiting for the dance!"

"I don't know. . . ." Moxie chewed her lower lip. She was already attired for the season in a red, 1950s wool coat with wide, bell-shaped sleeves and oversized black buttons. A pair of green, T-strap heels from that same era completed her holiday look. She'd probably been planning her Bark the Halls outfit since June. And I did see a flicker of interest in her eyes. "Maybe . . ."

Socrates, who didn't believe one should be bound by the past, gave a rare woof of approval, just as we reached the front of the line. Being much shorter than Moxie and me, he loped through the theater's glass door, which was propped open, and slipped under a silver turnstile that dated back to the theater's heyday in the 1920s.

I did my best to follow him, awkwardly lugging my sack of food, while Moxie slipped gracefully into the Bijoux behind me. Fortunately, the bins for donations were right by the door, and I gratefully relieved myself of my burden, while Moxie dropped off her bags, too.

Then I straightened and told Moxie, "You really should go. Don't let CeeCee French's possible presence deter you from attending one of the best events of the year!"

"You're probably right," Moxie agreed, sounding almost convinced. "I could make a point of steering clear of the punch bowl, in case I saw her and got the urge to dump it over again."

"Sounds like a plan," I agreed, taking a moment to gaze around the lobby, which never failed to impress me, although I'd been going to movies at the Bijoux since I was a kid. But there was something magical about the theater, which had been lovingly maintained since its heyday.

Art deco wall sconces cast a soft glow upon the walls, a dramatic, red-carpeted staircase led to a lavishly gilt balcony, and a massive Christmas tree, donated every year by Pinkney's Pines, dominated the lobby.

In fact, farm owner Brett Pinkney —

former quarterback of our high school football team and still ruggedly handsome in jeans and flannel shirt — was circling the tree, as if to make sure it was perfect.

"We should say hi to Brett," I told Moxie, just as our classmate disappeared behind the towering pine.

Moxie sucked in a breath. "Ooh . . . I don't know if he'd like that," she noted. "I bet he'd rather be left alone."

She was probably right. Brett had become something of a recluse since his high school glory days. He seemed to disappear in the months between the holidays.

"I'm not too eager to catch up with him, either," Moxie added softly.

That was when I recalled that Brett had dated CeeCee French off and on throughout high school. If I recalled correctly, they'd technically been "on" the night of the horrible holiday dance, making him another casualty of the soiree gone awry.

"Sorry, Moxie," I apologized, tapping her arm.

Thankfully, she was already distracted, gazing around the theater, which smelled like pine and freshly buttered popcorn. The classic movie snack was free that day, along with complimentary hot chocolate, courtesy of Oh, Beans, and adorable, snowman-shaped rice-and-marshmallow treats. I'd contributed some canine snacks, too. Not that many dogs, aside from Socrates, had the patience to sit through the entire Frank Capra classic.

In fact, scanning the crowd, I didn't see many other pets in attendance. But I did recognize lots of familiar humans, including Piper, who stood near the marble-topped concession stand, talking with her boyfriend, Roger, and my mother, who wore a Burberry plaid scarf and a red cashmere sweater — the holidays as interpreted by Talbots. They were joined by tall, skinny Norm Alcorn, owner of the Sylvan Creek Hotel and president of the chamber of commerce, which not only sponsored Bark the Halls, but supported the movie, too. I suspected that my mom was trying to convince Norm, who fidgeted with his trademark polka-dot bow tie, to highlight Maeve Templeton Realty's many contributions to the local economy in his annual welcoming remarks, which always preceded the film.

Behind the counter, frizzy-haired Bitsy Bickelheim, who wore an intricately patterned caftan with flowing sleeves, was serving up the cocoa and treats on behalf of her current employer. However, her gaze kept darting around the lobby, as if she was looking for someone. Or maybe I was imagining that she seemed edgier than usual, since I'd last seen her frozen like a mannequin, spilling coffee all over Gabriel Graham.

I hoped that poor Ms. Bickelheim, who'd drifted from odd job to odd job since leaving teaching, wouldn't lose her latest position for nearly scalding Gabriel, who was also there, snapping pictures for the *Gazette*'s society page.

Gabriel had wisely chosen to focus upon our town's most photogenic — and prominent — resident, Elyse Hunter-Black. Detective Jonathan Black's wealthy, gorgeous ex-wife posed on the carpet with her two elegant greyhounds, Paris and Milan, who, like Socrates, would have no trouble sitting through the film. The dogs were almost unnaturally well-behaved. As I watched, Elyse — dressed in tasteful black, her blond hair pulled into a sleek chignon — smiled, but with a wary look in her blue eyes, as Gabriel crouched down, trying to get the best angles.

I couldn't blame Elyse for feeling cautious while Gabriel snapped away. Like everyone else in Sylvan Creek, she'd no doubt seen unflattering shots in the *Gazette,* including a now legendary picture of me in her former husband's arms, being dragged from Lake

Wallapawakee during a polar bear plunge that had ended in disaster.

Shifting so I wouldn't accidentally end up in even the background of a photo, I next spied the new seamstress in town, Ivy Dunleavy, who appeared to be making stilted small talk with Tessie Flinchbaugh and her husband, Tom, who owned my favorite used bookstore, the Philosopher's Tome. The couple had apparently complimented the copper-haired town newcomer on her unusual, asymmetrical dress, because her fair cheeks flushed and she self-consciously smoothed her A-line skirt. Tom, meanwhile, had obviously spilled hot chocolate on his red-and-white plaid sweater vest, and Tessie wore one of her trademark seasonal sweatshirts, which featured a running wiener dog and the phrase DACHSHUND THROUGH THE SNOW.

I was about to note that I thought the pun wasn't the best when Moxie sighed and said, "I really am glad I came to the movie, at least, Daphne. The Bijoux at Christmas is like a movie set itself."

Before I could agree, someone sidled up to us and joined the conversation uninvited, noting, "Perhaps this could be the backdrop for some sort of maudlin, made-for-TV holiday romance, at best!"

I hadn't heard that voice in years. But I recognized it immediately. And all of the warm, fuzzy feeling I'd just enjoyed turned to a ball of ice in my stomach when Celeste French, who held the puffiest, whitest, snootiest poodle I'd ever seen, gave me and Moxie a once-over.

"Well, well, well . . . If it isn't Daphne Templeton — and Moxie Bloom!" Celeste said, in a silky yet snarky tone that was accompanied by a fake, lilting laugh. Then she dared to lightly touch Moxie's arm, adding, "You probably don't even remember, Moxie, it was such a silly, high-school thing. But I had a tiny fling with some boy you liked, a few years ago nearly to this day!"

CHAPTER 5

Moxie Bloom might've been caught off guard by the unexpected appearance of an imperious and wealthy, not to mention impeccably dressed and perfectly coiffed, high school bully, who wasn't supposed to arrive in Sylvan Creek before the ball, according to Moxie's rumor mill. Yet I had to give my best friend credit for grace under pressure when CeeCee French rudely brought up a topic that most people would've been ashamed to mention.

"How have you been, Celeste?" Moxie asked politely, her voice level, but her chin high. She wisely ignored CeeCee's reference to Mike Cavanaugh, whom Moxie certainly did remember. She forced a smile, trying hard to be kind. "It's been a long time."

CeeCee took a moment to coolly survey the lobby, her angular jaw jutting as she absently stroked the poodle with long, red-tipped fingers. Her toes, encased in sharply pointed, distinctive crimson shoes that contrasted with her black, formfitting shift, tapped the thick carpet, as if she was already impatient with the whole affair. I supposed that I should've been awed by our multimillionaire classmate, but, to be honest, I couldn't muster more than mild curiosity and a bit of disappointment to learn that she was still arrogant, and, let's face it, mean.

"Yes, it has been a while," CeeCee finally agreed, again looking Moxie and me up and down, her cool gaze taking in Moxie's vintage outfit and my old barn jacket. "And I find that nothing's changed." The corners of her lips twisted upward, and she got a knowing, almost secretive gleam in her dark eyes. "At least, nothing's changed *yet.*"

"What the heck does that mean?" I inquired, because that last word sounded almost ominous.

But before CeeCee could answer, and I wasn't sure she planned to, a short man in a gray suit, whom I hadn't even noticed before, drew closer and lightly touched her arm. Then he shook his head and whispered a soft, single-word warning. "CeeCee . . ."

I drew back, suddenly recognizing the man, whom I'd last seen at our high school graduation, where he'd been honored as salutatorian, right behind CeeCee, who'd been valedictorian. The tide had gone out slightly on his brown, bristly hair, and there was the hint of a paunch under his rumpled white shirt, but his ruddy cheeks and slightly bulbous nose hadn't changed. "Jeff! Jeff Updegrove!" I pointed to my chest. "Remember me? Daphne Templeton?" Forgetting CeeCee for a moment, I jabbed my finger at Moxie. "And Moxie Bloom?"

Sylvan Creek High wasn't a very big school, and it hadn't been *that* long since we'd all been students there, but I could tell that Jeff, who'd usually had his distinctive nose buried in a book, was searching his memory. "Umm . . ."

CeeCee also grasped that our former classmate was drawing a blank. "We were all just reminiscing fondly about our senior-year winter formal, when poor Moxie had a mishap with the punch bowl," she said dryly. "Perhaps you recall *that.*"

All the blood drained from Moxie's face, while the light of recognition finally dawned in Jeff's eyes. "Oh, yes," he said, clearing his throat, as if the mention of the incident made him uncomfortable, too. I still had no idea if he remembered me, but he nodded to us both. "Nice to see you again."

"What the heck are you doing here, and in a suit?" I inquired, as color slowly returned to Moxie's cheeks. "Are you back to visit family —"

"Jeff is my assistant," CeeCee said sharply, cutting me off. "He's been with French's Poodles nearly from the start." She smiled condescendingly at Jeff, whose jaw was visibly grinding, then used her free hand — the one not cradling the dog — to pat his arm. "Sylvan Creek people take care of their own, right?"

Jeff didn't respond to his boss. He tried to smile at me and Moxie, but it came out as a thin, grim line. "I'm actually chief operations officer," he informed us, his voice as tight as his grin. "Slightly more than an ass . . ."

"Jeff!" CeeCee's reprimand cut off the word "assistant" at an inopportune spot. She didn't seem to notice or care. And she quickly put her employee back in his place by asking, in a way that sounded like a command, "Will you *please* get me something to drink before this dog and pony show gets underway?"

Jeff hesitated for a long time, during which I half expected steam to start puffing out of his ears. Then he agreed, through gritted teeth, "Yes, of course, Celeste."

We all watched him thread his way through the crowd. Then Moxie said, "Umm, CeeCee? I hate to tell you, but there aren't any dogs or ponies in the show." My best friend might've been knocked for a loop, moments before, but she'd recovered enough to set her former rival straight about *It's a Wonderful Life.* "In fact, I don't think there's a single animal in the film. Although, Norm Alcorn will almost certainly mention pets in his little talk about all the wonderful things going on with Sylvan Creek's businesses."

I suddenly wondered if CeeCee French was scheduled to be part of that presentation, for some reason, while our former classmate rolled her eyes at Moxie's admittedly quirky comment and muttered, "Honestly. *Nothing* has changed in this town."

I glanced down at Socrates, expecting to find him observing Celeste with narrowed, disapproving eyes. But, to my surprise, he was focused on the poodle, who refused to meet Socrates's gaze. The smaller dog's dark, intelligent eyes were trained on the ceiling, and her nose was in the air. A collar studded with diamonds that I suspected were real circled her delicate throat, and she wore an elaborately pleated, red-velvet, fur-trimmed coat with what appeared to be pearl buttons.

I'd never seen anything quite like that dog jacket, but, all at once, recognition dawned on me again, regarding the poodle. Obviously, I hadn't attended high school with the dog, but I had seen her before, cavorting with children and doing tricks in television commercials for French's Poodles & More.

"Hey, you're Snowdrop!" I said, reaching out my hand to let the famously friendly pup take a sniff — only to have a set of razor-sharp teeth snap at my fingers. I yanked my hand away, just as those teeth grazed my knuckles. "Yikes!"

"Ooh, sorry," CeeCee sniffed, apologizing not to me, but to the dog, who watched me with what I swore was amusement in her dark, haughty eyes. CeeCee again stroked the poodle's silky-looking ear, this time to soothe her, while I checked to make sure my fingers were all still attached to my hand. "Snowdrop does *not* like to be touched by anyone except *professional* handlers and groomers, whom she can sniff out with her discerning little nose," CeeCee added, tapping the poodle's shiny black sniffer.

Snowdrop fairly beamed, while I had a feeling I'd just been insulted.

Then CeeCee turned to Moxie and arched a dark, dramatically plucked eyebrow. Apparently, she'd used some of her millions to buff away any soft edges that she used to have, back when we were teenagers. "Would you like to see if you pass Snowdrop's test, Moxie?" she inquired, holding out the dog. "Because I understand you own a *charming* little salon."

CeeCee hadn't just whittled away at her eyebrows, and, I thought, her nose, which looked more aquiline than I recalled. She'd also sharpened her always well-honed tongue.

"I think people do find Spa and Paw charming," Moxie said, quietly but firmly defending her beloved local establishment. I was very proud of her when she added, graciously, if through clenched teeth, "And you are welcome to stop by any time."

"Oh, I'll be sure to do that," CeeCee said, surprising me — and Moxie, who probably hadn't expected her offer to be accepted. "I always check out my competition!"

The funny thing was, CeeCee sounded almost serious, although I had no idea where the closest French's Poodles & More franchise was even located. We didn't have a lot of chain stores in Sylvan Creek.

But perhaps that was about to change,

because, without another word to us — or any warning for Norm Alcorn, who seemed unhappily surprised by what happened next — CeeCee French swept away from me and Moxie, mounted the Bijoux's gorgeous, grand, red-carpeted staircase, and summoned everyone's attention, merely by . . . existing. As she turned to face the crowd, with Snowdrop perched imperiously in her arms, the whole room went silent. Even the kids stopped running around.

"I know that I'm disrupting today's program," she said, with a funny smile on her face and a pointed glance at Norm, whose face was ashen.

Over at the concession stand, Bitsy Bickelheim seemed frozen in place, just like she'd been back at Oh, Beans, when she'd spilled coffee all over Gabriel.

I noticed that Brett Pinkney again stood by the tree he'd donated, his body as stiff as the pine's trunk and his cheeks as pale as snow.

My mother, Piper, Roger, and Elyse Hunter-Black appeared curious and, perhaps, cautious.

And Jeff Updegrove had stopped midstride, halfway across the lobby, the drink he'd been sent to fetch clutched in his hand and a look of dismay on his face — which wasn't turned toward his boss. He was looking in a different direction.

I was trying to figure out what, or who, he was looking at when movement outside the theater, just beyond the tall glass exit doors, caught *my* eye. Shifting, I glimpsed someone in a bulky, gray-green coat hurrying away from the Bijoux. In a split second, the person was out of sight, hidden by the ticket counter that extended onto the sidewalk.

Then I looked at CeeCee again and felt my heart sink as she announced, "A whole host of people will want to positively *kill* me for letting the cat out of the bag — pet pun intended — but I can't wait a moment longer to share *my* big gift to the town, this holiday season." Her smile widened, and I swore Snowdrop had a triumphant gleam in her eyes, too, when CeeCee informed us all, "I'm bringing my flagship store — the biggest and best French's Poodles & More franchise in the nation — to my beloved hometown of Sylvan Creek!"

CeeCee probably expected that news to be greeted with applause, but I didn't think any of the gasps, especially Moxie's high-pitched yip, signaled approval of the plan to build a pet superstore in our little community.

"What the . . . ?" Moxie muttered, turning to me, her thick lashes batting with confusion.

"I'm shocked, too," I whispered, my reply nonetheless too loud, because a hush had descended over the crowd.

The stunned silence, to which CeeCee, who gazed down upon us from her imperious perch, seemed oblivious, dragged on and on — until it was broken by me, when a little pug in a "bah, hum-pug" sweater dashed through the lobby and crashed into the back of my knees, causing them to buckle and sending me sprawling into a kid who held a bucket of popcorn, so the fluffy kernels flew everywhere, like a buttery blizzard. Then I cried out the word that was almost certainly on most people's lips.

"No!"

CHAPTER 6

"Did you know about CeeCee's plan?" I asked my mother, who was crammed with me, Socrates, Piper, and Roger Berendt into Flour Power's warm little kitchen, where we'd all retreated for coffee and, in Socrates's case, water, midway through *It's a Wonderful Life.* Quite a few people, including Moxie, had skipped the movie altogether after CeeCee French had dropped her bombshell on half the town. I was sure that by tomorrow, Gabriel, who'd snapped at least one hundred photos of Celeste and scribbled furiously in his reporter's notebook, would alert anyone who'd missed CeeCee's "dog and pony show" to the impending arrival of a gigantic pet superstore in Sylvan Creek. I watched my mother for signs of guilt as she pounded my poor, imported Italian coffee machine into submission, like she did every day when she snuck into my pet bakery for her evening caffeine infusion. "Next to Norm Alcorn, you're the most active chamber of commerce member," I added, continuing to study Mom. "You must've known what CeeCee was up to."

"Yes, Mom," Piper said, for once agreeing with me. She and my mother were usually two peas in a pod, but it was hard not to suspect that Mom had been keeping a pretty big secret from us. Taking a seat on one of the stools that ringed the kitchen's butcher-block island, where I rolled out dough for dogs and cats and occasionally baked for humans, too, Piper also watched our mother carefully. "Was the big announcement a genuine surprise to you, too?"

"Piper . . ." Roger seemed to caution my sister as he sat down next to her, while I leaned past him to light a pine-scented candle I'd set on the island. As he drew back, giving me room, he told Piper, "You sound as if you're accusing your poor mother!"

Socrates made a groaning sound deep in his dappled chest, and I stifled the urge to roll my eyes at Roger, who appeared to be currying favor with his likely future mother-in-law, who was anything but "poor," in any sense of the word.

Then again, if I'd been in Roger's conservative loafers, I would probably also take pains to get on Maeve Templeton's good side. I'd spent enough time on her *bad* side, as her own flesh and blood, to know that could be a very, very uncomfortable place. Perhaps, in spite of his mild manner and penchant for wearing argyle, the brown-eyed English professor, who was reaching for one of the double-fudge peppermint brownies I'd just pulled from the oven, along with some Nutty Bacon Wreaths for dogs, was actually a savvy strategist.

Whatever his motive, the comment earned Roger points. Mom turned from the coffee maker, which was hissing like a time bomb, and graced my sister's boyfriend with a rare smile. "Thank you for your vote of confidence, Roger," she said, before shooting me, and me alone, a dark look. "I only wish Daphne shared your faith in me."

I opened my mouth to point out that Piper had also expressed doubts, only to immediately give up. Placing two "wreaths" onto a festive, holly-patterned plate, which I set on the floor for Socrates, I took a seat and grabbed a brownie, myself. Then I asked Mom, point-blank, "Did you know about the plan or not?"

"No, I honestly didn't," she insisted, filling up four deep-red mugs that, like the coffee maker, were left over from the bakery's previous incarnation as an Italian bistro. Frowning — another rare show of emotion — Mom distributed the beverages, sliding a mug under each of our noses before climbing onto the stool next to mine with surprising grace, given that she wore a constricting black pencil skirt and four-inch-high, patent-leather Ferragamo heels. "And you can imagine that I am quite piqued with Norm Alcorn, springing this upon the rest of the chamber at a public event. We should have all been consulted months ago!"

Although I rarely attended meetings, I was technically a chamber member, and I hadn't even thought about that. But my mother was right. Then I pictured Norm Alcorn's face, as CeeCee had delivered her speech. I often watched Norm's ailing Newfoundland, Dunston — in fact, the big black dog was on my schedule for later that week — and I thought Norm had seemed more pale and agitated than usual, back at the Bijoux.

"Are we sure Norm even knew?" I ventured, through a bite of gooey, freshly baked brownie, topped with crunchy, crushed candy canes. "The chamber isn't really a governing body, right? It's more of a booster club for the town — albeit a powerful one."

"I agree with Daphne," Piper said, surprising me again by taking my side. It wasn't that we didn't get along. We just often viewed life from different perspectives. But apparently, we'd both observed the same thing at the theater. "I saw Norm, and he looked shocked."

Of course, a lot of other people had been stunned, too, including Moxie. And Ms. Bickelheim. Not to mention tree-farm owner and former quarterback Brett Pinkney, as well as CeeCee's own colleague, Jeff Updegrove, who couldn't have been surprised by the news.

So why had *he* looked startled?

And who had been standing just outside the theater, before hurrying away . . . ?

"Well, I remain very peeved," Mom said, with a sniff. She absently smoothed the slightly-too-asymmetrical bob that Moxie had convinced her was not a mistake, but rather a "signature look." "Obviously there was a substantial real estate deal involved," Mom added, sounding almost hurt. "And I was not a part of it."

"That's not necessarily true," Roger ventured, daring to contradict his potential relative. Perhaps his plan was to alternate between currying favor and speaking his mind when it counted. That seemed sound, to me. Resting his arms on the table, he leaned forward, frowning thoughtfully. "Maybe this Celeste person made the announcement on the spur of the moment. Maybe she doesn't have a plan in place yet."

"I don't know about that," I said, again thinking back to the lobby, where CeeCee had said Sylvan Creek hadn't changed — yet. "I think she at least went to the theater with the intention of making a big announcement."

"We'll probably know more tomorrow, when the *Gazette* comes out," Piper noted, sipping her coffee. Her cheeks were rosy and almost a little plump. Being in love was giving my cardigan-wearing, sometimes stern sister softer edges, while CeeCee had gone the other direction. "Gabriel was practically salivating while CeeCee was talking. I'm sure the front page will be dedicated to the story." Then Piper quirked an eyebrow at me. "And what happened to you, Daphne? Why in the world did you *fall down,* spilling popcorn everywhere?"

"The little pug . . . It was his fault," I defended myself, although I could tell that no one knew what I was talking about. My mother, my sister, and Roger were all giving me funny looks. "You know. The little dog in the red 'bah, hum-pug' sweater," I clarified, holding down my hand to indicate the pug's diminutive stature, although I didn't come even close to the floor. I looked to Socrates for support, but he shook his head, letting me know that he hadn't seen the impish canine, either. I turned back to the humans. "Seriously? None of you saw a pug?"

"Celeste was holding a poodle," Roger pointed out. "Maybe you're mixing up the breeds."

At the mention of Snowdrop, Socrates started, the tags on his collar rattling. I had no idea what that was all about. I only knew that I was insulted by Roger's comment.

"I'm a *professional pet sitter,*" I reminded him. "I know a pug from a poodle. Especially a famous poodle, like Snowdrop."

My mother set down the mug she'd already drained and waved a hand laden with large, but tasteful, rings. The gesture was dismissive. "You're debating dogs when there are huge things at stake here, Daphne. Like the future of Sylvan Creek." Roger had just been discussing canines, too, but she gave him a grateful micro-smile. "And real estate deals that might still be on the table!"

"How can you think about making money off a store that might destroy local businesses?" I asked Mom, setting down what was left of my brownie. I'd suddenly lost my appetite. "A pet superstore could mean the end of Moxie's salon and Tessie's boutique."

Every time that reality sank in, I felt a little sick, and I wished that Moxie hadn't insisted on being alone that evening. But she'd refused to join us for coffee, saying she preferred to spend some quiet time with Sebastian and a pint of ice cream in her garret.

"Competition is the American way," declared my mother, who only had one real rival for the local real estate market. And Reed Bynum — terrible slogan: "We're Bynum and Sellin' 'Em" — was also an independent operator, without the backing of a national chain. Mom reached for a brownie, then withdrew her hand, no doubt having mentally calculated the potential calories as she lectured me. "And I hope you are already strategizing to keep your share of the market, Daphne," she cautioned. "You will almost certainly be impacted, too. From what I understand, French's Poodles & More provides kenneling and, of course, sells pet treats at discount prices."

"People hire me because they don't want to kennel their pets," I reminded Mom. Needless to say, I'd considered the potential impact of CeeCee's plan on my own small enterprises, and, although I could see the potential for problems, I was trying to stay positive. "And my treats are organic and locally sourced," I pointed out. "They also appeal to a certain clientele. I think my 'market share' will be okay."

I could tell from their expressions that Piper and Roger were still concerned for the future of my businesses. But Piper, at least, seemed to agree that I produced a high-quality product at Flour Power, compared to the food sold at CeeCee's superstores.

"The products CeeCee stocks under the store's brand name are terrible," my veterinarian sibling said, with clear disapproval. She'd obviously followed the news about the scandal that Gabriel had referenced. "A few months ago, CeeCee French's company was in court . . ."

I wanted to hear the rest of that sentence, but at that moment, my cell phone rang with a custom tone that I'd never *really* expected to hear, and I was so intrigued that I popped off my seat and went to my jacket, which hung on a peg near the back door.

I'd missed the call, but there was a voice mail waiting.

Playing it, I then stuck my phone in my pocket, grabbed my coat from the peg, and told Mom, Piper, and Roger, "I'm going to trust you to blow out the candle and clean up when you're done, okay? Socrates and I have to leave now."

Roger appeared surprised, while Piper and my mother studied *me* suspiciously.

"Where are you headed in the middle of your *own gathering*?" Mom asked, as if we weren't all — or at least nearly all — family, and she didn't visit Flour Power all the time, uninvited.

"Yes, Daphne," Piper said, observing me skeptically from behind her wire-rimmed glasses. "It's pitch-black and practically freezing outside."

Although part of me was almost nervous, I couldn't help grinning at Socrates, whose keen ears must've picked up at least some of the message, even though the phone hadn't been on speaker. His tail twitched, just slightly. Then I turned back to the humans, telling them, "What better time for a stroll through Pettigrew Park!"

CHAPTER 7

"This was a good idea, right?" I asked Socrates, who was jumping down from my van, which I'd parked in front of the Sylvan Creek Public Library, at the edge of Pettigrew Park. The library was closed, but each of the ornate, Italianate building's many windows, including those in the pretty cupola that topped the roof, glowed with candles. The structure, which always reminded me of a wedding cake, was also bathed in spotlights that highlighted the elaborate woodwork on the wraparound porch and two gorgeous, oversized pine wreaths that hung on a pair of tall, arched main doors. Then I glanced behind us at the park, where the gazebo was outlined with white lights and Sylvan Creek's big community Christmas tree gleamed in the distance. But the town's namesake creek ran black and silent, and the paths were dark and quiet. I looked down at Socrates, who also seemed uncertain. "I didn't reply to the invitation, so we might actually be alone. . . ."

I had barely finished that thought, my words still hanging in the frosty air, when I heard claws tapping on pavement, followed by excited yips, right before a tiny dog darted around the corner of the library and launched himself directly at the basset hound by my side.

"Artie!" I cried, so the one-eared, drooling Chihuahua diverted for a second to wriggle against my ankles, his big eyes bulging even larger than usual with happiness. Then my favorite, most exuberant former foster scampered to his best, if completely opposite, canine buddy.

Moments later, another bigger dog loped in our direction, followed by a man who stepped from the shadowed paths.

"Hello, Daphne," Detective Jonathan Black said, grinning at me, his teeth white in the darkness. "I wasn't sure you'd come if I didn't promise you cheese — or a murder."

"I was half afraid there'd actually been a homicide, and I was somehow involved without even knowing it yet," I joked . . . or sort of joked . . . with Jonathan, who strolled next to me along the narrow footpaths that wound through Pettigrew Park. The sky had cleared, and the snowy grounds were bathed in soft moonlight. The dogs ran off-leash, Artie leading Socrates and Jonathan's chocolate Lab, Axis, on a merry chase — although, as always, Socrates slowed when he thought I could see him. I did my best to keep my focus on Jonathan, which wasn't difficult. The six-foot-something, ex-SEAL was as handsome as ever. Maybe even more so.

He continued to wear his nearly black hair a little longer than when he'd first moved to Sylvan Creek, a good look for him, and his changeable, often difficult-to-read blue eyes were practically the color of the starry sky that arched overhead. He wore a black down jacket, only half-zipped in spite of the cold, and worn jeans that he carried off as well as the tailored suits he favored when on duty.

I studied his face, my gaze shifting from a small scar on his jaw back to his eyes, and I suddenly recalled the illness he'd once suffered. The one that had caused him to leave the military, because there was a real risk of relapse. Given that Jonathan had never called me before to meet socially, I suffered a twinge of concern. "Is everything okay?"

Jonathan hesitated, and for a split second,

I thought something really was wrong. Then he smiled at me. "Everything's fine, Daphne. I just realized, this evening, that the dogs and I have spent a lot of time on our property lately. And, since you haven't stumbled across any bodies — thankfully — Artie hasn't had a chance to expend his considerable social energy on Socrates. I thought it might be nice for the dogs to see each other."

I couldn't resist nudging Jonathan with my elbow, since my hands, protected by soft, knitted mittens, were stuffed into my pockets. "Gee, I've missed you, too," I teased, trying not to be offended by Jonathan's failure to even mention me in his explanation for the unexpected outreach. "I kind of thought you'd extended the invitation to take a walk so *we* could catch up."

Jonathan laughed, his breath coming out as a puff of steam. "Okay, Daphne. Perhaps I was curious about what you've been up to." He seemed to grow more serious. "It has been a while."

I stopped joking, too, and spoke more softly. "Yes. I've noticed."

I didn't think I'd realized, until that moment, that I actually *had* missed Jonathan. I supposed I'd expected our paths to cross after we'd last parted. But they hadn't, and time had passed. . . .

"So, what's been happening with you, since you've apparently retired from doing my job?" he asked, lightening the mood again. We walked slowly past the gazebo, so I could better see his face by the garlands of white lights that were strung around the gingerbread structure, and I thought his expression didn't quite match his tone. "Is business good at the pet bakery?"

"First of all, thank you for dropping off the bamboo," I said, referencing a gift he'd somehow managed to leave at Flour Power's grand opening. I hadn't even seen him deliver the plant, which was thriving. "I could feed a panda with that thing, these days."

"You're very welcome." He lightly touched my arm for a moment, guiding me around a patch of ice, and our pace slowed to a crawl. "I hope it's lived up to its reputation for bringing good luck."

We'd passed into the darkness again, and a shadow crossed my thoughts, too. "Things have been going great. Although, I'll admit that I'm a little concerned for all the pet-related businesses in town, now that we're apparently getting a French's Poodles & More franchise."

"Yes, I heard about Celeste French's big

announcement," Jonathan said, as the three dogs tore past us, kicking up snow. Socrates didn't even try to pretend he wasn't having fun. His long ears flew back as he raced on his short legs. Jonathan and I paused for a moment to watch the trio disappear into the darkness, then we resumed walking, Jonathan bending to see my face. "How worried are you?"

"First of all, how do you even know about the announcement?" I asked, tilting my head, which was also covered by a fuzzy, knit cap with a pompom on top. "I didn't see you at the theater, and I don't think you follow the local gossip."

He smiled. "You're right. I normally don't. Unless Moxie Bloom has me hostage in her chair." He absently dragged a hand through his hair, and I made a mental note to tell my best friend that, while she'd really messed up my mother's look, she was doing a great job styling her crush. "But, as you can imagine, the arrival of a wealthy, powerful woman in this little town has not gone unnoticed by the other wealthy, powerful female, who *did* attend the movie."

For a second, I didn't know who he was talking about. Then I realized he was referring to his ex-wife, Elyse Hunter-Black, who was Sylvan Creek's richest, most influential

67

resident of either gender.

Elyse, who split her time between Manhattan and the lakeside mansion she'd purchased in Sylvan Creek — probably to be near Jonathan, if Moxie's guess was correct — was a high-powered producer for the Stylish Life television network. And, from what I understood, Elyse, like Jonathan, had some family money to burn, too.

"Elyse isn't normally the jealous type, but she is competitive," Jonathan added, grinning. "I don't think she's happy about being deposed, even temporarily, as Sylvan Creek's most accomplished woman, and she's keeping close tabs on Ms. French."

"Unless CeeCee has changed dramatically since high school, everyone should be on guard around her," I noted, kicking at some snow with one of my favorite oversized cowgirl boots, which was still stained with guacamole from another adventure in that very same park. "Which is not to say that CeeCee hasn't evolved. As Günter Grass once noted, our younger selves can seem like strangers, or aliens, to us."

Jonathan arched an eyebrow. "You usually reference Greek philosophers, not German novelists."

I pictured Jonathan's amazing A-frame cabin in the woods, where massive, well stocked bookshelves flanked an equally impressive stone fireplace. "Are you a fan?"

He shrugged. "I've read a few works."

I was pretty sure that if I ever got to check out those groaning shelves, I'd find a whole row of volumes by Grass — probably in their native German. I strongly suspected that Jonathan, who'd grown up, and then served, all over the world, had a few linguistic tricks up his sleeve.

But he probably wouldn't say more, right then, so I switched the topic back to Celeste French. "To be honest, based upon my brief conversation with CeeCee at the Bijoux, I have a feeling she's still not to be trusted. Especially around boyfriends."

Jonathan seemed intrigued. "I take it she stole one of yours?"

I shook my head. "No. The boy was Moxie's true love. And I'm not sure she ever got over it."

"Poor Moxie." I thought Jonathan sounded genuinely sympathetic. "And now it seems as if your former classmate intends to rob the whole town blind, if Elyse — and the *Gazette* — are to be trusted." The corners of his eyes crinkled with amusement. "Although, honestly, I only have faith in one of those sources, when it comes to accuracy."

We'd reached a fork in the paths, and I stopped in my tracks. Jonathan paused, too. Overlooking the fair joke about the *Gazette,* I asked, "Are you saying that Gabriel . . . ?"

"Has already posted a story on the online edition." Jonathan finished my thought. "I looked up the article after Elyse called me. It's a fairly comprehensive piece, given how quickly Graham slapped it together."

"Why do I keep forgetting the Web version of the paper exists?" I muttered, choosing the path that led toward the Christmas tree and resuming our stroll. The dogs darted by again, Artie's tongue flapping out over his recessive chin, Socrates starting to look tired, and Axis loping easily along. When they were once more out of sight, I shot Jonathan a wary glance. "Was there a picture . . . ?"

"You were only featured in one shot," he assured me. Having been the chiseled, heroic-looking half of the legendary image of me being hauled, bedraggled, from the lake, he clearly understood why I was worried. And my concerns were apparently justified. "You seemed to be picking yourself up after a fall," he added. "The caption read something about 'local baker for pets collapses in wake of devastating news.'"

Jonathan was trying hard not to laugh,

while I was not amused. "I was actually knocked over by a little, pranking pug in a red sweater with a grumpy logo," I informed him. "Not that anyone believes me!"

Jonathan seemed as skeptical as my sister, my mother, and Roger Berendt. In fact, he overlooked my comment about the dog and asked, more seriously, "Daphne . . . are you upset about the store, which likely *will* impact your bakery, if not Lucky Paws?"

We'd reached the massive tree, the boughs of which were iced with snow, so the lights glowed more softly, as if behind frosted glass, and I stopped us again, so I could study Jonathan's reaction when I ventured, uncertainly, "You . . . You called me because you're worried about me, didn't you? And not my safety, like when you put a lock on my door . . ."

"Which you don't use, I'm sure."

I ignored his attempt to laugh off the kind gesture. Plus, he was right. I never locked up Plum Cottage.

"And now, you wanted to make sure I'm okay in the wake of CeeCee's bombshell," I added, watching his blue eyes. "You didn't *just* want to get the dogs together. You're checking on me."

I expected Jonathan to deny that and distance himself from me, like he usually did when things got too personal between us. But, for once, that didn't happen. In fact, his expression softened, and my heart did a funny leap when his deep voice grew lower and quieter, too.

"Yes, I guess I am checking on you, Daphne," he admitted, stepping closer, so I could smell his signature spicy cologne on the crisp air. I was barely aware of the dogs playing near the creek — and a person who walked along the bank, too. My gaze was locked on Jonathan's eyes, which suddenly seemed even darker than the night sky. However, I was pretty sure the figure who had stopped, perhaps to stare at the water, had been walking unevenly, with a limp. I flashed back to the man I'd seen darting into Cherry Alley. The one I'd mistaken for Mike Cavanaugh. Then the individual moved out of my peripheral vision, and the dogs ran to the gazebo, so the night was almost silent when Jonathan said, "And I had a question for you, too. Something I've been meaning to ask."

I tucked the curls that peeked out from under my hat nervously behind one ear. "A question?"

"Yes," he said, although he didn't ask me anything right away. Instead he said, cryptically, "It's been a . . . *challenging* year, in some ways."

I had no idea what that meant, but I didn't interrupt him, for fear of shattering the always fragile bridge between us.

"I thought about contacting you, several times," he continued, surprising me. "But I wasn't sure if you and Graham . . ." He hesitated, and for the first time I could recall, Jonathan Black seemed unsure of himself. He dragged his hand through his hair again, then asked, "Are you two . . . ?"

The half-formed question — which may or may not have been the one he'd originally intended to ask, when he'd contacted me — caught me off guard. And I had no idea how to label my relationship with Gabriel — if that was, indeed, what Jonathan was prompting me to do.

Nor did I have a chance to form any kind of response before the snow at the base of Sylvan Creek's huge, pretty holiday tree was suddenly disturbed, and a small tan-and-black face poked out from under one of the lowest, drooping boughs. Big, round eyes gleamed at me, and a pink tongue darted in and out of a pushed-in muzzle.

Pulling my mitten-clad hand from my pocket, I pointed. "Look! There's the pug I was telling you about. . . ."

Then the words died on my lips and my

hand fell to my side when I realized that the splash of red I also spied under the tree wasn't just a glimpse of the dog's sweater. By lifting the bough, he'd also revealed a very distinctive crimson shoe.

One that I'd last seen at the Bijoux theater, on Celeste French's foot . . . which looked cold and blue, poking out from the snow, too.

CHAPTER 8

"Where is the hand-knit, free-range, yak-hair cardigan I bought for you when we need it?" I asked poor Artie, who was tucked into my barn jacket, shivering with either cold or happiness. Maybe both. Artie loved a free ride. His eyes were bulging again, and his tongue was hanging out, dripping little icicles of drool, as Socrates, Axis, and I walked from Pettigrew Park to Moxie Bloom's garret apartment, where Jonathan's partner, Detective Doebler, had agreed we could wait, in case Jonathan planned to question me about CeeCee French's apparent murder. I'd appreciated the offer, because it was getting late, and the temperature was dropping. "I can't believe I found another body," I grumbled to the dogs, echoing things Jonathan had said earlier, before the EMTs and coroner Vonda Shakes had arrived to claim his attention.

In fact, I hadn't spoken to him again, after

he'd gently, but firmly, turned me away from the Christmas tree, so he could confirm what I'd already suspected.

Celeste French was dead.

He hadn't told me anything else, but, as we'd both waited for the backup he'd called, I was pretty sure I'd seen one more red thing on the snow, when he'd pushed aside the low boughs.

Blood.

"Poor Celeste," I whispered, with a glance at Socrates, who was also somber. Axis was padding along quietly, too, his head lowered, as if he grasped that something bad had just happened. We'd almost reached the big, yellow Victorian building that housed the Philosopher's Tome bookstore and Moxie's apartment. Moxie's business, Spa and Paw, was tucked into a tiny storefront, right next door. Across the street, under the town clock, Brett Pinkney had set up a small, white wooden hut, which was surrounded by Pinkney's pines, for sale like they were every year. The scene, reminiscent of childhood holidays, gave me a rush of nostalgia, which was quickly tempered by the recollection of Brett's former girlfriend's feet sticking out from beneath Sylvan Creek's biggest Christmas tree. I sighed, my breath a puff of steam in the cold air. "I wonder how Brett will take the news," I added, shuffling past Spa and Paw. "I have no idea if they stayed in touch —"

"Woof!"

Socrates's soft, unexpected bark interrupted me. Looking down, I saw that he'd stopped in his tracks, and his nose was pointed toward the salon's door, which was slightly ajar. Just a crack.

Like me, Moxie wasn't very consistent when it came to using locks, and the door was old, so the sight didn't surprise me. But I told Socrates, "Thanks for pointing that out. Spa and Paw would've been freezing in the morning!"

He wagged his tail, a restrained gesture, then resumed walking, while I pulled the door shut, being careful not to let Artie slip down the front of my coat.

Then our chilly little party passed by a narrow, dark passageway that separated Spa and Paw from the Philosopher's Tome, and I opened the door — also unlocked — to a staircase that led to Moxie's apartment.

"Come on, guys," I said, leading the way upstairs.

I felt a little guilty, because it was late, and I knew that Moxie, who was likely already asleep, would jump out of bed — probably wearing vintage pajamas reminiscent of the Haynes sisters' attire in *White Christmas* — to make a fuss over us, even though she'd had a bad day, herself.

However, when we reached the landing, my ears caught the faint, but distinctive, sound of Dean Martin singing "A Marshmallow World."

"At least she's awake," I told the dogs. "And maybe feeling a little better."

Artie, who'd visited Moxie's place before and probably recalled having fun, yipped hopefully, while Socrates lowered his already drooping tail, as if to remind me that we weren't exactly bearing good news.

"You're right," I said, with a sigh.

Then I knocked on the door, and almost immediately heard slippers slapping against floorboards. A moment later, Moxie opened the door, clad in the exact pajamas I'd imagined, and wearing an equally anticipated look of surprise on her face.

I, meanwhile, gasped when I looked over her shoulder into the apartment.

"Moxie!" I cried softly. "What in the name of Burl Ives have you been *up to*?"

CHAPTER 9

"Oh, goodness," Moxie said softly, for at least the tenth time since I'd broken the news about CeeCee's death. Shaking her head sadly, she piped white royal-icing "snow" onto the pitched roof of an exact gingerbread model of the Philosopher's Tome, complete with a turret, her third-floor balcony, and melted-sugar "glass" windows that glowed from inside, thanks to carefully placed tea lights. The replica, and a towering pile of waiting gingerbread "walls," which Moxie planned to use to re-create Sylvan Creek's *entire main street,* had been the inspiration for my earlier gasp of surprise. She squeezed a pastry bag, and a perfect icicle dripped from the cookie structure's roof, echoing the jagged ice that ringed the real building. "I didn't like CeeCee," Moxie added, pausing to hand Sebastian a bite of broken cookie, which he nibbled gratefully. "But how awful, to be stuffed under a Christmas tree, like the world's worst present. No one deserves to meet her demise, or be remembered, like *that.*"

"No, I agree," I said, curling myself more tightly under a warm, fuzzy blanket Moxie had offered me, along with a small, but welcome, tumbler of hot buttered rum. I sat on a surprisingly comfortable midcentury modern Danish rocker, while the dogs, including the usually inexhaustible Artie, dozed near a white aluminum Christmas tree. I was warming up, and Moxie's apartment, strung with cheerful, antique — and probably slightly dangerous — colored Christmas lights, was reminiscent of Santa's workshop, but I shuddered. "It's a horrible homecoming."

"I'm so sorry you had to be the one to find her," Moxie said, offering me a sympathetic glance, even as she artfully piped icing snow around a sweet little chimney.

I often wondered why my best friend seemed capable of conquering every artistic endeavor she undertook, with the notable exception of the terrible painting on the side of my van. However, I couldn't ask what had gone wrong without hurting her feelings. Especially since I sometimes thought she considered the strange dog just fine.

And speaking of dogs . . .

"That little pug — the one that knocked me down at the theater — actually alerted me to CeeCee's presence," I told Moxie, as Perry Como began to sing the nostalgic classic, "Home for the Holidays." I pictured the bah, hum-pug standing in the snow and hoped he had a warm place to call home. Then I recalled that he'd been wearing a sweater, so someone must've looked out for him. "He was in the park, off-leash and maybe alone," I added. "And he popped out from under the tree, right next to CeeCee."

I kept explaining long after I realized Moxie was completely baffled. "What pug?" she asked, finally setting down the pastry bag and wiping her hands on a ruffled apron that covered her pajamas. Picking up Sebastian, she took a seat on a rocker that matched mine. "I didn't see many dogs at the Bijoux, except for Socrates, Paris, and Milan. I don't think many animals appreciate Frank Capra movies."

Socrates's tail thumped against the floor, as if his subconscious was grateful for the implied compliment.

"You really didn't see a pug in a sweater?" I asked, sipping my buttered rum, which perhaps I didn't need if I was hallucinating.

All at once, I again recalled how I thought

I'd seen Mike Cavanaugh limping away from me on Market Street. And I'd glimpsed a person with a similar gait in the park.

Was I imagining things?

I didn't think so.

In fact, I knew that I was right, at least about the pug. . . .

"Daph?" Moxie asked, breaking into my thoughts. I snapped out of my reverie to find her observing me with shrewd, curious eyes. Sebastian, sitting on her lap, blinked at me, too. "Why were you out walking with Detective Black, anyhow?" she asked, finally posing a question I'd been expecting since I'd arrived. "What was that all about?"

"I . . . I . . . ."

While my mouth opened and closed, repeating the same word over and over, I also thought back to the moments before the pug, and the body, had ended Jonathan's and my conversation.

What, exactly, had we been doing?

Moxie continued to watch me closely. "Was he finally telling you . . . ?"

The question, which sounded uncharacteristically serious, was interrupted by the sound of heavy footsteps coming up the stairs to Moxie's apartment. She and I jolted upright, and the dogs roused, too.

"I suppose that's for me," I said, standing up to answer a loud, solid rap on the door. I looked over my shoulder at Moxie, who seemed content to let me welcome the visitor to her home. "I guess I'm going to be questioned, after all," I added, grabbing the knob and swinging the door open.

As I'd anticipated, Jonathan Black was standing on the landing, filling the space in the way only he could manage.

"I'll get my coat," I told him, before he could even greet me. In fact, he didn't seem inclined to say a word, and he looked so grave that I got a different kind of flutter in my stomach, quite unlike the tickle I'd felt back in the park. This was a bad feeling, which was at odds with the scent of gingerbread wafting from the apartment, the colorful lights, and Gene Autry's jaunty version of "Rudolph, the Red-Nosed Reindeer," which was currently playing on Moxie's stereo. I swallowed nervously, then asked, "Should the dogs come, too . . . ?"

Jonathan was shaking his head — and looking right past me, even as he addressed me. "If you don't mind, could you please take all the dogs home with you, Daphne? Just for the night, because I may be working late."

Confused, I glanced over my shoulder at

Axis, Artie, and Socrates, who all sat up, uncertainty in their eyes. Even Socrates seemed unsure. Then I looked at Moxie, whose fair skin was ashen, and saw a flicker of fear in her green eyes as she half rose from her chair.

She must've grasped what was happening before I did. I was still struggling to connect the dots when Jonathan said brusquely, "I need Moxie to come with me. Now."

Spinning back around, I blinked at Jonathan. "What?"

He gave me an apologetic look. At least, I thought he did that. The glance only lasted a moment, and once Jonathan was in professional mode, he wasn't one to say he was sorry for doing his job. Then he looked past me again.

"Moxie," he repeated. "You need to get dressed."

"Why?" I asked on her behalf, stepping more squarely in front of Jonathan, instinctively protecting my best friend. I knew, by then, that he wanted to question Moxie about CeeCee's death, but I'd known Moxie Bloom since childhood, and she'd *never* be involved in a murder. The thought was ridiculous — even crazier than when Piper had been suspected of killing her ex-boyfriend — and I continued to block Jona-

84

than's path. "Why do you need Moxie?"

"She and I are going down to the station," Jonathan informed us all, in an even, measured, deadly serious tone. "And this might take a while."

CHAPTER 10

In spite of the fire that crackled softly in the
fireplace, casting the first floor of Plum Cottage, below my loft bedroom, in a warm
glow, and the gentle snores of three sleeping
dogs — not to mention the soothing cham-
omile tea I'd brewed after returning home
from Moxie's apartment — I had trouble
sleeping the night of CeeCee French's
death.

Wriggling carefully down deeper under
my warm, goose-down comforter, so I
wouldn't disrupt Tinkleston, who was curled
at the foot of the bed, I tried not to recall
the sight of CeeCee's foot in the snow.

But as soon as I'd banish that image, I'd
start worrying about Moxie, who would
never harm anyone, but who did have motive to kill our former classmate.

*A stolen boyfriend . . . A business in jeop-
ardy . . . People had likely killed for less
compelling reasons. . . .*

"Oh, Moxie," I whispered, hoping that Jonathan hadn't interrogated her too intensely, but knowing that he wouldn't go easy on her, either. Cringing, I recalled how he'd once questioned poor Piper to the point that she'd doubted her own innocence. And Moxie wasn't as hardheaded as my sister. "I am very concerned," I told Tinkleston, who'd crept closer, his orange eyes reminiscent of the fire downstairs. "*Very* concerned."

Tinks mewed softly, and I dared to stroke his head. For once, he didn't even complain. He just curled up by my side and yawned.

A moment later, I found myself yawning, too, as a bitter winter wind rocked the cottage, compelling me to snuggle even more deeply under my heavy blankets. And soon, exhausted by the day's events, I drifted off to sleep, my dreams set in a hazy high school gymnasium, where Moxie and Jonathan . . . or maybe it was Mike Cavanaugh . . . danced, the man's arm wrapped too tightly around my best friend's waist. I wanted to run over and help her, but my feet were stuck in a pile of snow, stained red with punch, or something else. . . .

"Moxie!"

I cried out loud and fought to sit up, but my feet, overheating in thick socks, really

87

were stuck in the blankets I'd twisted around myself.

Taking a few deep breaths, I untangled myself, observed by Socrates, Axis — and Artie, who'd somehow managed to climb onto my high bed and take the place of Tinkleston, who often wandered off in the middle of the night.

"How did you get up here?" I asked the Chihuahua, who wriggled with happiness and attempted to lick my face. I noted that he'd drooled all over one of my pillows. Sitting up straighter, I gently pushed Artie aside. "I bet you don't do this to Jonathan," I said, my eyes adjusting to bright sunlight that streamed through the circular window above my head. "I bet you sleep in your dog bed at his house."

Artie spun happily in place and yipped, as if he had no idea what I was talking about. But Axis barked deeply, presumably to let me know that I was correct, while Socrates shook his head, disapproving of his best canine friend's behavior.

"Well, you are probably going home any minute now, anyway," I told Artie, immediately suffering a twinge of disappointment. The exuberant little dog's questionable behavior aside, I wished Artie and Axis could stay longer.

And, apparently, wishes sometimes came true.

Reaching for my cell phone, which sat on my nightstand next to an ancient, rotary-dial landline phone, I tapped the screen and saw that I had three messages — including two from people who'd just made appearances in my troubled dreams.

First was a request from Jonathan Black, written in a way that told me he was in full detective mode, and probably wearing a suit.

Can you please keep the dogs until this evening, Daphne? If that's a problem, I will make other arrangements. But your professional help would be appreciated, if possible. And I will, of course, pay you for your trouble.

"Hey, Artie, you're staying!" I told the Chihuahua, who remained on the bed when he should've been on the floor. I overlooked the issue and smiled at Axis, too. "We have all day to hang out!"

Socrates's tail thumped once against the floorboards, although he was still trying to act disappointed with Artie's behavior.

No problem, I texted back. Then, because I still hadn't fully repaid Jonathan for a few meals and some outstanding library fines he'd covered, I added, And keep your $$! Still owe you!

Next, I checked the second message, which was from Gabriel.

Another body! When can we talk? Would like to go to press ASAP.

He might've been in a hurry, but I wasn't eager to be interviewed, and I clicked on the next message before I replied.

This text was from Moxie Bloom, and it said, simply, HELP — followed by seven sad-face emojis and a seemingly endless string of exclamation points.

Springing from bed, I let her know that I'd meet her at Oh, Beans in a half hour — an appointment for which I was unfortunately late, although it only took me a few minutes to toss on a pair of jeans and an oversized sweater, then rush downstairs to feed Tinks and the dogs.

However, when I reached the bottom of my spiral staircase, I discovered a "present" that someone had left me in the dead of the night.

A gift that, moments later, tried to *bite* me.

CHAPTER 11

"I can't believe you're watching Snowdrop," Moxie said, lacing her fingers around a steaming, candy-cane-striped mug of double-fudge hot cocoa topped with a melting mountain of Oh, Beans's house-made peppermint-swirl marshmallows. I'd ordered the same thing, as an antidote to the chilly day, which was clouding over, too. Moxie's bow-shaped mouth drew down with disapproval. "What kind of person leaves a dog on a doorstep?"

"Jeff Updegrove, that's who," I said. "And he actually left her inside the cottage, along with a note, scrawled on a big, manila envelope, that said he would've knocked, but it was very early, and my door was unlocked." I was glad Jonathan wasn't there to learn that I still wasn't using the lock he'd installed. "Not wanting to disturb me, he quietly placed Snowdrop's monogrammed, bejeweled carrier inside the door before racing off to the airport."

Moxie's mouth formed a perfect *o* of surprise. Then she said, "That all sounds suspicious!"

"I know, right?" I'd been debating calling Jonathan, but I assumed that he already knew about Jeff's hasty departure from Sylvan Creek, minus the dog, who wore what I believed to be a genuine cashmere, pastel-pink sweater with an ironic, 1950s-style embroidered black poodle on the breast. Not that I could get a good look at Snowdrop, who refused to leave her deluxe crate, and who'd bared her teeth at Artie, too, that morning.

The gregarious Chihuahua had clearly been shocked by Snowdrop's failure to fall for his relentless charms, a snub that had only made him more determined to win her over. He'd actually started dancing in front of her classy crate.

Axis, meanwhile, had wisely kept his distance. But Socrates had nudged a food bowl in Snowdrop's direction. The gesture had greatly surprised me. My baleful basset hound sidekick was always a gentleman, but he didn't suffer snobs. I could only assume that he felt badly for the newly orphaned, now abandoned pup and was temporarily overlooking her snippy attitude, just like I was doing. In fact, Socrates had remained behind with snooty Snowdrop and a very irate Tinkleston, instead of coming to town with me, Axis, and Artie. Both those dogs were testing out holiday treat recipes at Flour Power while I met with Moxie, who seemed more interested in discussing my new charge than unloading about her interrogation.

"So what was in the envelope?" she asked, dabbing at her mouth with a napkin. The cocoa was impossible to drink without getting a mustache. Her eyes snapped wide open as she was struck by a thought. "A confession? Because, in spite of being a meek bookworm, and one of those forgettable class officers like recording secretary, which makes me doubt he could kill anyone, Jeff really didn't seem happy with CeeCee!"

"To be honest, I haven't opened the envelope yet," I admitted, suddenly wishing I'd at least peeked inside. Then I shrugged. "I assume it's filled with paperwork. Snowdrop is a star. She's probably insured and requires special care." I wiped my sleeve across my own mouth, which felt a little sticky. "I was in a hurry to see you and decided to check it out later."

"Aw, thanks, Daphne." Moxie scooched forward in her seat, so someone could get past our table in the crowded room.

Glancing up, I recognized the young woman from Ivy Dunleavy's Custom Creations, who made a beeline for Bitsy Bickelheim, greeting her with a big smile.

Ms. Bickelheim, attired that day in a sequined, batwing-sleeved caftan, was struggling to fill a glass jar with loose tea, but she abandoned that endeavor and moved to the counter, where both women consulted a notebook that Ivy had pulled from a big tote slung over her small shoulder.

At least, I once again assumed the younger woman was Ivy Dunleavy, who seemed somehow familiar to me, upon closer inspection. There was something about the way she tilted her head when she smiled. Or maybe it was the unusual copper hue of her long, straight hair.

I wanted to point out the seamstress to Moxie, but she was still fixated on the Snowdrop situation.

"Well, when is Jeff coming back?" she inquired. "He can't expect you to watch Snowdrop indefinitely."

"I have no idea how long I'm supposed to watch the dog," I admitted. "Maybe that information is in the envelope." Then I reached across the table and gave Moxie's hand a quick squeeze, only to regret that, because I had sticky fingers, too, from the marshmallows I'd been picking at. "Forget Snowdrop and Jeff," I urged. "What the heck happened last night, after you left with Jonathan?"

"Oh, goodness." The light of curiosity flickered out in Moxie's eyes. "I have to admit you were right," she said, dipping her head sheepishly and wiping her fingers with her napkin. "You tried to tell me that being interrogated by Jonathan Black isn't exactly pleasant." Then she quickly brightened, her cheeks getting pink spots that matched the hand-embroidered poinsettias on her vintage, cream-colored sweater. "Although, he looked *so* sternly handsome when he basically accused me of murder!"

I wasn't sure how to respond to that, but I was glad she was at least smiling after fighting off allegations of homicide.

"So, maybe it wasn't quite as bad as I feared when I read your text?" I asked hopefully, grabbing a napkin from the holder on the table, too. The paper stuck to my fingers. "Because your message seemed a little desperate."

Moxie sighed. "I suppose I might've sent *one* too many sad-faced emojis, before I could get some sleep and put things in perspective. Because, honestly, once Detective Black and I got past the part about how I never forgave CeeCee for stealing away Mike Cavanaugh . . . And the stuff about how she *was* going to destroy Spa and Paw, so, at the very least, it would just be 'Spa,' with no paws to speak of . . ." Moxie shrugged. "After that, things weren't so awful. I think he's only ninety-percent convinced I killed CeeCee, when he started at one hundred."

I took a moment to digest all that, while picking gooey scraps of paper from my hand.

"You, er . . . seem to have moved past CeeCee's demise," I finally observed, hoping she hadn't been glib with Jonathan.

"No, I haven't done that," she said, more seriously. "I still feel terrible about what happened to her. But I can't mourn her like I would a friend, or even acquaintance. In fact, I feel almost as if a stranger has died."

That was valid. I also felt badly about CeeCee's death, the same way I felt whenever I heard about someone who'd died too young. But I wasn't consumed with grief.

"Umm, Moxie?" I didn't want to put my best friend through a second interrogation at my hands, but I had one more important question regarding CeeCee's murder.

"Yes?" She'd been eating a marshmallow,

too, and she licked her fingers.

"Did you have an alibi to share with Jonathan? Anything, beyond Sebastian's squeaky word, to prove that you were really home the night of CeeCee's death?"

"Oh, I wasn't home," Moxie said, frowning.

I was pretty sure she'd told me that she planned to stay in her apartment, eating ice cream with her rat, when we'd parted at the Bijoux. "Really, because I thought . . ."

"I know what I told you at the theater," Moxie said. "But after CeeCee's awful — and very smug — announcement, I decided I shouldn't sit home sulking. So I walked around town, well into the night, taking pictures for my gingerbread village."

I wasn't sure I understood. "For the *village*?"

"Yes." Moxie nodded. "I want the cookie version of Sylvan Creek to be as accurate as possible. And it *is* a night-time scene. So I strolled through town, snapping pictures for reference."

I fought the urge to groan. "So, you basically *recorded proof* that you were wandering around town, alone, the night of Cee-Cee's death?"

Moxie seemed proud of me for catching on. She grinned. "Precisely!"

I wanted to *thunk* my head against the polished, wooden table, because, from my perspective, it didn't seem like things had gone very well during her interrogation. But I didn't want to alarm Moxie, or ruin the positive spin she was putting on her discussion with Jonathan.

Plus, my attention was suddenly drawn to something I'd noticed outside. A little dog in a red sweater, who darted down the street on stiff legs, his tongue lolling from his mouth and a mischievous look in his round, bulging eyes.

"Hey!"

I started to rise from my seat, just as someone else came hurrying along the sidewalk. A man with an uneven, lurching gait whose shoulders were hunched under a heavy, grayish-green coat with an upturned collar that all but obscured his features.

As he moved quickly past Oh, Beans's windows, he turned slightly, just enough for me to see his eyes, which locked with mine for a split second before he moved on.

"Daphne? What's outside?"

Moxie spun around in her seat, and, on instinct, I grabbed her hand again. "Nothing," I assured her, settling into my chair once more and compelling her to face me. I wanted to mention the pug and the man, but for some reason, I simply smiled. "Nothing important."

Moxie rested back into her seat, too. "Oh. Well, I was just telling you that I do wish Detective Black had worn a suit last night. I always imagined him being impeccably tailored when he finally questioned me." Hesitating, she licked one finger, growing thoughtful. Then she ventured uncertainly, "Daphne, has Detective Black said anything . . . ?"

Moxie didn't have a chance to finish that question, which reminded me of something she'd started to say the night before, in her apartment. While she was still choosing her words, someone interrupted us, asking in a timid voice, "Did . . . did one of you just say *tailor*?"

"Oh, your designs are just lovely," Moxie said, brushing a finger lightly over the pages of the sketchbook that Ivy Dunleavy — who'd joined us at Moxie's insistence — had reluctantly opened on the table. Moxie's eyes gleamed, while fair-skinned Ivy blushed to the tips of her ears. "You are very talented, at least on paper."

"I'd like to think I'm as good with a needle and thread," Ivy said, but humbly, her pale lashes lowered over her blue-gray eyes. "I've been sewing for a long time. And I attended the Fashion Institute of Technology."

"Wow." Moxie nodded, clearly impressed, while I dared to glance at Ms. Bickelheim, who had spilled a container full of sugar across the counter.

"Are you sewing something for Ms. Bickelheim?" I asked, continuing to observe the flustered barista in the sparkly shirt. Given that she was at least as klutzy as me, and more scattered, to put it kindly, I wasn't sure how she managed to make such wonderful drinks. I was also eager to know if Ivy was responsible for any of her clothes. Not that Ms. Bickelheim wasn't pretty. Back in the day, she'd been quite striking. But her wardrobe seemed to be growing increasingly flamboyant as her personality became more erratic. "I saw you talking with her," I added, facing Ivy again. "Is she a . . . umm . . . client?"

Ivy seemed to grasp what I was trying to ask. She laughed, a soft, pretty sound. "No, I am *not* responsible for that interesting caftan." She hesitated. "Although, Ms. Bickelheim did hire me to make the costumes for the Sylvan Creek Players' production of *A Christmas Carol.*"

"Oh, how fun!" Moxie clasped her hands.

Apparently, she wasn't overly worried about being a suspect in CeeCee's death. She beamed at me. "Daphne is a veteran of that production, herself!"

Before meeting Moxie at Oh, Beans, I'd promised myself that I would politely but firmly say no if Ms. Bickelheim approached me about playing a ghost. And perhaps the role had finally been filled, because she'd made no attempt to offer me the part. I was pretty sure I was off the hook. Yet I suddenly grew edgy, just to be in the director's presence. "We don't really need to talk about that. . . ."

Moxie spoke right over me. "Have you heard about Daphne's outstanding portrayal of the Ghost of Christmas Present, a few years back?" she asked Ivy, even as she continued to flip through the sketchbook. When she turned a page, I spied a very unusual drawing. I couldn't imagine how a person would even wear the tartan-plaid garment, and I tilted my head, trying to imagine where I'd put my arms and legs. But before I could ask Ivy about the strange cross between a kilt and a cloak, Moxie flipped to another page, adding, "You must know the story about how the harness broke when Daphne was flying, right?" My best friend apparently still found the incident, which had terrified me, quite thrilling in a positive way. "No one had ever soared like that on a local stage!"

Ivy grinned at me. "I'm sure that was quite a sight. And it's a brand new tale, for me. Having just moved to town, I don't know many local legends, or people, yet."

I took a moment to look closely at Ivy again, which caused her to blush once more. Then, just as I was about to ask where she was from, and if there was a chance we'd ever met, Moxie turned another page in the sketchbook and cried, "Oh, Daphne! You *must* wear this to the ball!"

I wanted to see what Moxie was pointing to, but at that inopportune moment, Ms. Bickelheim fluttered over to us, her batwing sleeves flapping, and asked, in an excited voice, "Is Ivy showing you your costume, Daphne? Because I think it's going to be *just marvelous*!"

CHAPTER 12

"I have no idea why Ms. Bickelheim believes I've not only agreed to play the Ghost of Christmas Future, but actually *auditioned* — in costume," I told Artie, who was strapped into the front seat of my VW. Axis sat in the back, weaving sleepily after eating quite a few snacks at Flour Power, where I'd worked most of the day after leaving Oh, Beans. Glancing in the rearview mirror, I saw Axis's sleek, brown head bob, then jerk. I didn't know why he didn't just lie down. Then I returned my attention to the road and the Chihuahua, who was drooling right where Socrates usually sat, when he didn't inexplicably choose to stay home with a surly Persian cat and a snobby poodle. I'd stopped by Plum Cottage after leaving the bakery, to check on everyone, and he'd again refused to take a ride. "I never showed up at the high school auditorium wearing a black cloak and a skull mask," I added, again addressing Artie. "I think I'd remember that!"

"Yip!" Artie barked shrilly and wriggled on the seat, his brown eyes bulging with excitement. He loved costumes, even scary ones, and probably thought I should've dressed like the personification of Death and strolled onstage, seeking a role.

"Well, I think I'm stuck doing the play now," I informed him, steering the van carefully down the dark, narrow country road, which was lined with snow-covered pine trees. The VW's unpredictable heater was working overtime that night, and I tugged at my plaid scarf, feeling too warm. "I can't let Ms. Bickelheim — and the whole community — down!"

That was probably an exaggeration. The annual production of *A Christmas Carol,* always held at the high school, was probably the least popular of the town's many holiday events. Still, if Ms. Bickelheim honestly believed I'd accepted a key, if tiny and wordless, role, it hardly seemed nice to leave her high and dry.

"I'm not sure about the gown, either," I noted, turning off the main road onto a path that was nearly hidden by the trees. The van jolted and bumped, which caused one of the headlights to blink out, just for a moment. "It really is gorgeous on paper, but don't you think hiring someone to create a dress I'll only wear once is a little extravagant? It's not like when Moxie alters something for free."

Artie yipped again, and I could tell he thought I should commission Ivy to make the gown, which really had looked amazing. I was downplaying how pretty the dress had been — and how much I wanted to wear it to Bark the Halls.

"Vanity blossoms, but bears no fruit, as the old Nepalese proverb says," I reminded Artie, who strained at his harness when we drifted to a stop, right behind a black truck that was parked where the lane dead-ended. The Chihuahua paused in his attempt to slip out of his safety gear to bark at me again. "I know," I agreed, unclipping the harness. "That quote wasn't very relevant. I'm just trying to convince myself not to spend a lot of money on a frivolous outfit."

Artie, who had a short attention span, had lost interest in the conversation, so I got out of the warm VW, cringing when the cold air hit me. Then I went around to the passenger side and released both dogs, who bounded toward an A-frame log cabin that loomed against a sky dusted with swirling stars and smudged with smoke from a big stone chimney.

Seeing lights on inside the house, I followed Axis and Artie, my feet crunching loudly in the snow on that still night. Clomping up onto the porch, I pulled off one of my mittens and raised my hand to knock on the door, only to hesitate when my ears picked up another faint and unexpected sound.

As Jonathan Black opened the door before I could even rap, I asked him, with confusion, "Do I hear *sleigh bells?*"

CHAPTER 13

"Jonathan, this is amazing," I said, leaning against a split-rail fence he'd built behind his house — along with a rustic, pine barn that was the perfect complement to the cabin. The homespun, honey-colored structure replaced ugly, warehouse-like, corrugated-metal buildings that had housed a dog-training academy run by the property's former owner. It was difficult to believe those oversized sheds had ever existed on the snow-covered clearing where *three blanketed horses* — and two dogs — now played under the moonlight. And parked just inside the long, low-slung barn, visible under a soft spotlight, was a lacquered, black, old-fashioned sleigh, with a velvet seat and curved, red runners. I looked up at Jonathan, who was observing the horses with a half-smile on his handsome face. "When did you do all this? And I didn't know you rode!"

"Yale equestrian team," he said, surprising me with a glimpse into his past. Jonathan Black almost never referenced his personal history, unless I dragged the information out of him. I nearly fell over when he added, unprompted, "That is, I rode competitively before I dropped out of college to join the Navy."

I wanted to ask for more details, but before I could pick up my jaw, which had thudded to my boots, he answered my question about the renovations. "I built the barn and fencing piecemeal, with the help of two former convicts who needed work experience as they transition back into society."

I wasn't surprised that Jonathan had given ex-prisoners an opportunity. He was something of a mentor to a young, troubled, former murder suspect, who considered Jonathan like an older brother. "That was a really nice gesture," I told him.

He shrugged. "If you put people away, you probably have a responsibility to help them when they get out." His smile faded, and he looked out over the pasture again, speaking more softly. "The project ended up taking quite a while. Much longer than anticipated."

I felt like there was something he wasn't telling me. Something related to the delays.

"Jonathan . . . ?"

"As for the horses . . ." He spoke over me, pointing at the animals, two of which were lean and long-legged, standing at least eighteen-hands high. The other steed was a jet-black draft horse with a flowing mane and tail. When he pranced in the snow, he raised his hooves high, his steps exaggerated. Axis and Artie darted in and out between his legs, making me a little nervous, but it was obvious they all enjoyed the game. "The gray and chestnut thoroughbreds are mine," Jonathan explained. "But the draft horse — the Friesian — is on loan to pull the sleigh."

"Umm . . . pull the sleigh where?" I inquired, thinking I'd like a ride in the pretty vehicle.

Jonathan grinned at me, the corners of his eyes crinkling. "Sorry. I've said — and you've seen — too much." He lightly touched my arm and nodded toward the house behind us, where, through a wall of windows, I could see his floor-to-ceiling bookshelves and the fire roaring in the fireplace. "Plus, you're shivering. Let's go inside. Where you'll promise me that you won't mention the horse or the sleigh to anyone, quite yet."

I had no idea what the mystery was all

about, but I would do my best to keep my mouth shut until instructed otherwise. Then I realized that I shouldn't make any promises until I received something in return.

Pulling back slightly, I told Jonathan, "I'll keep quiet about your secret sleigh and horse, if you'll answer my questions about CeeCee's murder — and Moxie Bloom."

Jonathan hesitated for a long moment. So long that I thought he was going to tell me to trudge back to my van and be on my way.

Then he took my arm again and said, quietly and seriously, "Come on, Daphne. For once, I think we should discuss a murder — and the fact that your best friend seems determined to get herself convicted of the crime."

CHAPTER 14

"Is Moxie in serious trouble?" I asked Jonathan, who was opening a bottle of merlot. I sat across from him at his poured-concrete breakfast bar, perched on a surprisingly comfortable wood-and-metal, rustic-meets-industrial-chic stool. He hadn't put up a tree or set out any holiday knick-knacks, but the house — decorated by his professional-stylist ex, Elyse — was a winter wonderland in its own way, between the blazing fire, the hundreds of books waiting for snow-day reading, and the inviting, butter-soft, worn-leather furniture. Artie and Axis, tired from their adventures, were already curled up and sleeping on matching beds, which awaited them on a huge, faded, antique Turkish carpet that anchored and warmed the space. The scene was cozy, but I couldn't relax as I accepted the tumbler of deep-red wine that Jonathan slid across to me. "It sounded as if her interrogation went poorly."

Jonathan had been about to sip his own drink, but he set down the glass and dragged one hand down his jaw, which was stubbled. I could barely see the scar that always intrigued me. "Honestly, I shouldn't tell you any of this. But I suppose I'm starting to accept that the rules I learned at the police academy don't always — perhaps shouldn't always — apply in Sylvan Creek."

I grinned at him. "In other words, you're becoming a 'local'!"

"Let's not go that far," he said, resting back against the counter and crossing his arms over his chest. He wore a long-sleeved, pale-blue T-shirt that made his eyes look even deeper blue than usual and accented his biceps pretty nicely, too. A shock of his dark hair fell over his forehead. Moxie would've swooned and fallen off her stool, if she'd been there.

The thought of my friend brought me back to reality. "So, what's happening with Moxie?"

Jonathan inhaled deeply, then let out his breath with a sigh of frustration. "She would not stop incriminating herself. No matter how I tried to help her — which I have never done, with any other suspect — she kept rambling on about how CeeCee French had wronged her in high school, and how Spa and Paw would have been . . . maybe still will be . . . destroyed by the new store, if the plans go through."

I sat up straighter, while my heart went in the opposite direction, sinking fast. "You think we might still get a French's Poodles & More? Because I'd assumed that, with CeeCee gone, that plan would vanish, too."

Jonathan had opened his stainless-steel refrigerator and stuck his head inside, but he withdrew from the chilly compartment to shoot me a funny look. "Should I be questioning *you*?"

"Ha . . ." I started to laugh, only to realize that he was serious. "No. No, you shouldn't," I assured him, as he began searching the fridge again.

A few moments later, he emerged once more, this time with several varieties of cheese and a bunch of red grapes balanced in his hands. Setting all those items on the counter, he pulled a plate down from a cupboard. "French's Poodles is more than just CeeCee," he reminded me. "It's a national chain. I doubt that decisions about locating stores were — are — made on a whim. The plan that was unveiled at the theater had likely been in the works for months, if not longer. And her death probably won't signal the end of the company or the new store."

I hadn't considered any of that. CeeCee was such a force of nature that I'd imagined her running her stores like I ran Lucky Paws and Flour Power, making decisions alone and sometimes quickly. But, of course, that wouldn't have been the case with a national, publicly held corporation.

All at once, I realized that CeeCee's death's potential failure to impact the establishment of the Sylvan Creek franchise could be a good thing for Moxie and other local merchants, at least in terms of making them less likely suspects in her murder.

"So, it wouldn't make sense for Moxie, or Tessie, or anyone else to kill CeeCee to stop the store from coming here," I noted, watching Jonathan wash the grapes and add them to the plate. "It probably won't change anything."

His back was to me, and he shrugged his broad shoulders. "I can't assume that the killer thought things through. *You* assumed that Ms. French's death would signal the end of the store. And it's quite possible that whoever committed the crime was acting on pure impulse. From what I understand, based upon Elyse's report and other accounts, Celeste French knew that she was dropping a bombshell on the whole town, and she appeared quite pleased with herself."

That was all true.

Sipping my wine, I pictured chamber of commerce president Norm Alcorn's pale face when CeeCee had commandeered the Bijoux. "Still, how could Norm not have known anything?" I muttered softly. "Especially if the store had been in the works for months . . ."

"What's that?" Jonathan inquired, setting the plate, now laden with a richly veined blue cheese, a creamy wedge of goat cheese, a variety of crackers, and the grapes, onto the counter before me. "What did you say?"

"Nothing," I fibbed, but only because I didn't want to cast suspicion on Norm without real reason. I wasn't going to bring up the man I was almost certain I'd seen around town lately, either. Not until I was 100 percent sure of his identity, at which point I'd probably have to tell Jonathan — and Moxie. In the meantime, I reached for a knife that Jonathan had also provided and cut myself a sliver of the pungent Roquefort, adding that to a cracker. Then I smiled at my host, who was well aware of my fondness for cheese. "It's almost like you knew I was coming."

"Someone's been murdered, and, as usual, members of your cohort are involved," he reminded me, leaning back again. "Even if you hadn't watched the dogs — whom I should've picked up earlier . . . my apologies — I knew you'd show up at some point."

I spoke through a mouthful of the best blue I'd ever tried, covering my mouth so I wouldn't spray him with cracker crumbs. "This really was for me?"

"I *do* owe you for taking care of Artie and Ax when I was in a bind," he said, downplaying his thoughtful gesture. "So I thought I'd pay you in your favorite currency — curds — and knock fifty more dollars off your debt, too."

"Aw, thanks," I said, smearing another cracker with goat cheese and topping that with a grape. "We must be about even, by now."

He picked up his glass and raised it to me. "Let's call the debt settled."

"Deal," I said, lifting my glass, too. We clinked and sipped. "And I don't think I'll be borrowing from you again, any time soon," I noted. "Along with selling a lot of pet treats this year, and keeping my books, with the help of Fidelia Tutweiler . . ."

Jonathan lowered a skeptical eyebrow at the mention of my part-time accountant, who was also one of his former murder suspects. However, I trusted Fidelia and didn't acknowledge his obvious doubts.

". . . I also have a very exclusive client right now," I informed him. "And I expect that I'll be paid handsomely to watch her."

Jonathan had been popping some grapes into his mouth, but he paused, his eyebrows arched. "You've got the poodle from the commercials?"

I nodded and took another sip of the wine, which was smooth, earthy, and warming. "Yes, Jeff Updegrove dropped off Snowdrop — who is as icy as her name — sometime this morning. I found her . . ." I suddenly realized that I was about to admit that my door had been unlocked, and quickly skipped ahead to, ". . . with an envelope full of what I assume are instructions and paperwork related to her care."

Jonathan glanced at Axis and Artie. "So, Socrates stayed home with the cat whose name I'd rather not speak, because it makes me feel ridiculous, and a high-strung canine celebrity, rather than come here with Artie and Axis?"

"I thought it was weird, too," I agreed, reaching for more of the blue cheese. Jonathan wasn't indulging, and I wouldn't want it to go to waste. "And speaking of weird . . . Don't you think it's odd that Jeff had to race off, right after his boss's death?"

"Yes, I agree," Jonathan said. "And his alibi, which places him alone in a room at the Sylvan Creek Hotel, isn't exactly airtight — unlike your friend Tessie Flinchbaugh's. You'll be happy to know that Tessie was at that new coffee shop, Oh, Beans" — he rolled his eyes at the name — "where her laptop records and the barista —"

I sat up straighter. "Bitsy Bickelheim? My former English teacher, now director?"

Jonathan appeared confused. "No. Her name was Jane Landon. And what do you mean by 'director'?"

My cheeks flushed with more than the wine. "I might've agreed to play the Ghost of Christmas Future in the Sylvan Creek Players' production of *A Christmas Carol.*"

I could tell that Jonathan was picturing me in a big, black robe, because he covered his mouth and pretended to cough, to hide his laughter.

I waved my hand, urging him to move past the image. "Anyhow, about Tessie . . ."

"Oh, yes," he said, his eyes still gleaming with poorly concealed mirth. "It seems pretty clear that Tessie Flinchbaugh was

118

shopping extensively on a Web site called 'seasonal sweaters dot-com' at the time of the murder."

"That makes sense," I said, with a rush of relief on Tessie's behalf. She and Tom had already endured one emotional homicide investigation. "Getting back to Jeff," I said. "Did you know that Moxie and I went to school with him?"

Jonathan nodded. "Yes. He mentioned that you were all classmates. Which didn't surprise me in the least, since you tend to have a history with every suspect, in every homicide I investigate." He paused for a long time, and I could tell he was debating whether to ask me for background on Jeff. Then he sighed again and said, "Go ahead. Tell me what you know about him."

I grabbed a grape and popped it into my mouth, talking while I chewed. "First of all, I don't think he remembered me at all, when I saw him at the Bijoux, which was kind of insulting."

"And surprising, if not exactly pertinent," Jonathan noted.

I wasn't sure if he thought I was memorable in a good way or a bad way, so I forged ahead. "But from what *I* recall about *Jeff,* he was always the guy who tried really hard, but never quite excelled."

Jonathan took some more grapes, too, and tossed them absently in the palm of his hand. "How so?"

"He was on student council, but, while CeeCee was president, Jeff held one of those offices nobody even understands, like sergeant at arms."

Jonathan finally swallowed the fruit. "Or parliamentarian."

I nodded briskly. "Yes! Exactly! I think he was that . . . thingy."

Jonathan, who'd probably been class president in a string of foreign schools, leaned forward, resting his arms on the counter, so we were eye to eye. "Go on."

"And while CeeCee was valedictorian, Jeff was . . ." I couldn't recall the title of the person who came in second, in terms of class rank, either.

Jonathan supplied the word. "Salutatorian."

I snapped my fingers. "Yes! That was Jeff. Always striving, but never quite matching up to CeeCee, especially."

Jonathan leaned back again and frowned. "Yet he took a job with her company, right out of business school, and *did* work his way up. . . ."

"But not to the top," I noted. Outside, one of the horses whinnied. The happy sound contrasted sharply with a dark thought that had just crossed my mind. "Maybe CeeCee hired him because she liked keeping Jeff under her thumb. Maybe it amused her, on some level, to dangle promotions in front of her old rival, keeping him with the company, but knowing that he'd never be in her top spot, as founder of the French's empire."

"That would be diabolical," Jonathan observed, picking up his wineglass and swirling the liquid as he considered my theory. "And slightly farfetched."

"Maybe so," I agreed. "But I will say that she seemed happy to wield power over her 'assistant.' "

Jonathan rubbed the back of his neck with his free hand. "Yes, and Updegrove was quick to admit that there was no love lost between him and his boss."

I shifted on my seat, growing intrigued. "How about an alibi?"

"He *claimed* he was alone in the Sylvan Creek Hotel, watching Snowdrop, at the time of the murder," Jonathan said. "Not exactly an airtight story. Especially since he says he had no idea where Celeste was going when she asked him to keep the dog for a few hours."

"Where do you think she was going?"

"I haven't pieced that together yet," Jonathan admitted. "And without a real timeline, or a weapon, I didn't have enough evidence to force Updegrove to stick around. I had no choice but to let him leave town. However, his parents still live in Sylvan Creek, and I have an address for him in California. Hopefully, I can find him if necessary."

"If he doesn't fly off to some foreign country."

"Believe me, I've thought of that," Jonathan agreed. "But for now, he's assured me that his next trip will be back to Sylvan Creek for holiday celebrations with his family and French's memorial service."

Jonathan didn't sound convinced that Jeff would return, and I again wondered how long I'd be watching Snowdrop. I hoped the answer lay in the envelope that was waiting at Plum Cottage, where I needed to return — after trying one more time to get some assurance, regarding Moxie.

"Jonathan?" I ventured. "When you said you tried to help Moxie . . ."

He frowned. "Please, don't ever mention that outside of this house. Doebler already thinks I've lost my edge."

"My lips are sealed," I promised, although I couldn't imagine Jonathan's partner ever losing respect for his younger, but more assertive, colleague. "But, just between us, about Moxie . . ."

Jonathan lowered his head for a moment and rubbed his eyes, as if he was getting tired. Then he met my gaze again and said, "I know she has motive, and her alibi is . . . nothing. But I can't help but find it difficult to believe that Moxie Bloom could kill anyone."

"Yet, you thought Piper —"

He raised one hand, silencing me. "I was new to Sylvan Creek then. And I'm not telling you that I'm dismissing Moxie as a suspect. But, to some degree, I trust my gut when it comes to killers." He dragged one hand through his hair, a gesture that made me think he was a little frustrated with himself for not being completely objective. Or maybe he was just thinking about Moxie's haircuts and shaves, because he added, "And the woman who cried once when she nicked me with a razor . . . the one who loves a *rat* . . . It's honestly almost impossible for me to believe she committed homicide."

I felt another rush of relief, until he concluded, grimly, "Although, I won't rule out that possibility if the evidence leads that way."

I knew that he was just being honest, and, with one last, wistful glance at the cheese, I hopped off the stool. "Thanks for at least admitting that it's hard to imagine Moxie as a killer. That's reassuring."

Jonathan followed me to the door. The dogs were so tired they didn't even rouse when the wide-plank floors creaked under our feet. We paused in the foyer, and I reached for my coat, which he'd tossed onto a bench. "Remember," Jonathan said, "nothing we discussed this evening — neither the sleigh nor the case — should be mentioned once you leave here."

Folding the coat over my arm, I looked out the window and saw that snow was falling softly on the pasture and the horses were gone, likely seeking shelter in the barn. Then I met Jonathan's eyes again, and I saw that he appeared concerned.

"I never asked if you were okay, after finding CeeCee," he said quietly. "All joking aside, I know that discovering bodies isn't something you ever really get used to." A dark shadow formed in his eyes. "Especially when the deceased is someone you know and have a history with." I was sure a part of him was back on a battlefield. "I wanted to check in with you," he continued, "but I went straight to work, and then had to deal with Moxie."

"I'm fine," I assured him, although I had been unnerved by the sight of CeeCee's corpse. I shook off the memory of her red shoe, and the red blood, in the snow. Then I recalled a little red sweater I'd spied, too. "Whatever happened to the dog at the scene?" I asked. "Did you try to catch him? Or did he run away?"

Jonathan gave me a sharp look. "If you saw Snowdrop — who is female, right? — that would poke a big hole in Updegrove's story."

"No, not the poodle," I said. "The pug. In the 'bah, hum-pug' sweater."

He clearly wasn't following. "Pug?"

I nodded. "Yes, the small, tan-and-black dog with the mischievous eyes." He continued to look askance at me, so I gave up. "Never mind. I seem to be the only one who can see him!"

I thought Jonathan was going to rest the back of his hand against my forehead, checking me for a fever. He actually raised his hand — then dropped it to his side. He didn't seem to know what to say, and we stood in silence for a moment, the only sound in the house the crackling fire, while I again flashed back to the previous night, when we'd stood before the town Christmas tree. Only this time, I wasn't thinking about murder. I was recalling the mixture of warmth and anticipation and nervousness I'd felt when we'd been close to each other in the frosty park.

He'd wanted to ask me a question then. One that was still on his mind. I could tell by the way he was looking at me that he had something to say.

"Jonathan? You wanted to ask me something, on our walk," I prompted softly, studying his expression. "What was it?"

He opened his mouth to reply — just as *both* our phones started making noise.

"Sorry," he apologized, pulling his cell from the back pocket of his worn jeans. He checked the screen. "I have to take this. It's Vonda Shakes."

"Sure. Of course." While he turned away, speaking quietly with the local coroner, I retrieved my phone, which was stashed in my pocket, and read a text from Gabriel.

Meet me at town tree, half hour.

As always, fate had intervened to put a stop to whatever had been about to transpire between Jonathan Black and me. As I tucked my phone away, I wondered if the universe knew best. And when Jonathan tapped his screen, ending his call, I knew that we weren't going to resume our discussion. Clearly, something had gone wrong.

"What's the matter?" I asked, worried about his very grim expression. "What happened?"

He stared out the window for a moment, as if he couldn't decide whether he should confide in me. Then he faced me again and said, "Vonda believes that her team has matched the wounds that Celeste French suffered with a type of tool, if not the exact weapon used in the crime."

I swallowed thickly, not liking the grave tone of his voice. "And that weapon would be . . ."

"Scissors," he said. "Perhaps the kind a beautician — or dog groomer — might use."

CHAPTER 15

"Sorry I've been out of touch," I told Gabriel, who was pacing just beyond a line of yellow crime scene tape that ringed the Christmas tree in Pettigrew Park. The snow around the tree was trampled down and muddy. And, down the street, a dark sedan and Jonathan's truck were parked across from Moxie's apartment, near the Pinkney's Pines hut, where Brett Pinkney was unloading a truck full of trees to sell the next day. A fourth deceptively nondescript vehicle sat in front of Spa and Paw.

I assumed that Moxie was being taken in for questioning again, and her business, at least, scoured for a possible weapon. Moments after getting the call from Vonda Shakes, Jonathan had walked me to my van, his hand lightly, perhaps apologetically, on my back while he made phone calls, telling someone he needed a warrant, right away, to search Moxie's salon and apartment.

Then, after taking a momentary break to let me know that he'd follow me, to make sure my old VW didn't break down halfway to Sylvan Creek, he'd called Detective Doebler, too.

They'd still been talking when he'd climbed into his truck, headed to Moxie's to meet his partner.

I stared down Market Street, hoping Moxie's prized tools wouldn't have to be confiscated, and wondering when the detectives and my best friend would emerge into the frosty, moonlit night.

I was also trying to figure out why Jonathan had told me about the coroner's findings, and I thought I knew the reason.

He wants me to protect Moxie. He'd never admit that, or urge me to investigate, but it's true. . . .

"You're right here, but still 'out of touch,' " Gabriel said, lightly tapping my shoulder to get my attention. I turned to see that he was grinning at me, the corners of his dark eyes crinkled with amusement. Then he looked past me and frowned. "What's going on over by the Philosopher's Tome and Spa and Paw that's got you so distracted?"

I *hated* lying, but I didn't want news of Moxie's second interrogation winding up in the *Gazette,* so I crossed my fingers inside my big, knitted mittens and said, "Nothing important, really."

That was hopefully *kind of* true. The actual questioning would almost certainly take place at the police station, and there was no way the murder weapon was at Moxie's home or business.

"So, why are we at Pettigrew Park after dark?" I asked Gabriel, stepping around him, so he'd follow me and stop watching Moxie's home. I knew he'd dart off if Jonathan, Detective Doebler, and Moxie emerged while he was still looking in that direction. "Why did you ask me to meet you here?"

"I know that you're going to investigate CeeCee French's murder, if you haven't already started on behalf of your best friend," he told me, jerking his head in the direction of the Philosopher's Tome, where colored lights glowed in the third-floor windows. I suspected that Moxie had been working on her gingerbread re-creation of Sylvan Creek when Jonathan and Detective Doebler had arrived. I'd tried to text her, to warn her that they were coming — Jonathan hadn't made me promise to do otherwise — but she hadn't answered. I knew my best friend well, and I was almost certain that she'd been too busy piping white icing and propping up cookie walls to bother with her phone. "There's no way you're going to let Black railroad Moxie Bloom," Gabriel noted, surprising me by adding, "especially since she's being taken in for a *second* round of questioning."

I felt my cheeks get warm, in spite of the fact that the temperature seemed to be dropping. Our breath came out in puffs. "How did you know?"

Gabriel, who'd no doubt faced a lot of competition for scoops, back when he'd been a top crime reporter in Philadelphia, didn't seem to mind that I'd misdirected him. He continued to smile. "Let's just say I have sources."

"Who . . . ?"

He didn't answer the question. Instead, he told me, "Plus, I saw Black and Doebler go into Moxie's building, right around the time you arrived. I don't think they're buying old books after hours, or making a social call on a murder suspect. And I spied two uniformed cops, who pulled up in a plain car and entered Spa and Paw — where I'll be headed next. Although, I'm not in a huge hurry to get stonewalled by any of the local law enforcement professionals."

My heart sank. "You're not going to

print . . ."

Gabriel raised both of his hands, one of which held his trusty Nikon. "I make no promises. Especially since some *huge* news outlets are about to swoop down on this town at any moment. While I can't imagine Moxie Bloom hurting a flea, and think everyone down the street is barking up the wrong tree — forgive the two pet-related clichés — this story is pretty big, Daphne. Most people didn't know CeeCee French from Adam, but she was rich. And rich counts with the media."

"I know," I agreed, my shoulders slumping with resignation. The rational part of my brain understood that Gabriel was a journalist and had to report every development in such an important story — just like Jonathan had to follow every lead, even though he didn't believe Moxie was a killer, either. Still, it was sometimes difficult to separate the men I knew personally from the jobs they had to do. "I'm glad I'm a pet sitter," I muttered. "There are fewer conflicts of interest."

"You're also an amateur detective, who was practically at the scene of the crime," Gabriel pointed out. He cocked his head. "What did you see? And what have you dug up so far?"

"All I saw were CeeCee's shoes — and a naughty little pug, who seems to show up everywhere, although only I ever see him."

"You . . . You're seeing another ghost dog?" Gabriel asked, referencing a spectral Saint Bernard who was said to haunt the woods around Lake Wallapawakee. For a moment, I thought Gabriel might reach out to rest the back of *his* hand against my forehead, checking if I had a fever. But, like Jonathan, he refrained. "How many canine phantoms can one town handle?"

"The bah, hum-pug is a real dog," I insisted, immediately wishing I hadn't used the pun from the pup's sweater. The reference only seemed to baffle Gabriel more. "And he's more like a canine elf on the shelf — showing up and doing mischief — than a haunting poltergeist."

" *'Elf on the shelf'?"*

I'd completely lost him, and I gave up. "The point is, I didn't see much of anything, the night of CeeCee's murder. And I haven't done any investigating. Yet." As the icy breeze off the creek riffled Gabriel's dark, longish hair, I watched him for some sign of secrecy, or smug superiority. "How about you?"

"I've just started digging around, quite literally." Before I could ask what he meant, he gestured around the park. "I've been searching high and low for the murder weapon, which gut instinct tells me was ditched here."

I tilted my head and felt the puffball on the top of my knit cap jiggle. "Why do you think that?"

"This is a dark but public place to commit homicide," he pointed out. "I think there's a good chance someone would toss the weapon and run." He nodded toward the creek, which ran like a black slash through the park. "I wouldn't be surprised if the knife is in the water."

"Knife?" I realized that I probably had a bit more information than he did. "How do you know that's what you're looking for?"

"Well, the weapon was something with a blade," he said. "I understand that French was stabbed." He hesitated, then asked, almost too casually. "You saw blood on the snow, right?"

"I don't want to be interviewed," I told him, folding my arms around myself.

Gabriel narrowed his eyes at me. "Do you know something you're holding back, since you're pretty tight with Black? What are the cops searching for at Moxie's salon?"

As he asked that, he glanced past me, and I turned to catch a glimpse of Jonathan entering Spa and Paw, while Detective Doebler's sedan rumbled to life. I wondered if Moxie was inside the car, because the windows of her apartment were now dark. Brett Pinkney was gone, too, and the trees he'd dropped off were still baled, as if he'd been in a hurry.

Meeting Gabriel's gaze again, I decided I wouldn't lie a second time. But I wouldn't tell him everything I knew, either. "I do know a little bit about what's happening tonight. But you'll have to ask your other 'sources' for details. I don't think I'm supposed to divulge anything."

Gabriel might've left Philadelphia because he was tired of constantly covering homicides. But a part of him still enjoyed the challenge of solving crimes. However, the spark of friendly competition I'd seen in his eyes suddenly flickered out. "All joking about you and Black aside," he said, "what's going on there?"

I couldn't help looking down the street one more time. Jonathan's truck was still there, along with the unmarked car. Either he was supervising the uniformed officers in the salon, or he'd ridden with Detective Doebler, and probably Moxie, to the police station. Detective Doebler's sedan was gone. Then I turned back to Gabriel, who'd slung his camera around his neck and buried his hands in the pockets of his rust-colored down vest.

"There's nothing 'going on' with me and Jonathan," I said, not quite sure if that was true. At least, I thought something might've happened . . . something small, like an invitation to lunch or a movie . . . if our phones — and destiny — hadn't seemed determined, as always, to keep us apart. Then again, I still had no idea what, if anything, was transpiring between Jonathan and his ex-wife, nor why his year had been "challenging," and I shrugged. "There's really nothing but a fits-and-starts friendship between me and Jonathan. Not that it's really any of your business. You and I aren't exactly a couple, either!"

I kept that reminder light, and I was glad Gabriel laughed. "You're right. My questions were nosy and out of line."

"So, do you want to keep searching for the weapon?" I suggested, because that activity intrigued me. In fact, finding the scissors used in the murder might help me clear Moxie's name. I knew that she was very particular about the tools of her trade. Then I thought about Snowdrop, Tinkleston, and Socrates, all waiting at Plum Cottage, and added, "Although, I can only stay for a few minutes."

Gabriel didn't jump to accept my offer to help with his search. Nor did he ask why I needed to rush off. Instead, by the light of the same, now somewhat disheveled, Christmas tree where I'd recently stood with Jonathan, he posed a different question. One that caught me off guard more than it should have.

"Forget the murder for a minute," he said. "I really called you here to finally ask a question I tried to get out the other day, only to get coffee spilled down the front of my pants."

I couldn't help grinning at the image, which was comical, in retrospect. "What did you want to ask?"

Gabriel assumed a mock air of formality, but I sensed that he was serious when he inquired, "Will you do me the honor of attending the Bark the Halls Ball with me?"

"I guess I will need a dress without a tomato-sauce stain now that I have a date," I whispered under my breath as I walked down the dark street toward my van, which I'd parked near Flour Power. I'd intended to stop in the bakery, just for a moment, to stock the glass case with some treats I'd left cooling in the kitchen, but I really needed to check on the dogs and Tinkleston, so I abandoned that plan in favor of heading straight home.

As I crossed the street, headed for the VW, I saw a faint light gleaming in the window of Ivy Dunleavy's shop, and I wondered if she was working on the big, black cloak I'd soon wear onstage.

I also couldn't help noting that Jonathan's truck was still parked on the otherwise empty road, near the trees Brett Pinkney had hastily dumped by the hut, without setting them on their display stands.

Jonathan *must've* ridden to the station with Detective Doebler and Moxie. And apparently they weren't done talking yet. Moxie's apartment was still dark.

"Poor Moxie," I mumbled, digging in my pockets for my keys. I stepped up to the VW. "I hope she's . . . Hey!"

My soft-spoken comment ended in a shout as a little pug in a red sweater darted out from beneath my van. The adorable, if troublemaking, dog gazed up at me with his bulging eyes, and his curly tail whipped back and forth on his wriggling behind. His pink tongue darted in and out when he breathed.

"Who in the world are you?" I asked, bending to let him sniff my hand.

That was when I realized he'd dropped an object at my feet. Something shiny and silver, which lay right in front of my favorite cowgirl boots. Then, yipping three times, his voice high and excited, he scampered away on his stubby legs.

I wanted to chase the pup and check for a collar under his high-necked sweater, so I could possibly help him get home, but my feet seemed rooted in place.

It was almost as if they'd been speared to the ground by the *razor-sharp scissors* that glittered on the pavement, the menacing-looking blades twinkling like the bulbs that were strung in the bare branches above me.

But those scissors . . . They didn't fill me with holiday cheer.

On the contrary, as I stared down at them, I suffered an icy, growing sensation of dread, deep in the pit of my stomach.

Chapter 16

The whole time I was creeping down the alley that ran behind Flour Power and Spa and Paw, I could hear Piper's voice in my head, telling me to contact Jonathan immediately about the scissors, which I'd carefully tucked into one of the clean plastic doggy-doo bags that I kept in my van.

"Don't meddle, Daphne," my sensible sister kept saying in my imagination, as I nevertheless approached the back door to Spa and Paw, which was dark and silent in the wake of the officers' departure.

"This will only take a minute," I continued the one-sided conversation, trying to convince imaginary Piper — and myself — that I was doing the right thing. Then I twisted the knob, which spun, allowing me entry to Moxie's shop.

Moxie Bloom was better than me when it came to locking up, but not by much, and I wasn't surprised that the door was open.

Needless to say, the police officers, under Jonathan's supervision, had locked the front door, which I'd tried first.

Slipping inside the retro space, I inhaled the familiar odors of dye and bleach and the peppermint-scented shampoo that Moxie always used during the holidays, for people and pets. Then I absently reached for a light switch on the wall, only to catch myself at the last moment. Instead, I dug into one of my barn jacket's pockets and pulled out my cell phone.

Swiping the screen, I found the flashlight app and shined the beam toward the floor, moving quickly to the cheerful, red 1950s metal cabinet Moxie used to store all her prized styling tools. Using my sleeve to cover my hand, I opened the narrow, top drawer, which held an array of scissors arranged carefully by size on a black velvet cloth.

"Oh, no," I whispered, shining the light into the drawer. It was quite obvious that one of the larger pairs was missing. There was a distinct empty spot on the velvet.

I knew that my best friend was innocent, but my hands still shook as I set down the phone and pulled the plastic bag from my pocket, knowing that I shouldn't handle potential evidence. But I had to know if the scissors the pug had dropped at my feet matched the set that was missing from the drawer, at least by my layperson's estimation.

The bag crinkled loudly when I uncovered part of the shiny, silver tool, being careful not to touch it, and my heart was thudding in my chest, too. Which was probably why I hadn't heard a car pull up outside and found myself standing there, caught red-handed, when Jonathan Black opened the back door and stepped into the salon, joining me.

Switching on the light I'd avoided using, so I could see his grim expression, he said, in a low, grave tone of voice, "Please tell me you're not holding a previously *missing* pair of Edelstein 'ultimate curved' shears featuring Japanese molybdenum alloy blades that are cryogenically tempered for long-lasting durability."

Fingers still trembling slightly, I took a moment to look carefully at the object in my hand, noting the maker's name, engraved in tiny letters on the handle.

Then I swallowed thickly and told Jonathan, "I'm not sure about the molybdenum or the cryogenic part, but I'm afraid these do match at least part of your description."

He didn't say a word. He just kept staring

at me, until I broke the silence, asking, hopefully, "I don't suppose you'd believe that a troublemaking, elfin pug in an anti-Christmas sweater delivered these to my feet, would you?"

Jonathan still didn't speak. Yet it was clear, from the set of his jaw, that the answer was no.

CHAPTER 17

"This is not good," I said, shaking my head and tramping up onto my porch at Plum Cottage. The temperature felt like it had dropped about ten degrees during the ride home, probably because the VW's heater was being temperamental again that night. I still suffered an icy feeling in my core, too, as I relived my attempt to convince Jonathan that my tale about the pug was true. We'd parted with Jonathan telling me to leave Spa and Paw, so he could think about how to explain the sudden appearance of Moxie's previously missing scissors without having to take me in for official questioning — which was not an option he'd ruled out. "Nope," I sighed, opening my front door. "Not good at all!"

Truer words were never spoken.

Stepping inside my snug, toasty home, I took a moment to let my eyes adjust to the surprisingly dim room, which was lit only by some embers glowing in the fireplace, although I'd been pretty sure I'd left the Christmas tree plugged in.

Then I spied a sad heap in the corner of the living room and cried, "Oh, you poor thing!"

"Well, we'll definitely need a new tree," I told Socrates, Tinkleston, and Snowdrop. Not that Snowdrop would acknowledge me. While I had freed Tinks from the mangled pine, where I'd found him tangled up in the lights, just like Moxie had been, the haughty poodle had retreated to her posh, oversized carrier. She sat just inside the arched entrance with her nose in the air — although I was pretty sure I caught her eyes rolling in my direction now and then.

Socrates, meanwhile, kept pacing back and forth, his head low and his ears swaying, as if he were trying to shake off the evening's events. And Tinks, once liberated, had leapt onto the mantel, where he was hissing like a broken teakettle. His back was arched and his tail stood straight up, so my festive display of greenery and deep-red candles took on a Halloween air.

"Enough," I chided him, but gently, because I was pretty sure he'd been provoked into destroying the already woebegone tree. Propping my broom near the fireplace, I paused in cleaning up the last needles and dared to stroke his back, a gesture he endured, for once. "Calm down, okay?"

Tinks seemed to heed my advice. Hopping down from the mantel, he retreated on his puffball paws to his usual spot on the kitchen windowsill without so much as a glance at Snowdrop, who made a point of not looking at the cat, either.

"This must've been quite an evening," I told Socrates, who'd finally sat down near the fire. "I know you're not to blame, but maybe you can offer some insights into what really happened . . . ?"

My voice trailed off, because I realized that Socrates wasn't listening to me. His gaze was trained on Snowdrop, and he had a funny, dreamy look in his droopy eyes.

I nudged him with my leg, compelling him to look up at me. "You're not star struck, are you?" I teased. The comment was ridiculous, because Socrates was not impressed by fame nor fortune. Still, he'd been so lost in thought that I joked, "You looked a little bit like a teenager with a crush on a pop star!"

Socrates could contain his emotions better than Jonathan Black, which was saying something, but I swore that my favorite baleful basset hound looked sheepish when I said that.

"I'm just kidding," I assured him, with another nudge. Then I moved to Snowdrop's carrier and knelt down. The pampered poodle edged around, showing me her back, but I knew she was listening. "Hey," I said, in a soothing voice. "Are you sure you don't want to come out and eat something? I'm not a fancy Beverly Hills chef, but I do make my own food. It's good."

I could barely see Snowdrop's face, but I was pretty sure I glimpsed a pink tongue licking her muzzle, like she was hungry.

However, she wasn't about to deign to eat whatever I cooked yet, let alone socialize.

"Suit yourself," I said, rising and nearly bumping into the small table that held the manila envelope, which I still hadn't opened.

"Maybe there's something in there about your diet," I said, again addressing Snowdrop, while I snatched up the envelope and tore open one end, messing up the note that Jeff Updegrove had hastily scrawled before disappearing. "Or, at the very least, I'll find some information that will tell me how to take care of you."

Needless to say, Snowdrop didn't reply from her crystal-encrusted cave, so I went to the kitchen and dumped the envelope's contents onto the slightly bigger table there — only to discover that Jeff hadn't provided me with any instructions related to the persnickety pup, or even contact information, in case I needed to get in touch with him.

The only things he'd left — aside from the dog — were a key, stamped with a tiny number 37 and attached to a thin, burgundy velvet ribbon, and something I already owned, but had lost track of ages ago. A puzzling artifact, which he'd likely taken from his parents' garage or attic — because, no matter how strong Jeff's school spirit might've been, back in the day, I doubted he traveled with his copy of the Sylvan Creek High *Magical Memories* yearbook, dating back to our senior year.

Turning over the familiar, nostalgia-inducing volume, I discovered a sticky note, which didn't exactly explain why he'd given me a book filled with old pictures.

In fact, all it said was, *"I believe you may find this helpful."*

Which really wasn't helpful at all.

CHAPTER 18

"I hate to admit it, but it sounds as if Moxie is in deep trouble," Piper said, unwrapping one of the tamales she'd purchased at my favorite Mexican restaurant, Casita Burrito.

Chef and owner Sofia Medina only made the time-consuming treats at Christmastime, and the batches usually sold out shortly after noon each day. Fortunately, my sister had swooped in early that snowy morning and bought a half-dozen of the pork and vegetarian varieties, as well as three cups of Sofia's special *ponche navideño,* which was a hot, holiday fruit punch made with Mexican hawthorn, apples, guava, and cinnamon. The small feast was set up at Flour Power, where Mom had also joined us for lunch.

The storm outside was bad enough that Piper's appointments and Mom's showings were being canceled, and my shop's door hadn't opened in over an hour. Still, we ate gathered at the counter, instead of in the kitchen, so I could keep an eye out for customers. Plus, the view of Market Street, out my front window, was quite charming as the snow frosted the town.

"I wish Moxie — and Socrates and Snowdrop — would've joined us," I said, pushing aside a basket of Christmas-tree-shaped dog cookies, so we'd have more room for our plates. The treats, studded with tiny dried-cranberry "ornaments" reminded me of the Charlie Brown tree that I'd returned to the forest near Plum Cottage, and I momentarily crossed my fingers, hoping everything would be okay while I was away for the day. I also made a mental note to stop by Brett Pinkney's lot, down the street, to pick up another pine on my way home.

"Where are Moxie and the dogs?" Piper asked, untying a thin strand of cornhusk from around one of the tamales, which looked like rustic, wrapped gifts. "I hardly ever see you without Socrates!"

"Moxie understandably claimed she was too tired after defending herself to Jonathan and Detective Doebler last night," I informed Piper and my mother, who was picking delicately at the masa and meat on her plate. Mom was always wary of "foreign food," even if it was made a few blocks away. "She wanted to use her snow day cancellations to stay home and work on her elaborate, nighttime, gingerbread re-creation of Sylvan Creek."

Since no one even bothered to raise an eyebrow over my comment about the cookie village, I moved on to answer Piper's question about the dogs. "As for Socrates and Snowdrop — when the poodle refused to come along, by burrowing into her posh crate, Socrates decided to stay behind, too. He seems to have some sort of clinical fascination with our resident star."

"Hmm . . . Do you think it's just clinical?" Piper mused, a funny smile tugging at the corners of her lips.

I had no idea what she was talking about. "What?"

"I saw Socrates gazing raptly at Snowdrop, at the theater," Piper said, breaking into a full-fledged grin. "And, while I don't normally ascribe human feelings to canines, I'll admit that Socrates is rather special —"

"What are you getting at?"

"I think Socrates is in love," Piper said, her eyes twinkling behind the lenses of her wire-rimmed spectacles. "To the degree that dogs are capable of romantic feelings."

I couldn't believe my sensible sibling had just admitted that animals might fall in love

— something I was convinced was true. But she was dead wrong about Socrates and Snowdrop.

"You have got to be kidding!" I cried, through a mouthful of masa. I raised my hands to my lips, but kept talking. "Those two are complete opposites!"

Piper's gaze cut to the bamboo plant. "Yes," she noted slyly. "Those types sometimes attract."

"You and Roger are cut from the same cloth," I pointed out, knowing full well that Piper was talking about me and Jonathan. I appreciated that my newly-in-love sister wanted me to find the type of happiness she shared with her boyfriend. But, honestly, I almost wished she'd go back to rolling her eyes at my strange relationship with Jonathan Black, and I shifted the conversation back to the dogs. "And we're talking about Socrates, here. There's no way he has the slightest interest in a snobby canine actress!"

"Your dog is not in love, Daphne." My mother ended the debate with a firm pronouncement that overlooked the fact that Piper had made that claim, not me. She waggled her fingers dismissively. "The whole idea is ridiculous!"

Maeve Templeton didn't care about canines, who couldn't sign leases or apply for mortgages. She was, however, concerned about me — or, more accurately, about how my increasing involvement in CeeCee French's homicide investigation would reflect upon her.

"Poodles and scissors and yearbooks from classmates!" she added, sounding like a disgruntled Julie Andrews, singing "My Favorite Things." But clearly, those items did not please my mother at all, and I regretted an earlier mention of the curious objects Jeff Updegrove had given me, one of which was in my pocket. For some reason, I was carrying around the key, although I still had no idea what it was supposed to unlock. Then Mom shook her head, her too-asymmetrical bob swinging. "Why must you be involved in such strange, and public, mysteries, Daphne?"

"I'm honestly trying to stay out of this, publicly," I said, sipping the punch. The blend of exotic and familiar flavors momentarily whisked me away to a Christmas I'd spent in the pretty Mexican town of Zacatecas. I set down the paper cup. "I haven't even spoken to Gabriel about the case."

"Well, he's still covering it extensively," Piper said, reaching for her phone, which she'd set on the counter near her paper plate. She tapped the screen a few times and held it out for Mom and me to see. "There's a picture of poor Moxie exiting the police station last night."

"Oh, no," I groaned, studying the image, in which my best friend was descending the steps at the station. She wore a pair of elvish, red-and-white-striped tights, fur-topped boots, and the vintage green coat she'd worn to the Bijoux. "Do you think the fact that Moxie's smiling and waving — no doubt greeting Gabriel — makes her look innocent, or like a heartless killer?"

"Hmmm . . ." Mom's lack of an answer spoke for itself, and, although I knew that Gabriel was just doing his job, for a split second, I suffered a flash of frustration with him. We seemed much more compatible when he wasn't covering murders that involved people I loved.

"I honestly don't know if the shot does Moxie a disservice or not," Piper said, setting down the phone and picking up her fork. She scooped up a healthy bite of her tamale. "It could go either way. But I do think she should get a lawyer about now."

"Yes, you're probably right," I reluctantly agreed. I'd been so reassured by Jonathan's belief in Moxie's innocence that I hadn't thought much about lawyers, even when she'd been questioned a second time. I'd

154

kind of assumed that Moxie would be fine, and that her guilelessness might actually help her. After all, if she simply stated the truth in her quirky but straightforward way, she'd be hard not to believe. But perhaps it was time to encourage her to consult with a legal professional. "Mom, you deal with lawyers all the time," I noted. "Do you know anyone who does criminal law?"

"*I* do not get involved in crimes!" Mom said, drawing back like I'd smacked her. She'd obviously, or conveniently, overlooked the fact that she had been a prime suspect in a recent murder. Then she smoothed her scarf — a subtly Christmasy red-and-green geometric print — getting herself back under control and speaking more calmly. "However, I will make some inquiries on Moxie's behalf," she assured me. "And because I fear that *you* will need a lawyer soon, Daphne."

I started to insist that I wouldn't need an attorney, only to realize that my mother might be right. I half expected Jonathan to walk through the door at any moment, telling me that it was my turn under the interrogation spotlight. Not that he had a real spotlight. It just felt that way when he was trying to get answers.

Perhaps my sister and my mother, who'd

both endured Jonathan's scrutiny, too, were recalling their own interrogations, because we all got quiet for a moment, the hush intensified by the blanket of snow piling up outside.

Inside, Flour Power was as cheerful as always, thanks in large part to the mod, pink flowers Moxie had painted on the walls. I'd decorated for the holidays, too, placing colorful lights around the window and door and setting a Santa hat on the cat-shaped wall clock with the swinging tail and shifting eyes. I'd even hung a few small, cute dog and cat-shaped ornaments on the thriving bamboo plant that Jonathan had given me. But I couldn't help feeling uneasy, and the comfort food on my plate and warming drink didn't taste as good, either, when I pictured the scissors, glinting on the street.

My sister, at least, was on board my train of thought. "Tell me again," she urged. "How in the world did you end up holding what is likely CeeCee French's murder weapon?"

I set down my fork, prepared to tell that tale again, when all at once something banged against the door, and I spun around, pointing and speaking before I even had a chance to think.

"Him! That little pug, with his paws

against the glass!" I whipped back around, facing my mother and sister, who were looking at me like I was crazy. "Please, tell me you see him, too!"

CHAPTER 19

"Come back!" I begged the pug, stumbling through the snow and struggling to put on my coat, which Piper had shoved into my arms, after promising to watch Flour Power while I was out. The dog — whom my sister and mother had seen, thank goodness — trotted ahead of me. I almost got the sense that he wanted me to follow him, because he wasn't darting away at his usual pace. His red sweater bobbed steadily in front of me, a beacon in the storm. Then all at once, he did vanish, around a corner.

"Wait!" I called, skidding when I tried to follow him. I was glad that Sylvan Creek had become a ghost town as the storm grew more intense, because I must've looked very strange. But I felt as if I had to catch the dog if I was ever going to convince Jonathan Black that the pug had brought me the scissors. I picked up my pace, running after the pug down the alley I'd sneaked through the night before. However, we weren't headed toward Spa and Paw. He was leading me in the other direction. "Come, please!"

The dog didn't listen. Instead, he continued his purposeful journey, making one more turn down a narrow lane I probably hadn't visited ten times in the whole time I'd lived in Sylvan Creek, because it was a dead end, almost like a miniature, half-block neighborhood unto itself.

I slowed down, not sure where the dog would take me next, and hoped he wouldn't disappear between two of the adorable tall, narrow houses that lined the street. Fortunately, he stopped in front of a lovely, lilac-colored home with gingerbread trim. Then the pug turned, looked me straight in the eye, and yipped loudly. The sound was definitely a summons.

"I'm coming," I promised, as he hopped up onto the house's porch.

I hurried up the steps, too, just as a cheerful, red door swung open, and a man bent down to pick up my guide, scolding him gently and affectionately. "Tiny Tim, where have you been this time?" Straightening, with the dog wriggling happily in his arms, the man smiled at me, the expression in his brown eyes warm enough to ward off the chill of the snowflakes landing on my bare cheeks. "Thank you for bringing him. . . ."

His voice died off, and the warmth flickered out, replaced by something like *fear* when he recognized me. I could feel my own eyes growing wide, because I knew him, too.

"Da . . . Daphne?" he stuttered, while I pointed and exclaimed, "Mike Cavanaugh! I *knew* you were in town!"

CHAPTER 20

I was pretty sure Moxie's former boyfriend wasn't rich in terms of money, but his nook-sized efficiency apartment, which consisted of a few small rooms on the first floor of the pale-purple Victorian house, was more appealing to me than the biggest penthouse Manhattan had to offer.

Not that I'd spent a lot of time . . . or any time . . . in penthouses. I just knew for a fact that Mike Cavanaugh had created a welcoming home for himself and the dog named Tiny Tim.

At least, I thought Mike and the dog were the only residents of the apartment, where I stood in the living room, warming myself by a fireplace with a crisp, white mantel while Mike brewed some coffee. The hearth was flanked by two overstuffed chairs that looked like they would swallow someone up, in a good way, if he or she sat down with a book and a cup of tea. An old-fashioned braided rug, placed between the seats, would be the perfect spot for a dog with wanderlust to snooze after a snowy adventure. And the small kitchen, visible through an arched doorway, was painted a soft and cheerful shade of yellow that brought some sunshine into the gloomy day.

"Mike, this place is wonderful," I said, as he stepped under the arch, joining me in the living room.

"It's not much," he said, with the slightest shrug. He carried two mismatched mugs, and he was being careful not to spill, because his limp was pronounced — and the pug kept darting between his feet, twirling and prancing with excitement.

I was starting to think Tiny Tim was high-spirited, like Artie, as opposed to a trouble-maker.

Well, maybe the pug was a bit of a scamp.

"Settle, Timmy," Mike urged, placing both mugs on a small end table between the chairs. He smiled at me in a lopsided and somewhat nervous way, as if my presence still made him uneasy. But he'd insisted that I come inside for a quick drink, so he could thank me for escorting the pug home. I'd texted Piper, telling her to put a "back in 15 minutes" sign in the window, then accepted, because I had *a lot* of questions for

Moxie's high school love. "I apologize for Timmy's behavior," he added, gesturing for me to take a seat. "We don't get many visitors, and I think he's excited."

"I take it he's not a fan of the holidays," I noted, pointing at the pup's red sweater with its play on the quote from Scrooge. "Assuming that's really his motto."

Mike laughed, seeming more relaxed. "He actually has five of those sweaters, which Tessie Flinchbaugh sold me at a discount. She bought a few too many, overestimating how many pugs live in Sylvan Creek — and probably how many people like bad pug puns."

That explained why the dog always wore the same outfit.

"I make sure he's always dressed for the weather," Mike added, shooting Tiny Tim a frustrated but loving look. "He's such a little escape artist that I want to make sure he's at least warm when he *somehow* manages to sneak out."

Tiny Tim spun a few circles on his short legs, as if his escapades delighted him, at least, and I sat down, sinking into a chair that was as soft as I'd expected. Getting myself situated, I asked, "How long have you had him?"

Mike took a seat, too, and Tiny Tim

thunked down on the rug, his wrinkled head between his black-tipped paws and his round eyes rolling restlessly, as if he was ready to pop up again at a moment's notice.

"I adopted Timmy about a month ago — right before I moved here," Mike said, his gaze suddenly fixed on the fire. His mood had shifted, and he hunched his shoulders, sinking deeper into his chair, as if he wanted it to literally swallow him. "I've been trying to keep a low profile, but I know you saw me a few times."

"Yes. Near the theater, right? Twice. Including the day CeeCee French addressed the whole town."

He nodded. "Yes. I'd heard she was in town, and I wanted to see her after all these years. Not speak to her. Just see how time had treated her."

I wasn't sure what to make of that comment. "So, why'd you dart off?"

He finally met my gaze. "I've been trying to steer clear of everyone from high school." We hadn't mentioned Moxie yet, and he still didn't speak her name. But I was pretty sure she was the main person he'd been trying to avoid. "I know that's ridiculous in a town this size," he added. "And I know I can't hide out forever, because I don't have plans to leave Sylvan Creek . . . don't have anywhere else to go, really . . . since my Uncle Jack was kind enough to give me a job at his garage, out on Pine Road." He shrugged. "When options run out, I guess we turn to the familiarity of home."

I'd forgotten that Mike's family owned a garage and auto body repair shop, just outside Sylvan Creek. "I've readopted the community, too, after being a bit of a nomad," I noted. I thought about how happy I was with my friends, family, cottage, and businesses. "Coming home can be a good thing."

"Yes, I may come to see things that way." Mike tapped his bad leg. "And I'm lucky that my uncle lets me work behind a desk most of the day, keeping the books, doing invoices — things like that. I'm pretty good with engines. But standing too long is still painful, since the accident."

Tiny Tim raised his head and yipped, as if he wasn't happy with who or whatever had harmed his person. And I dared to venture, tentatively, "Do you mind if I ask what happened?"

Mike smiled again, but wryly. "It was a car accident, in a war zone. Syria. But not a battle-related injury." His grin was extinguished, replaced by a haunted look. "I saw enough combat, though." Then he obviously shook off whatever dark memories had just haunted him and clapped a hand on his leg again. "But this thing was just dumb luck on a dangerous road, a few days before I was shipping home for good."

"I'm so sorry," I said, thinking Mike had several things in common with Jonathan Black — including good looks. Moxie's old flame had grown into quite a handsome man. He still had his thick head of dark-brown, wavy hair and an athletic build. Back in high school, he'd been a star multisport athlete, so, while he hadn't rivaled CeeCee and Jeff Updegrove for top spots in our class, he'd won a Wynton scholarship, nonetheless, because he'd been so well rounded. Age, and no doubt experience, seemed to have added an appealing gentleness to Mike, too. It was just a feeling I got, sitting next to him.

And yet, a tiny part of me couldn't help wondering if he'd had something to do with CeeCee French's murder.

After all, Mike's dog had shown up with what was likely the murder weapon. And Mike had said that strange thing about wanting to see Celeste, who had played a role in his breakup with Moxie . . .

"We're both thinking about Celeste, aren't we?" he asked, softly and seriously. "About her murder."

I swore, the storm seemed to intensify in response to his mention of CeeCee's death. Wind rattled the tall, narrow windows on either side of the fireplace, and snow swirled past the panes.

"You're thinking about how I ran away from Sylvan Creek and abandoned my scholarship to Wynton," Mike continued, "only to end up battle-scarred and beaten up, sharing a few rooms with one terribly behaved rescue dog for a friend. And it's probably crossed your mind that the . . . *incident* with CeeCee French, back at a holiday dance, set so much of that in motion."

Tiny Tim yapped loudly. I felt like he was letting Mike know that he, at least, was grateful for their circumstances and the chance at a home.

In spite of his bad behavior, the pug was quickly winning my heart, too. I could think of worse friends.

In fact, a girl who'd behaved questionably toward others, back in high school, was on my mind, right then. Mike had guessed correctly.

"Yes, I was thinking about CeeCee," I admitted, settling deeper into the chair. "I'm actually interested in getting to the bottom of the crime. Because right now, it seems as if Moxie is a prime suspect. And we both know she couldn't hurt, let alone kill, anyone."

Moxie Bloom's name was finally out there, the elephant in vintage clothing unleashed upon the snug room, and Mike again looked pained. Maybe more so than when he'd recalled his time in battle. He leaned forward, twisting his hands, and the pug whimpered.

"I've been reading about Moxie and CeeCee in the local paper," he said, his voice hitching when he spoke both those names. "And I don't care what the police or reporters think." I didn't interrupt to tell him there was only one reporter. Gabriel Graham. "There's no way Moxie murdered CeeCee," he continued. "I might not have seen her for years, but nobody changes that much. She'd never harm a living thing. And I'm sure *she* forgave CeeCee, ages ago, for everything that went wrong."

Mike again had trouble getting his words out. And it was clear that *he* hadn't managed to forgive CeeCee yet. He obviously still hadn't absolved himself, either, for his role in the high-school-dance debacle.

"Mike . . ." My mind was spinning in so many directions that I didn't know where to steer the conversation next. I finally settled on the weapon. "Do you know about Tiny Tim and the scissors? Did he bring them here, before leaving them with me?"

I could tell, before he even responded, that Mike had no idea what I was talking about. He continued to lean forward, his hands clasped between his knees and a frown dragging down the corners of his mouth. Then he glanced at the pug, who watched us, his head still between his paws and his eyes still rolling. Mike looked at me again, his expression guarded, as if he already suspected what I was about to say. "What scissors? What are you talking about?"

I believed that he was genuinely clueless. Either that, or he should join the Sylvan Creek Players. Maybe take my spot in the rehearsal I was scheduled to attend the following night.

"Daphne, the scissors — and Timmy," Mike said, making a rolling motion with his hand. "I'm getting concerned, here."

"Oh, yes," I said, getting back to the matter at hand. "From what I understand, the coroner thinks CeeCee's killer used a pair of scissors," I explained, hoping that information wasn't confidential anymore. I doubted that I was sharing a secret, but I added, "Please keep that to yourself for now, okay? I'm not positive that news is public yet."

Although I could tell that he had no idea where I was headed with the discussion, Mike nodded gravely. "Sure."

"Anyhow, I was out last night, and Tiny Tim ran up to me and dropped a pair of scissors right at my feet." I paused for a long time, letting Mike digest that strange story, while I tried to figure out what to say next. "I'm pretty sure the scissors belonged to Moxie, and I know for a fact that the detective who's investigating the case had been looking for them. There was a pair missing from the drawer where Moxie keeps all of her instruments."

All the color drained from Mike's face as he quickly grasped what I was saying. "The detective . . . Black, that's his name, right? The one who always refuses to talk to reporters."

Jonathan's silence was probably another reason Gabriel sometimes got prickly about him. I nodded. "Yes. Jonathan Black."

"He thinks Moxie killed CeeCee with a pair of scissors that *my dog* was, for some reason, carrying around?"

Tiny Tim whined, as if chastising himself. But his curly tail was wagging.

Mike groaned. "Timmy, what have you done?"

The bah, hum-pug yapped again, shrilly, defending himself.

Then Mike turned miserable eyes on me. "I suppose I'm mixed up in this whole mess now, too. And, to make matters worse, everyone around here knows there was no love lost between me and Celeste French." He drew back slightly, frowning as he tried to piece things together. "Why hasn't Detective Black contacted *me*?"

"If he even knows who you are, I doubt he's aware that you're in Sylvan Creek," I pointed out. "*I* wasn't sure you were really in town, before today. And I certainly didn't know that you and Tiny Tim were connected."

"But the police must be looking for him."

"I doubt it," I said. "I couldn't get anyone to believe Tiny Tim even existed, let alone that he'd delivered a potential murder weapon to me." Reaching for my mug, I sipped my coffee, which was strong and black. A preference for dark roast was apparently something else Mike shared with Jonathan. Fighting the urge to wince, I swallowed the bitter brew, adding, "I was honestly starting to wonder if I'd dreamed the dog up. Because a mysterious pug who always wears a 'bah, hum-pug' sweater, causing trouble, then vanishing . . ." I shook my head. "It seemed unlikely, even to me, who kept seeing him!"

"Wait a second." Mike's gaze darted back and forth between me and Tiny Tim, who had squeezed his eyes shut and hunkered down even lower to the floor, if that was possible. I swore, he was cringing in anticipation of his person's next question, posed to me. "Where else have you seen Tiny Tim?"

I didn't want to get the little dog in too much trouble, so I didn't mention how he'd knocked over a charity kettle, nor how he'd pushed me. However — cringing, myself, and shooting the pug an apologetic glance — I told Mike, "He was at Pettigrew Park the night of CeeCee's murder. In fact, he popped out from under the tree where her body was found, only to run away before anyone else saw him."

Flopping back in his chair, Mike dragged his hands down his face. "Oh, Tiny Tim . . ."

The little pug rolled over, playing dead about as well as I would in a few days, onstage. I wanted to smile at Tiny Tim's pathetic attempt to avoid a scolding, but I had a serious question on my mind. One that I was half-afraid to ask, even though I couldn't really believe Moxie's former love was a killer.

"Mike," I nevertheless ventured, gently. "You were at the park, too, weren't you? Not long before the body was found. I'm pretty sure I saw you walking near the creek."

Mike's whole body stiffened, and he didn't respond for a long minute. The only sound in the room was Tiny Tim's rapid, snuffling breathing. Then Mike sat up, looking at me again and nodding gravely. "Yes. I had hoped you hadn't seen me. You seemed very focused on the man you were with."

I felt warmth creep into my cheeks. "That was actually Jonathan Black."

Mike nodded. "Yes, of course. I forgot that the *Gazette*'s first story mentioned that a detective had been among the first on the scene."

I wondered, for a moment, if I had been identified in that article. I'd left the park before Gabriel had arrived, and Jonathan didn't make a point of sharing information if he could help it. But Gabriel had texted me that quick note — Another body! — so he must've known about my role in the grim discovery soon after it had happened. Making a mental note to check the paper's online archives, I returned my attention to

173

Mike, who had finally sat back in his chair, although I wouldn't have called his posture relaxed. "Why didn't you tell the police you were there?"

"I wasn't doing anything wrong," he said reasonably. "I was looking for Tiny Tim, who had disappeared *again.*" Mike nudged the dog with his foot, and the pug popped to his feet, then jumped up on the chair with Mike, who stroked him absently. "I was gone before anything really happened, and — like any normal person — I don't want to be involved in a murder investigation, so I never came forward. Never thought I had a *reason* to come forward."

I hoped he was telling the truth. I hoped he really didn't have cause to speak up. Yet, I thought he should talk to Jonathan. In fact, that was probably unavoidable.

I rose, thinking it was time for me to leave soon. Right after I urged him to do the right thing. "Mike . . ."

"I know," he said, his jaw clenched with resignation. Setting Tiny Tim on the floor, he stood up, too. It was getting late, and the fire cast shifting shadows on his face. "I'll talk to the detective. Not only because I am involved, at this point. But because it might help Moxie."

I'd been slipping on my coat, which I'd

set down near the fire, but I jerked to a stop with only one arm in a sleeve. "How so?"

"Suspicion will be shared with me," he said. "I'll make it clear that I had no fondness for CeeCee French."

"You'd do that for Moxie?" I asked, stunned by the gesture. "But . . . ?"

"Of course, I'd do that." Even in the dim room, I spied a faint flush on *his* cheeks. "I owe her that much. And more." He hesitated, as if considering whether to tell me something. Then he confided, quietly, "I sometimes walk around in the evening, trying to build up strength in my leg. I often pass through the alleys — keeping that low profile — and I stopped one time at the back door to Spa and Paw, telling myself I should go in. At least let Moxie know that I was in town, so she wouldn't get an unpleasant surprise in a more public place."

I had no idea where he was going with the story. And I wasn't sure if muddying Jonathan's pool of suspects was a good idea, even if Mike's heart was in the right place. Not that I hadn't interfered in a few investigations, myself, with similarly good intentions. Regardless, I stayed quiet, letting him finish his anecdote.

"I actually twisted the knob, and the door was open, but Moxie wasn't there," he continued. "I think she was gone for the day, because the place was very quiet." He shrugged. "I suppose, if she makes a habit of leaving Spa and Paw wide open, it would be easy enough for *anyone* to take something from the salon."

That was true, and I felt a surge of hope that, if the scissors did turn out to be Moxie's, it would also be easy to prove that someone else had removed them from her shop. Then I realized how badly Mike would be implicating himself, if he related his tale and theory to Jonathan, and I said, firmly, "No, Mike. Don't tell Detective Black that story. Don't make yourself look guilty, unless you . . ."

The words tumbled out almost before I could stop them. I hadn't even realized I'd been about to say "unless you are guilty" until it was too late.

Mike knew where I'd been headed with my comment, but he didn't say a thing. He just took a few steps toward the door.

Tiny Tim and I followed, the pug attempting to trip *me,* while I tried to figure out if I should apologize, or if it was too late for that.

All three of us stopped at the threshold, and I bit my lip, then decided I had to try to fix my error. "I'm really sorry, Mike," I

176

said. "I *don't* believe you killed CeeCee."

He tried to smile, but it was bitter. "Well, I am a cheater. It probably doesn't seem like that big a leap to killer."

"No, it's not like that." I heard the misery in my voice. "That dance was years ago. We were all kids, and we all did stupid things."

He didn't respond right away, and I said, "You really should reach out to Moxie. Tell her, yourself, that you're back in Sylvan Creek. Because you *will* see her sometime, in a town this small," I reminded him. "Especially if you're both mixed up in a murder case. So why don't you just contact her? It might go well. And, like I said, coming home can be a good thing." I gestured around his small home. "But not if you lock yourself away, no matter how charming the space."

He was shaking his head, his attempt at steeling his eyes failing miserably. "No. I don't think contacting Moxie is a good thing. I've been glad, ever since I stopped by her salon, that she wasn't there."

I didn't see why they couldn't at least have a cup of coffee. Unless he was hiding something, perhaps related to the mysterious circumstances surrounding that long-ago dance. I kept watching his eyes, which weren't meeting mine. "Mike, what really happened at the formal? Why *did* you cheat with CeeCee? Because I know you really cared about Moxie."

He jerked, like I'd slapped him. Then he said, through gritted teeth, "I *didn't* actually cheat, Daphne. And I *loved* Moxie. But I'll never share what really happened that night. Ever."

I couldn't believe that the story I'd assumed to be true, for years — the tale that had messed up Moxie's and Mike's lives — might not be accurate. And I suddenly felt this surge of hope that two high school sweethearts, both of whom almost certainly still carried, at the very least, flickering little torches for each other, might get another chance at love.

But that hope was quickly dashed when I asked, "Why not tell the truth, Mike? Why not just set the record straight?"

He shook his head again, the gesture more vehement. "No, never," he said. "Because the truth involves people I haven't seen nor heard of in years. And it's much, *much* worse than what anyone — discounting one living individual and one who's dead — imagine."

CHAPTER 21

By the time I returned to Flour Power, after convincing Mike that we, at least, should exchange contact information, there was no sense in keeping the bakery open. Sylvan Creek was basically deserted, the sidewalks were deep with snow, and fat flakes continued to fall hard past the streetlamps that were flickering to life as night fell.

Removing Piper's neatly hand-lettered sign from the door, I made sure the ovens were turned off, then switched off most of the lights, too, with the exception of the holiday bulbs around the window and door. Then, bracing myself, I stepped back into the storm and locked the door behind me.

When I turned around, I took a moment to look up and down Market Street, in spite of the wicked weather. In fact, the town looked especially pretty as the snow settled on the bare branches of the trees, muting the canopy of white lights, while the windows of the otherwise dark storefronts glowed with holiday color. The Bijoux's marquee was lit, advertising *White Christmas,* but showings had been canceled for the evening, and someone had spelled out, STAY WARM & SAFE! where the show times would normally be posted. Even Gabriel, who usually worked almost around the clock, had called it a day. The offices of the *Weekly Gazette* were shuttered for the night. And Brett Pinkney must've assumed that no one was going to buy Christmas trees in a near blizzard. I saw him down the street, climbing into his old-fashioned pickup truck, his shoulders hunched against the wind.

I tried to wave to him, but I was too late. The taillights of his truck lit up like Rudolph's nose, and a few seconds later he was gone, swallowed by the swirling flakes.

Pulling my knit cap down over my ears, I started wading toward my VW, which was the only vehicle parked for the length of the block, only to notice that one local business owner hadn't given up and gone home to weather the storm.

A light burned in Ivy Dunleavy's tailoring shop, and, as I watched, a slender, shadowy form flitted quickly past the single, small window.

I stood on the sidewalk for a long moment, picturing the dress Ivy had shown me in her sketchbook. The gown I didn't really need, and which would be an unnecessary extravagance.

Then I dug my mitten-clad hands into my pockets, ducked my chin against the rising wind, and trudged across the street.

"I know I don't need a fancy gown, but I couldn't resist," I confessed to Socrates, as I prepared a bedtime snack for him and Snowdrop, who, to my knowledge, continued to fast.

I'd arrived safely at Plum Cottage after lingering in Sylvan Creek a little too long, given the conditions outside. I still wasn't sure what had compelled me to rap on Ivy Dunleavy's window and hire the very eager seamstress, last minute, to sew the gown I'd first seen in her sketchbook. Vanity, I supposed. A weakness that had been punished immediately with a harrowing drive up Winding Hill in the continuing blizzard. I was happy to be home in my flannel jammies and fluffy slippers, puttering around my warm, safe cottage, where, thankfully, creatures hadn't stirred too much in my absence. The Christmas lights were in place, the greenery on the mantel was undisturbed, and Tinks was on top of the icebox, eating a Cranberry-Chicken Stocking Stuffer, made from rolled oats, dried cranberries, and boiled chicken breast.

Snowdrop had poked her head out of her crate when I'd opened the front door, only to shoot me, then Socrates, disappointed and disdainful looks before retreating into her private domain.

"Has she been in there all day?" I asked Socrates and Tinks, while I placed two Snicker-Poodles dog-friendly cookies onto white, snowflake-shaped plates. I hoped the pretty presentation — at least, the plates, while flea market finds, were pretty in my opinion — would meet Snowdrop's high standards and convince her to dine with us. I set the treats on the floor in the kitchen. "Does she *ever* come out?"

Tinks stopped eating long enough to hiss, which I thought meant Snowdrop had, indeed, trotted around snootily while I'd been away.

Socrates didn't respond. He looked despondently toward Snowdrop's snazzy lair, then wandered over to his rug by the hearth, where he lay down with a thud, without eating his snack. It was not like Socrates to break his nightly routine, and I took a moment to watch his doggy eyebrows twitching, while his gaze remained fixed on the standoffish poodle's abode.

"Oh, goodness," I muttered softly to myself. Then I grabbed a mug of tea I'd brewed, joined him by the fireplace, and sat down cross-legged on the edge of his rug. "Hey." I bent slightly to nudge him with my elbow, getting his attention. And when the basset hound I'd known since his puppyhood met my gaze, I knew that Piper had been right all along. Socrates was lovesick for a dog who wouldn't give him the time of day. I could see the mixture of confusion and misery — topped off with a heaping pile of self-reproach — in his normally wise, stoic brown eyes.

"Apparently, Snowdrop doesn't have such great taste, after all, if she's snubbing you," I whispered. "She might have a diamond collar and a cashmere sweater, but she doesn't recognize *real* quality when she sees it."

I'd kept my voice low, and the wind was rattling the shutters loudly, but Snowdrop must've heard. At the very least, she'd picked up her name, and the disapproving tone of my voice, because a bark of disagreement echoed from inside her lair.

I ignored her, figuring two could play at that game.

"And everybody falls for a complete mismatch at some point," I added softly, nudging Socrates again. "It just . . . happens."

Lying beside me, Socrates drew a deep breath and huffed, as if he wished that weren't the case.

We all got very quiet then. Even the wind died down, and the sounds of the night were muffled by the falling snow, which was piled at least six inches high on the windowsills and the branches of the plum tree, which dripped with lacy icicles, too. The crackling fire warmed my back, and I sipped my tea, thinking about what I'd just told Socrates — and, for the first time, fully admitting to myself that Piper had also been right about *me.*

I was drawn to Jonathan and scared to admit it, because we were total opposites. Plus, early on, he hadn't given me any reason to believe he had any interest in me. I *still* wasn't convinced that he saw me as more than an amusing, sometimes frustrating friend.

However, as I sat there next to Socrates, who approved of Jonathan Black, I knew in my heart that, if Jonathan and I ever did move beyond friendship, I wouldn't be able to keep the relationship casual and noncommittal, as I'd done with surfer and vet tech Dylan Taggart, and like I was doing with Gabriel Graham, who didn't want or expect more than a date for dinner or a dance, now and then.

"I've been a big commitment chicken," I told Socrates, who raised his head and shot me a sympathetic glance. Then I reminded myself that, while Jonathan and I had shared some charged moments, he wasn't exactly busting down my door to ask me out, and I added, "But, in my defense, Jonathan *wasn't* the guy who invited me to Bark the Halls. Only Gabriel asked me to be his date."

Socrates gave me a funny look, like he knew something that I didn't, as I believed was often the case. Unfortunately, our conversations were always somewhat one-sided, and I couldn't ask what was on his mind.

Resisting the urge to pat him, because he would've hated that, even in his confused state, I stood up and shuffled to the kitchen, where I set my empty mug in the sink before giving Tinks, who was curled up on the windowsill, a quick scratch behind the ears. I was pretty sure he purred.

Not wanting to press my luck by trying again, I withdrew my hand and padded over to the small table by the door, where I'd placed Ivy's sketch of my dress. She'd loaned me the drawing so I could plan for shoes and accessories while she hopefully delivered on her promise to whip up the gown in record time.

Picking up the paper, I saw the yearbook, too, with its strange note — *I believe you may find this helpful* — so I also grabbed that and went to the loveseat, where I curled up, pulling a soft throw over my legs.

Opening the annual to a random page, I sucked in a sharp breath, even though I shouldn't have been surprised to see Cee-Cee French smiling at me, in a group photo of class officers.

Needless to say, CeeCee's image would be all over a compendium of high school memories. Yet I briefly wondered if Jeff Updegrove had looked at that particular page often, since the book had naturally opened to that spot. Then I studied the image more closely, noting CeeCee's dominant posture — and parliamentarian Jeff's sweater vest and bad case of acne.

Again, nothing unexpected.

"It would be 'helpful' to know what I was looking for," I noted quietly, with a glance at Socrates, to see if he was listening.

His eyes were closed, but I suspected that he was awake and meditating upon our recent talk, so I didn't bother him and flipped a few more pages.

All at once, I broke into a wide grin, having spotted an image of me and Moxie washing dogs in the school parking lot to raise money for Sylvan Creek High Shelter Partners — a club I'd completely forgotten organizing, in an early attempt to support local pet rescues. I wore a flannel shirt, unbuttoned to reveal a "Fur-Ever Friends" T-shirt, and ripped denim shorts over leggings. I looked like a cross between a roadie for a Seattle grunge band and an extra from the TV show *Blossom,* while Moxie was primly attired in vintage pedal pushers and a blouse with a Peter Pan collar.

"You are always timeless, Moxie," I whispered, turning to another page, where Bitsy Bickelheim was shown in what passed for a classroom action shot. She stood before a whiteboard, holding a pen and gesturing broadly to students who were slumped over their desks, failing to match her enthusiasm.

Although not *that* many years had passed, Ms. Bickelheim appeared dramatically younger in the photo. Her hair — now gray and usually wild — was dark and pulled into a sleek chignon, and my mother would have approved of my former instructor's pencil skirt and silky-looking blouse, which was open perhaps one button too low, given the situation. That was the only minor, and perhaps accidental, thing I could find to critique regarding her appearance.

"Ms. Bickelheim was really pulled together — and pretty," I said, addressing Tinks, who'd levitated up behind the loveseat in his spooky way to peer over my shoulder. "I bet some of the guys secretly drooled over her."

Tinks reached out one of his puffball paws and swatted at Ms. Bickelheim, perhaps offering his stamp of approval.

"What do you think happened with her?" I mused, meeting Tinks's orange eyes. "Why'd she quit teaching?"

Unlike Moxie, who could probably tell me the whole story in detail, the prickly Persian had no answers for me. He jumped down next to me, curling up to sleep on the edge of the throw, while I turned yet another page, heading into unfamiliar territory, where I knew Moxie and I wouldn't make an appearance: sports.

The section's very first page — titled SYLVAN CREEK'S FIGHTING SQUIRRELS SUPERSTARS! — featured standard group shots of the four most prominent teams: girls' softball and basketball and boys' football and baseball.

I quickly found Mike Cavanaugh and Brett Pinkney on the football team, because they'd been co-captains. They stood in the foreground with their arms draped around each other's shoulders, big grins on their youthful faces and swagger in their postures.

I'd forgotten that they'd been friends, because they hadn't socialized much off the field. Probably because Mike had spent most of his free time with Moxie, and Brett had dated CeeCee, who hadn't exactly been in our social circle. Sports had been the nexus of Brett and Mike's relationship.

And yet, when I scanned the photo of the baseball team, Mike's posture was different — shrunken — and Brett wasn't there at all.

That was strange, because, while I hadn't followed the Sylvan Creek Squirrels very closely, or at all, I knew that Brett had been a star athlete in every major sport.

"Did he just miss picture day?" I mused aloud, tapping the pages with my fingers. The innate sleuthing sense I seemed to possess was starting to tingle. "Or was something else going on?"

No matter how hard I stared, the photos didn't seem to yield any more answers, so I turned to the next page, where I again encountered CeeCee French, this time in full cheerleader regalia, standing triumphantly atop a human pyramid.

CeeCee wasn't the most petite girl in that stack of teen females, but I couldn't imagine her accepting a lower role on the totem pole.

As the snow continued to float past the windows and the fire flickered softly, I studied CeeCee's face. Her dark eyes gleamed with whatever victory she'd just achieved, or perhaps with the anticipation of inevitable victories to come. Her then-chestnut hair was long, slicked into a high ponytail held in place with a scrunchie in Sylvan Creek's signature green and white. Her nose was definitely broader than when I'd seen her at the Bijoux, so I was pretty sure my guess about plastic surgery had been correct. And her smile was wide and . . . hungry. Even at seventeen or eighteen, CeeCee French had looked ready to take big bites of the world and swallow them whole.

Regardless of how I felt about the questionable methods I suspected she'd used to reach the top of the *corporate* pyramid — the scandal I needed to look into came to mind — I had to admit that CeeCee had gone after whatever future she'd envisioned, standing atop that heap of girls, and made her dreams come true.

"I'm sorry, CeeCee," I said, suddenly suffering a genuine pang of loss as the years seemed to melt away. The icy wind blowing outside was forgotten, and I could almost feel the late-summer air and smell the freshly cut grass on the athletic fields that stretched behind the cheerleaders. The fields were crowded with football players and coaches, the scene full of life. It was easy to imagine the girls in the foreground — maybe even CeeCee — giggling and gossiping right before the photo was snapped. "What a shame."

All at once, I heard a soft, whining sound right next to me, and I looked down to discover that Snowdrop had emerged from her crate. She'd padded across the room on silent paws and was watching me with alert and, I thought, disappointed eyes. But I didn't think she was judging me again. I was pretty sure she'd heard me mention CeeCee's name, and perhaps thought her person had returned.

"I'm sorry," I apologized to Snowdrop, too. The sweater she was still wearing was rumpled, and her fur wasn't as fluffy as before. "This is difficult for you, isn't it? A big change?"

Her eyes flashed, like she couldn't drop her attitude and let me in, even for a moment. Then her tail, with a slightly matted puffball on the end, drooped.

"I honestly don't know what kind of gourmet food you're used to, but I really am a decent cook," I told her, moving to shut the yearbook. But at the last moment, I noticed a figure in the field behind the cheerleaders. One of several people I recognized, but an unexpected presence, nonetheless. *Ms. Bickelheim.* I wanted to check the photo again, but I didn't want to ruin the moment I was sharing with Snowdrop, so I shut the annual and carefully extricated my legs from the throw, without moving Tinkleston, who was sound asleep. Standing up, I set the yearbook on my steamer trunk coffee table. "Please, let me get you a fresh treat, okay?"

Snowdrop blinked at me, and I thought she was going to assume her haughty, defiant air again. I was pretty sure we'd all see that side of her in the future. But she was also confused and hungry, and, after a moment's hesitation, she followed me to the kitchen, where I retrieved a fresh Snicker-Poodle cookie, replacing the perfectly good one that was already on the plate. I would try to meet her royal highness halfway.

Snowdrop sniffed the snack for a long time, then she took a few delicate nibbles before finally digging in with gusto.

As she ate, I smiled at Socrates, who was observing his crush from his spot near the fire.

"Your snack's waiting, too," I reminded him, with a nod to the plate next to Snowdrop's.

Socrates hesitated, then rose and joined Snowdrop, who looked up at him, challenge in her eyes, as if she couldn't believe he'd dared to dine with her. Socrates didn't back away. Nor did he fawn and act lovestruck. He merely watched her with the intelligent, impassive gaze I knew and loved. Apparently, our discussion and some meditative time had helped to center him again. A moment later, they both began to eat, as if, at the very least, an accord had been reached.

I kind of wanted a snack, too — there were some freshly baked sugar cookies calling my name — but I quietly backed out of the kitchen and headed upstairs, grabbing the yearbook on my way to bed, in case I wanted to keep paging through, either to solve a mystery, or to see what other interesting fashion choices I'd made back in high school.

In fact, I opened the book before I was halfway up the spiral staircase, and I stopped in my tracks, my eyes widening with surprise as I spotted something intriguing on the very last page — and it *wasn't* a photo.

CHAPTER 22

"So, Jeff Updegrove forgot you, after you promised never to forget him in a yearbook inscription," Piper said, helping me haul a tarp off an old, red truck with wooden slats around its bed, the day after the storm.

The vehicle, which had belonged to Winding Hill's former caretaker — who was currently in prison — had been parked in the barn ever since the day Mr. Peachy had been arrested. Since no one seemed to be claiming it, Piper sometimes used it to run errands, and she was loaning the truck to me, because the plow she'd hired to clear the main road up the hill hadn't been able to fit down the narrow access road to Plum Cottage. The trees were too close to the lane, leaving no place for the snow to go. At a certain point, the plow driver had given up, meaning the VW might be stuck for several days — which was fine. The truck was cute, especially since Piper had affixed a pine wreath with a red bow to the old-fashioned grill. And both Piper and Mr. Peachy were fastidious about maintenance, so I trusted that the tires would be in great shape for winter driving.

"I don't see why you're insulted," Piper noted, dragging the tarp to an unused stall, where she tossed it so it hung over a low wall. She brushed off her hands, while I cleaned mine on my jeans. "He didn't make any promises in *your* yearbook, did he?"

"I lost mine years ago, but, no, probably not," I admitted, thinking that perhaps I had overreacted, upon spying my handwritten pledge in Jeff's annual. I pulled my mittens from my pocket, because the barn wasn't heated. When I did that, the key I was still carrying in my pocket came out, too, and fell to the floor. I bent to pick it up, telling Piper, "But his expression was *completely* blank when I greeted him at the Bijoux."

My sister wasn't listening. She was frowning at the shiny object in my hand. "Why don't you put your keys on a ring?" she suggested. "You're going to lose that, too."

Tucking my mittens under my arm, I held up the key, letting it dangle from the ribbon. "I don't even know what this unlocks," I said. "It's the key Jeff Updegrove left me, with the yearbook — and without a way to contact him."

"Can't you just call French's headquarters?"

"I tried that." I stuffed the key into my pocket again and slipped my mittens over my frosty fingers. "Jeff is on leave, and the person who answered wouldn't give me his personal number or e-mail, even."

Piper pursed her lips. Then she said, "Jeff's not coming back, is he? You're going to watch that poodle forever."

"Socrates would be fine with that," I noted, smiling. "You were right. He's fallen hard for Snowdrop — who has at least emerged from her royal castle to mingle, now and then, with us peasants."

In fact, when I'd left Tinks and the dogs, who couldn't enter some of the places I needed to visit that day, Snowdrop and Socrates had been eating breakfast side-by-side.

Piper, who was *always* correct, jabbed a finger at me and grinned triumphantly. "I told you he was in love!"

"I just hope he doesn't get his big, basset heart broken," I said, more seriously. "Because eventually someone will come to claim Snowdrop. She's a valuable, trained dog with acting experience. I'm sure Cee-

Cee left some provision for her in her will."

"I wouldn't count on that," Piper disagreed, grabbing a broom that rested against a wall and sweeping the floor, which was already clean, for a barn. "CeeCee almost certainly has legal documents drawn up, in the event of her demise, to protect her business empire. But I bet they don't cover small, personal things like Snowdrop. Because I recall CeeCee French from high school. I bet, deep down inside, she thought she'd defeat the Grim Reaper, just like she won every competition she entered."

"Speaking of the personification of Death, I really need to get going," I noted, with a glance out the barn door, which was open to reveal sunlight glittering on a snowy field. "I have to deliver dog cookies to the hotel for Bark the Halls, then hopefully get a Christmas tree before rehearsal tonight."

Piper paused in mid-sweep and furrowed her brow. "Rehearsal?"

I reached for the silver handle on the truck's front door. "Didn't I tell you that I'm the Ghost of Christmas Future in Ms. Bickelheim's production of *A Christmas Carol* this year?"

Piper blanched, no doubt recalling how I'd flown across the stage the last time I'd played a holiday spirit.

"There's no flying," I assured her, hauling open the door, which squeaked with age and the cold. "I just have to stand there in a big, black cloak and point."

"Good luck," Piper muttered doubtfully, leaning on the broom. "Break a leg."

"Thanks." Climbing into the truck, I slammed the door, only to hear a rap on the window. Using the old crank, I rolled it down, so I could hear Piper, who looked concerned again. "What's wrong?"

"Why are you carrying around that key, anyhow?" she asked. "What's the point, if you don't know what it unlocks?"

My cheeks got warm. "I'm not sure, myself."

Piper narrowed her eyes at me. "You're investigating CeeCee's murder, aren't you?"

"Moxie's potentially in big trouble," I reminded my sister, fumbling for the truck's key, which was already in the ignition. Piper might've been more cautious than me, but she was still a lifelong resident of Sylvan Creek, where crime was practically non-existent. Discounting the occasional murder. I twisted the key, and the engine turned over. "Now, I've really got to get going."

"Just be careful, Daphne," Piper said, as I rolled up the window. "Don't end up a real ghost this Christmas!"

"I won't," I promised, although I wasn't sure she heard me. I'd managed to crank the window up, and I put the truck in gear, steering it carefully through the wide door into the sunny but still frigid day.

Driving past Piper's farmhouse, I looked in the rearview mirror and was surprised to discover that my sibling had followed me outside, where she stood waving, making big sweeping gestures with her arm.

I thought the farewell was a little over the top, given that I was only going to town, a trip I made nearly every day.

It wasn't until the truck was skidding on a patch of ice at the very bottom of the hill, where the private lane met the main road into Sylvan Creek, that I realized she'd probably been trying to warn me that the tires weren't *quite* as good as I'd expected.

CHAPTER 23

Resting my head against the steering wheel, I closed my eyes for a moment, regrouping after the crash.

Well, what I'd suffered hadn't been so much a collision as a slow, but relentless and somewhat unnerving, slide across a rural road, until I came to a halt in a wide, deep gulley, where I sat at a weird angle, trying to figure out what to do next.

Luckily, I was about to have help.

For the second time that morning, someone rapped on the driver's side window. However, when I opened my eyes, I discovered not my sister, but a tall, handsome detective, who looked me up and down, scanning for bumps and bruises before asking, "What do you need more after your slow-motion mishap? A trip to the ER — or a tall stack of pancakes?"

"The whole thing was scarier than it

looked," I told Jonathan, who was laughing at me from across a table at the Silver Moon Diner, just outside Sylvan Creek.

Needless to say, I'd chosen hot cakes over a hospital visit, and I'd hitched a ride with Jonathan to the restaurant, which served the best breakfasts around. The towing service I'd called, after Jonathan and I had determined that the truck was fine, if stuck, had promised to drop the vehicle at the diner, which was housed in a 1950s, silver trailer, where locals gathered at the counter on red-upholstered swivel seats. Silver garlands, dripping with metallic red Christmas balls, were draped in the windows, and the jukebox played a steady, soft string of holiday hits by the Andrews Sisters, Dean Martin, and Frank Sinatra.

I could feel my Christmas spirit returning as I poured warm syrup over a fluffy stack of pancakes, piled six high. The sweet-smelling maple waterfall melted a big pat of butter, which dripped down the sides of the tasty pile. Picking up my fork, I waved it at Jonathan. "Things could've gone worse!"

"Yes, I know," he said, the mirth in his blue eyes flickering out. "I actually felt helpless when I saw you skidding." Then the corners of his mouth twitched. "Very, very slowly —"

"Enough!" I told him, although I was close to laughing, too. I had to admit that the image of the old-fashioned truck drifting across the road, with me frozen at the wheel, was funny in retrospect. Picking up my knife, too, I cut through the stack. "I suppose I'll never live this down."

"I'll probably mention it now and then," Jonathan agreed, dipping a slice of wheat toast into the bright yolk of one of his three sunny-side-up eggs, which shared a crowded plate with a tangle of crispy bacon and a pair of golden hash browns. "I need something to tease you about, now that you don't owe me any money." He hesitated, frowning. "Unless, of course, you forgot your wallet today."

For a moment, I nearly panicked, until I recalled that I'd stuck my wallet into my coat pocket, along with the mysterious key and my cell phone, before leaving Plum Cottage. And my barn jacket hung on a hook attached to the booth we shared. "Actually, I can treat today."

Jonathan, who was the only customer wearing a dress shirt and tie — Moxie's dream outfit — grinned. "No. This is on me. I invited you, remember?"

I speared a big bite with my fork. "Rescued me is more like it."

"My pleasure. As always."

Before I could thank him again, a waitress, clad in a pale-blue polyester smock and Santa hat, stopped by to refill our mugs with fresh coffee. As Jonathan and I both leaned back, giving her room, I quickly recalled several occasions when he'd shown up on the scene at precisely the right time.

Well, maybe a few minutes too late, in the case of my entrapment in my own walk-in refrigerator.

I supposed he was reliving those instances, too, because after we'd thanked the waitress — Imogene — and she'd sashayed off, he leaned forward again, his voice lower. "Daphne, I admire the fact that, any time you've gotten into trouble, it's happened while you've been protecting your family and friends. You take risks on behalf of the people you love. And I know that you are quite capable of taking care of yourself. I wasn't there for all of your adventures overseas, and you came through just fine."

Swallowing some pancakes, I opened my mouth to assure him that I really was able to fend for myself. But before I could speak, he raised a hand, requesting permission to continue.

I closed my mouth and nodded, granting it.

"That said, I'm going to ask you to back away from any private investigation of CeeCee French's murder that you might be conducting. Because the case is growing more . . . complicated."

I didn't like the sound of that. Syrup dripped off my fork, which I held in midair. "What does that mean?"

Jonathan leaned back and reached for his mug, absently tapping the smooth ceramic. "When I told you about Moxie's interrogation, I honestly believed she'd be exonerated almost immediately. But that hasn't been the case."

My breakfast suddenly felt like a lump in my stomach. "The scissors . . ."

Jonathan nodded, but spoke obliquely in the public space. "Moxie's identification of the pair was positive. And Vonda Shakes couldn't rule them out."

He was trying to tell me that Moxie had confirmed that the scissors the pug had brought to me belonged to her, and that the coroner considered them a likely match with the wounds.

"Was there any trace of — ?"

"I can't tell you more," Jonathan interjected, before I could ask about blood or fingerprints.

"Okay." Then I jerked upright, struck by a

sudden thought. "What about the photos Moxie took that night for her gingerbread village? They must be time-stamped on her phone, right? You should check those. They can prove where she was all evening."

"First of all, I'm insulted that you think I hadn't already considered that," Jonathan said dryly.

I shrunk down in the booth, because it had taken me quite a while to make that connection.

"And, not surprisingly," Jonathan continued, "Moxie chose to capture Sylvan Creek's holiday glory with a *1960s Polaroid Land Camera,* the film for which is apparently still available from some online retailers. But there is, obviously, no time stamp."

"Oh, that's not good." My shoulders slumped even more, and I took a moment to think, wanting to choose my next words carefully. Jonathan gave me time, slicing into one of the hash browns while Bing Crosby crooned about silver bells and Christmastime in a city. Then I asked, "Has anyone else come to talk with you . . . ?"

Meeting my gaze, he nodded. "Yes. And Cavanaugh told me he'd already spoken to you." I couldn't tell if Jonathan was irritated by that fact. His tone was neutral, as professional as his shirt and tie. We still sat in the cheerful, retro diner, but he was slipping into detective mode. "So, I assume you know about his visit to Spa and Paw?" Jonathan added. "Through the back door *you* also used."

How could my cheeks feel hot and my stomach ice over, all at the same time? "Mike did tell me about that." I lowered my voice and leaned over my plate, which was nearly empty. "I don't know if I should tell you this . . ."

"Is it pertinent to the investigation?"

My immediate thought was, yes. But I also knew that the information I had might make things worse for my best friend. And yet, having been through a few murder investigations — and believing that honesty would lead to the best outcome — I made up my mind to tell the truth.

"Mike told me that he was happy to implicate himself, to take some of the focus off Moxie."

I'd been convinced I was doing the right thing, but I felt sick after those words came out of my mouth.

Jonathan seemed to understand what I was feeling. He spoke gently, more like a friend again. "It's okay, Daphne. I already suspected that, from speaking with Cavanaugh. Nothing you just said makes things worse — or, unfortunately, better — for Moxie. And just because he's trying to muddy the waters on behalf of a former girlfriend doesn't mean he didn't commit the crime, himself. He hated Celeste French, and he's carrying a lot of guilt around. For all I know, some of that's related to a homicide."

"Did he confide in you, regarding any of that guilt?" I inquired, a bit too casually. "Maybe related to the old high school dance I told you about?"

Jonathan didn't answer directly. "We mainly spoke soldier to soldier," he said. "There was plenty of ground to cover there. As is probably the case for anyone who's seen combat."

"Sounds like it was a half questioning, half counseling session."

Jonathan shook some pepper onto his eggs. "He needed someone to listen."

I wanted to ask him what, exactly, they'd discussed, and whether *he'd* shared anything with Mike. But he wouldn't tell me more. I could tell by the way Jonathan had shrugged off his last comment and averted his gaze. Instead, I turned the conversation to another topic that was beginning to worry me: myself. "Given that I was holding the murder weapon, how bad are things for me?" I asked. "Am *I* a suspect?"

"Cavanaugh did help you by corroborating — to the extent that he could — your story about the dog, which he confirms has a Houdini-like ability to get loose and cause mischief. But, honestly, your lack of real motive — and your strong alibi for the night of French's death, as confirmed by Piper, your mother, Roger Berendt, and *me* — are the only things keeping you on the sidelines." He shot me a warning look. "For now."

I didn't like the sound of that, although I appreciated that he was vouching for me, probably with more conviction than my mother had done.

I was about to thank him when all at once my cell phone pinged in my coat pocket. Given that I had quite a few things going on, I excused myself with a raised finger, twisted around, and reached to dig it out. Checking the screen, I saw a message from Ivy Dunleavy, who must've been working around the clock, because she'd typed, Dress is ready for fitting!

She'd also attached an image of the gown I'd commissioned, draped on a dressmaker's dummy.

My free hand flew to my mouth, and I gasped, "Oh, goodness!"

"Is everything okay?"

I looked up to see Jonathan watching me with concern.

I quickly tapped the screen and tucked the phone away, hiding the picture. "Yes. Sorry. Everything's fine. And thanks for verifying my whereabouts."

Jonathan didn't acknowledge the comment. He shook his head, and — even as he set one of the hash browns, which I'd been eyeing, onto my plate — complained, "I don't know why no one around here locks their doors. It would save so much trouble."

All at once, I flashed back to the night of CeeCee's murder, when Axis, Artie, Socrates, and I had walked to Moxie's apartment. As we'd passed Spa and Paw, Socrates had barked, the rare sound meant to alert me to the fact that the salon's door had been open a crack.

My arm shot across the table, and I grabbed Jonathan's wrist, causing him to drop his fork. "Sorry," I said, quickly withdrawing my hand. "I just remembered something, and I got excited."

Jonathan didn't pick up the utensil. He watched me closely. "What is it?"

"Spa and Paw's front door was open the night of CeeCee's murder. Socrates noticed when we were walking to Moxie's. I pulled the door shut."

Jonathan took a long moment to digest that information. I could tell that he was at once intrigued, but also exasperated by the fact that I'd forgotten that detail — and inadvertently handled a potential clue, if by accident.

When his silence continued, I said, "There's no way you could've lifted prints off a doorknob that hundreds of people have used over the course of years, right?" He did not confirm nor deny that, so I added, "And everybody forgets to lock up in Sylvan Creek. It didn't really seem odd for me to shut the door. Not a detail worth noting."

I could tell that Jonathan wanted to mention the merits of police academy training, but he simply picked up his last piece of toast, dipped it into the remaining egg, and said, "Thank you, Daphne. Better late than never, I suppose. Although, really, you've just reinforced my comment about the *importance of locking doors.*"

"This is a small and usually safe town," I reminded him. "Even Piper, who is at least as responsible as you are, leaves the keys in the truck I drove today."

"Speaking of which . . ." He was looking out the window, where a tow truck was unloading the red pickup next to Jonathan's shiny black one. The wreath looked a little worse for the wear. "You should go settle up with the towing service," he suggested. "I'll pay for breakfast." He checked his wristwatch and arched his eyebrows, as if the time surprised him. "Then I need to get going."

I'd wanted to tell Jonathan about the key in my pocket, and the yearbook Jeff had left with me, but that discussion would have to wait for some other time, because I was running late, too. Still, I hesitated, not wanting to be in his debt again. "I'd really like to treat this time."

Jonathan reached for his wallet. "Maybe next time. You probably have a bigger bill to pay outside."

That was likely true, because I didn't have AAA coverage, which I planned to finally sign up for, after the day's close call.

"Okay, thank you," I said, slipping out of the booth, pulling on my coat and hurrying outside, where I paid a gruff, older man thirty-five dollars for the actual tow, plus twenty more for a "hook up" fee.

As the driver pulled away, his truck sounding worse than my van, Jonathan joined me by our waiting vehicles.

I turned to look up at him. "Thanks again for helping me, back in the ditch, and for breakfast," I said, wrapping my arms around myself to ward off the chill. "Is there anything I can *do* to repay you? Like watch the dogs again?" I grinned. "Or dress up Artie for Bark the Halls? Because you *are* taking him, right?"

Jonathan wore a gorgeous wool overcoat, unbuttoned in spite of the low temperature, and he slipped his hands into the pockets. "I've been meaning to ask you about the ball," he said, studying my eyes. For once, I didn't feel like he was boring into my soul, trying to determine if I was guilty of something. He wanted to gauge my reaction when he asked, "Are you going with Graham, as I assume? Or is there a chance you're free?"

My heart started racing and sinking at the same time, which was a wonderful, yet unpleasant feeling. I couldn't believe I was probably about to turn down a date with Jonathan Black for Sylvan Creek's biggest event of the year. A party to which he would almost certainly wear a *tux.* Then, realizing that he hadn't asked me yet, and might just want me to take his dogs, for crying out loud, I ventured, uncertainly, "Umm . . . Why do you ask?"

A big grin spread across his face, making him almost impossibly handsome. Moxie would've passed out, if she'd been there.

"I wanted to ask you to be my date, Daphne," he explained. "Sorry that I wasn't clear."

My heart thudded to my cowgirl boots. "I'm sorry, too," I said, hearing the profound disappointment in my voice. And it wasn't just because I had to reject an offer from someone I cared about. I realized that I really would've loved to have attended the dance with Jonathan. I would need to figure out what that meant for me and Gabriel. "I wish I could say yes," I added. "But I can't."

"I assumed as much, but I had to try." Jonathan was a confident man, and he didn't seem embarrassed in the least to have been turned down. But he did stop smiling. "You and Graham . . . Is it so serious that I can't ask you for one dance, at least? Or would that be overstepping a boundary?"

Smiling, I tucked some curls behind my ear, because my hair was starting to whip around in the wintry breeze. "I think a dance will be okay," I assured him, feeling lighter. "I think that would be fine."

He grinned again. "Good. I'll see you there."

"Do you want me to dress up Artie and Axis, beforehand?" I offered. "I wouldn't mind."

"Believe it or not" — Jonathan sounded like he couldn't believe *himself* — "I got them both bow ties, at Fetch!" As if reading my mind, because I was concerned that he'd bought flashy Artie basic black, he added, "Artie's is paisley. With a matching vest and cummerbund. And I'd rather not discuss any of that further. Or ever again."

"Fair enough," I said, as Jonathan reached outward, opening the door of my borrowed truck for me. Stepping on the old-fashioned runner board, I climbed behind the wheel. "I won't say a thing, except that I think you made a great choice."

Jonathan moved to close the door and end the conversation, but he stopped at the last moment. "Daphne," he said. "Moxie will be fine. I'm doing my best to watch out for her, to the extent that I can. Just try to trust me, okay?"

Then he slammed the door before I could respond, and I turned the key that would probably always be in the ignition, because we lived in Sylvan Creek, where the only crime seemed to be murder.

And maybe the occasional well-intentioned, impromptu break-in. Because, while I did trust Jonathan Black, if push came to shove, he would have to arrest my best friend, while I had no obligations,

beyond doing everything I could to keep
her out of jail.

CHAPTER 24

"The truck is fine," I assured Piper, who was fretting on speakerphone, while I was scurrying around Flour Power, trying to pack up twelve-dozen pet treats shaped like Christmas trees, tiny wrapped gifts, and snowmen. I'd painted the cookies with a dog-friendly "icing," made with a Greek yogurt base and tinted with natural colorings, so they looked quite festive. Carefully placing a half dozen into a bakery box stamped with Flour Power's peace sign-and-paw logo, I closed the carton's lid. Then I glanced at the cat-shaped clock, which told me I needed to transport the treats to the Sylvan Creek Hotel soon, while volunteers would still be decorating the ballroom for Bark the Halls. "I'm running a little behind, though, due to the *slight* accident — and a subsequent hour-long breakfast with Jonathan Black," I added. "Would you please let Socrates and Snowdrop out for a romp at some point? I don't think I'll be able to stop home before rehearsal."

There was a long silence, during which I feared Piper was going to refuse my request. Then she said, "I don't mind walking the dogs, assuming Snowdrop will get her paws wet. But are you sure you should play a ghost again?"

"No, I am not sure of that," I said, sealing the box with peace-sign washi tape. "But Ms. Bickelheim is counting on me. And maybe has been, for weeks. I have no idea how long ago my imagined audition even took place!"

"And I have no idea what you are talking about," Piper said. Her voice became muffled, and I assumed she was talking to someone else when she added, "No, it sounds crazy to me, too."

"Who's there?" I asked, adding cookies to another container. I hoped I'd baked enough. "Who are you talking to?"

"Roger," Piper explained. "And he also thinks you're making a mistake, performing in a play directed by someone whose behavior seems increasingly erratic."

"Oh, hey, Roger," I said, greeting Piper's boyfriend. I could picture them snuggled up on the couch at the farmhouse, sipping wine and admiring my sister's eight-foot-tall tree, which she always decorated with rustic ornaments and popcorn garlands. "Sorry I bothered you two," I told them. "And thanks for the advice, which I'm afraid I can't take at this late date."

Then I tapped the screen, prepared to end the call. But first, I sneaked a quick peek at the picture of my commissioned ball gown, which was currently undergoing minor nips and tucks, after a quick fitting at Ivy Dunleavy's shop that morning.

"Daphne, are you there?" Piper asked, interrupting my thoughts, which were filled with philosophers' quotes about the dangers of being seduced by material goods — sage advice that I seemed incapable of heeding, right then. "What are you doing?"

"I'm hanging up so you and Roger can enjoy your day," I said, putting the last few cookies into the final box. "Thanks again for taking care of the dogs, and please don't worry about the truck. The wreath is a little smooshed, but everything else is fine."

"Daphne . . ."

I again tapped the screen, this time really ending the call, before Piper could tell me that she was coming to town to check on her spare vehicle, and maybe her sister, too, although, I swore she'd been more concerned about the truck than me.

Tucking the phone into my pocket, I scooped up the tower of boxes, stumbled my way out the door, and maneuvered awkwardly down the street, my vision largely obscured. Fortunately, I was able to look downward, so I could keep an eye out for Tiny Tim. I was more than a little concerned that he would dart out of nowhere and knock me down again, costing me an entire day's work.

Thankfully, the pug never showed up, and I reached the hotel without incident. Fumbling blindly with one cold hand, I managed to open that door, too.

However, just when I thought my delivery had been a success, I nearly dropped everything when someone grabbed two boxes from the pile and exclaimed, in a booming, bass voice, "Ho, ho, hold on there, young lady! This looks like a disaster waiting to happen!"

CHAPTER 25

"Thanks for the help," I said, following hotel owner and Sylvan Creek chamber of commerce president Norm Alcorn through his inn's historic lobby, which was decorated in classic Victorian fashion, with burgundy ribbons, spicy-sweet-smelling orange pomanders, and flickering candles on the elaborately carved fireplace mantel. A fire popped and crackled in the hearth, which was surrounded by velvet chairs, where guests could relax and drink complimentary *glögg,* a warm, Swedish spiced wine, after shopping and exploring the town. Norm, who was going above and beyond as Sylvan Creek's holiday cheerleader, wore a full Santa suit, which he couldn't quite fill out, even with the help of the pillow that was obviously stuffed into the jacket. I nevertheless gave him an *A* for effort. "I love the suit!"

"I feel like we have to go all out this year

to promote Sylvan Creek as a safe, happy destination," Norm said, stopping at the front desk, which was currently unmanned. He set his share of the boxes onto the gleaming, mahogany counter, so I did the same, pushing aside an old-fashioned, pearl-handled letter opener and a stack of mail. I didn't understand why we were pausing there, when the ballroom was right ahead of us, behind two tall, arched wooden doors. "As you, of all people, should know, we're in danger of being best known for *murder,*" Norm added. He no longer seemed holly jolly, like when he'd greeted me with a belly laugh, and he twisted his hands. "And between CeeCee French's death, and the continued threat of a Poodles & More franchise here — which would be disastrous — it's not the happiest of holidays for pet-friendly merchants like yourself."

"I'll be okay," I assured him. "I think the whole town will be fine."

Norm didn't seem convinced. He raised one hand to fiddle with his omnipresent bow tie, only to realize that, for once, he wasn't wearing one. Instead, he smoothed the strip of white fur that ran down his red, fuzzy jacket. "I hope you're right."

"As the Dalai Lama once said, 'There is no benefit in worrying whatsoever.' I trust that things will work out." I moved to pick up my boxes. "In the meantime, if there's anything I can do . . ."

Norm rested one hand on my arm, stopping me. The overly familiar gesture came as a surprise, and I inadvertently withdrew a step.

"Sorry!" Norm said, quickly pulling back his hand. His pale blue eyes darted around, as if he was checking to make sure we wouldn't be overheard, then he lowered his voice. "There is something. . . . If you have any influence over Gabriel Graham, and could encourage him to tone down his coverage of, how shall we say . . . *less savory events,* that would be much appreciated." Norm smiled nervously. "You know, convince him to restore the *Gazette* to its kinder, gentler days, when every *tiny* flaw in the community wasn't exposed."

I didn't always agree with Gabriel's journalistic methods, but I didn't think people should be kept in the dark, either. Moreover, some of the things Gabriel covered weren't exactly "tiny." Last, but not least, there was no way anyone — let alone me — would ever convince Gabriel to make the *Gazette* "kinder and gentler."

"I'm sorry, Norm," I said. "But I don't have any influence over Gabriel, and I really

223

think the paper, while not perfect, is better since he took over."

"Oh, you can't think that, Daphne," Norm countered, rolling his eyes. "Surely, things were better when certain stories were swept under the carpet. Not every little secret needs to be exposed!"

"Of course not," I said. "But big stories need to be told. And, like I said, Gabriel is very independent —"

"But you two date."

"You're getting very personal," I said, taking another step backward. I felt like I was under attack. "Who I date, or don't date, is really none of your business, no offense. And, I'm telling you again, I couldn't — and wouldn't — try to tell Gabriel how to run his newspaper."

All at once, Norm's eyes grew flinty, his expression a strange contrast to the benevolent character he was playing. "I'm sorry to hear that, Daphne," he said. His voice had hardened, too. "Most local merchants agree that Graham's coverage of certain events — including stories on local murders that have been picked up nationally — has become detrimental to our community's image."

"The national media are already here about CeeCee," I reminded him. I'd seen a CNN truck parked near the Bijoux. "You can't avoid that type of coverage."

"CNN will be here and gone in a day," Norm said. "Graham keeps the stories going, digging up embarrassing details about decent citizens. Sometimes with your help, we all fear!"

"Who is 'we' . . . ?"

Norm didn't let me ask who else believed Gabriel's decision to actually print news in the *Gazette* — with or without my "help" — had harmed Sylvan Creek's reputation. He spoke right over me.

"It's nice when local merchants work together in unison," he said. "Supporting one another. Such gestures are reciprocated, which can be crucial in today's difficult business climate."

"I'm always supportive," I said, taken aback by his tone. I gestured to the boxes full of dog treats, which I'd donated for the ball. "I do my part."

Norm smiled, but there was no warmth behind it. "Of course, of course, Daphne. I hope you'll continue to prove that we can count on you."

I was standing in a lovely hotel lobby, talking with a man dressed like Santa Claus, but I felt increasingly uneasy. Almost like I was being threatened, in some vague way that I didn't understand.

Was I being warned that the chamber, which *was* influential in Sylvan Creek, would work against me if I didn't follow the majority on every issue?

It seemed that way, and I suddenly recalled my mother talking about a clothing boutique owner who'd run afoul of the chamber. The woman had been quietly left out of networking and promotional events targeting locals and tourists — her store basically made invisible — and the shop had shut down so quickly I couldn't even recall its name.

"It's very difficult to go it alone in Sylvan Creek," Mom had said, basically forcing *me* to join the chamber when I'd launched Lucky Paws, which had benefited from the organization's support.

Still, I set my jaw, refusing to be bullied.

Norm stared back at me, so suddenly we were in a standoff.

"I'll help you take the treats into the ballroom," I finally said, breaking the tense silence. "I need to get back to Flour Power."

I started to reach for some of the boxes again, only to feel Norm's hand on my wrist, gripping me more firmly. Once more, I pulled back, and he again released me, with another smile and another apology.

"Sorry, Daphne," he said, jerking his

thumb over his shoulder, gesturing to the closed doors behind him. "No one outside the decorating committee is allowed into the ballroom at this point. Elyse Hunter-Black, who has kindly agreed to lend her talents to our humble event, wants to have a big reveal this year."

"No problem," I said, as Norm gathered up all the boxes.

"Thank you for agreeing to walk Dunston later this week," he added, sounding more normal again. I almost wondered if I'd misconstrued his tone, moments before. But I didn't think I had. And I'd nearly forgotten that I was caring for his big Newfoundland soon. "I'll be very busy in the next few days, with both holiday bookings and the ball," Norm noted, backing away from me. The twinkle in his eyes made me doubt myself again. "And you've been so good with Dunston as he's recovered from his illness."

"He's a great dog," I said absently. I wasn't really thinking about the once ailing pup. As Norm used his foot to open one of the doors, I finally asked a question that had been bothering me since before CeeCee French's murder. "How long ago did you know about the franchise, Norm? When did you first hear about it?"

I knew that Norm heard my question, but he didn't respond. He slipped into the ballroom, managing to carry all the treats without giving me more than a glimpse of Elyse's handiwork.

Once again, I wasn't sure I trusted my senses, because what I'd seen was *very* different from the usual Bark the Halls décor.

I shook my head, trying to sort out my thoughts, then turned to leave the hotel — only to spy something behind the desk.

A wall of old-fashioned, brass keys, probably dating to the inn's establishment more than a century ago.

And each of those keys — presumably to the rooms on the floors above — hung from a velvet ribbon in the hotel's signature burgundy hue.

CHAPTER 26

Climbing the carpeted stairs to the inn's third floor, I fidgeted with the key in my pocket, wondering why Jeff Updegrove had left it with me. Technically, hotel guests were supposed to leave their keys at the desk when they went out. Hence the wall that was full of shiny brass at that time of day, because Sylvan Creek's many tourists were either skiing at nearby Pocono resorts, visiting the locally famous toboggan run that plunged from Bear Tooth forest and spun out over the ice on Lake Wallapawakee, or shopping downtown for gifts for their pets and people.

I needed to return to my business, but I couldn't resist at least opening the door to whatever room the key unlocked — and I assumed it would be Jeff's — because he had to have left me the curious object for a reason.

Padding quietly down the silent hallway,

which was dimly lit by gleaming brass wall sconces, each festooned with a ribbon and a sprig of mistletoe, I found room 37 and inserted the key into the lock.

At the last moment, I slipped my sleeve over my hand before touching the doorknob, although I doubted the maids who were probably cleaning the room every day were worried about leaving prints. And the knob, like the one at Spa and Paw, was likely handled by multiple guests between cleanings.

Still, just to be on the safe side, I made sure my fingers were covered. Twisting the knob, which was difficult, I finally managed to open the door. Then I crossed the threshold, only to discover that I wasn't exactly where I'd expected to be.

And the room, curtained off, dim, and cluttered, was filled with surprises, too.

Some of which I really wanted to take home.

I was debating whether I'd get in trouble for borrowing a few items, since Jeff had almost certainly left me the key so I could do just that, when my cell phone pinged with four messages.

The first was from Bitsy Bickelheim — which was a surprise, since I didn't have her in *my* contacts.

Rehearsal canceled tonight! Extra shift at Oh, Beans. So many peppermint mochas!! Meet tomorrow 7 p.m. at high school.

I hadn't been overly eager to spend my evening with the Sylvan Creek Players, but I was a little concerned about the fact that I'd only have one chance to practice pointing at Scrooge's grave. However, there was nothing I could do about the local run on seasonal coffee drinks, so I checked the next two texts, which were from Ivy Dunleavy, who had sent photos.

One image featured my completed gown, on a dressmaker's dummy, with the exclamation, Tada!

The second picture showed my Ghost of Christmas Future costume, above the word, Yikes.

"Yikes, indeed," I muttered, clicking onto the final message, which was from Moxie and consisted of a string of emojis that I immediately translated, although I kind of wished I hadn't:

Chapter 27

"Moxie, you know I won't stay upright for two minutes," I pointed out, nevertheless lacing up a pair of mismatched ice skates I'd rented for fifty cents from a hut on the banks of Pinchwater Pond, a pretty little body of water in the woods near Sylvan Creek.

The town didn't have an official skating rink, but every winter, local residents pitched in to ring the pond with Edison lights, fill the lean-to shed with hand-me-down skates, and stoke a bonfire that would blaze each night for as long as the water was frozen solid enough to support a lighted pine tree, always placed in the middle of the ice. Most evenings, volunteers from scout troops sold hot cocoa, as well as hotdogs and marshmallows, which skaters roasted on whittled-down sticks, gathered from the surrounding woods. And, of course, it being Sylvan Creek, everyone brought their pets.

Socrates and I often visited the pond during the winter months, but we didn't venture onto the ice. We just liked to soak up the atmosphere, while Socrates enjoyed a hot-dog or two and I scorched some marshmallows. However, once each year, Moxie managed to convince me to turn a few slow, clumsy circles with the other skaters, until I inevitably fell on my butt and retreated awkwardly back to the same rickety wooden bench I was sitting on right then.

"Winter sports never go well for me," I reminded Moxie, just like I did every year. I tugged on a lace, which broke in my hands. "Don't you remember what happened when we tried cross-country skiing?"

Moxie, who had managed to dig a pure white, Dorothy-Hamill-worthy pair of skates from the otherwise random, beat-up pile, took a break from looping her own laces around shiny, silver hooks. "Oh, I do remember," she said brightly. "We were having a wonderful time, until you went over the edge of that little hill —"

"Big Drop." I supplied the name, thinking the hill was far from little.

"Yes!" Moxie bent again and tied a perfect bow, while I tried to stretch my broken lace far enough to make a tiny knot. "Then you rolled to the bottom, where old Max Pottinger found you, gave you some herbal tea — and tried to kill you and bury you in a shallow, snowy grave. None of which can happen here. The pond is flat, there's no tea, and I haven't seen Mr. Pottinger here in years."

She was kind of missing the point, and exaggerating the part about the shallow grave. I'd merely feared that reclusive Mr. Pottinger had intended to kill me. He'd actually turned out to be quite nice.

However, I didn't bother correcting Moxie, who was standing up, not even wobbling on the gleaming blades beneath her feet. I struggled to rise, my knees knocking.

"I should point out that I really can't stay long," I said, grabbing Moxie's arm as we moved slowly toward the ice, which glistened under a full moon. The bonfire blazed cheerfully, and the sound of children's laughter filled the air as kids and a few adults zipped around, playing tag and crack-the-whip. A bunch of dogs were skidding around, too, trying to keep up and barking merrily. "I need to get home to Socrates and Snowdrop."

"I can't believe Jeff Updegrove left you a secret key to CeeCee's room, which turned out to be full of custom-designed poodle outfits," Moxie said, stepping onto the ice

234

first, followed reluctantly by me. She peeled my fingers off her arm and performed a quick twirl, while I flailed to stay upright. When she stopped spinning, and I'd managed to steady myself, she added, "And you really didn't take any?"

"I thought I should ask Jonathan first, and I didn't want to text him and let him know I'd visited CeeCee's room."

"I think, for once, your snooping was legitimate," Moxie said, gliding in a circle around me. She wore a knit beret with a pompom on top, plaid leggings, and a chunky, vintage men's fisherman's sweater, an outfit that would've fit right in at Pinchwater Pond circa 1959. "Jeff left you a key, with no explanation. Any sensible person would assume that the key was meant to be used. And since you're watching the poodle, it stands to reason that he expected you to pick up some of her belongings."

"When you put it that way, I almost wish I'd borrowed a few things, to get Snowdrop out of her rumpled cashmere sweater," I said, while two kids and a border collie zoomed past, nearly knocking me down. I got control of my feet again and said, "Still, I think I should consult with Jonathan first."

"Probably wise." Moxie pushed off, floated to an open spot near the tree, and proceeded to complete what I thought was a double axel. A few people applauded. Then she glided back to me and slid to a stop, kicking up ice. Holding out her arm, she kindly offered to let me lean on her again. I gratefully accepted. "Why do you think Jeff had *CeeCee's* key?" she mused, raising a question I hadn't really considered. "Wouldn't CeeCee have kept that with her when she went out?"

I understood what Moxie was saying. That CeeCee's key should have been on her body, if she wasn't killed at the hotel. Which mustn't have been the case. It would've been impossible to get her corpse from one of the rooms to the town tree without anyone noticing. The Sylvan Creek Hotel was always booked solid near the holidays. Which meant that someone almost certainly would have heard the murder taking place, too.

But Moxie's theory did have one flaw.

"Technically, guests are supposed to drop off their keys at the front desk when they leave the hotel," I pointed out, squeezing her arm when we hit a bumpy spot. "There's a place to hang them, behind the counter."

"And yet, the key left the premises in somebody's possession. Either Jeff's, or Cee-Cee's."

I looked sideways at Moxie. "Do you really think he might've taken the key off her body?"

"I think it's possible. Especially since he hurried out of state so quickly."

"Interesting."

We'd completed my obligatory single turn around the pond, and I tugged on Moxie's sleeve, indicating that I wanted to head toward the edge of the ice. She reluctantly followed, and I was relieved when my blades connected with snowy ground. Even so, I had to wobble my way back to the benches, choosing one by the bonfire. As soon as we sat down, two kids in scout uniforms approached, handing us sticks and offering us snacks. Digging into my pocket, I pulled out a dollar, the standard donation for a paper bag full of marshmallows.

When Moxie and I were both situated, sitting side by side, our sticks in the fire and gooey treats toasting in the popping flames, I finally asked, "Are we ever going to talk about the scissors?"

Her marshmallow had turned golden brown and puffy, and she pulled it back, plucking it from the stick while it was still hot. "There's not much to say," she told me, with a tiny shrug. "Somehow, a pug got scissors that belonged in my drawer, and that I didn't know were missing until after CeeCee's murder. I have no idea what really happened."

"You . . . you know who the pug belongs to, right?" I ventured, as my marshmallow erupted into flames. I yanked the stick back, blowing on the sugary torch, but it was too late. Shaking the stick, I flung the mess into the fire.

Moxie, who'd downed her snack in two delicate bites, seemed oblivious to my continued troubles. She licked her sticky fingers, staring into the flames, and I couldn't read her expression, nor her tone of voice, when she said, "Mike Cavanaugh. The last time Detective Black and I discussed the scissors, he told me that Mike is back in town. And that you spoke with him."

"Yes," I confirmed. "The pug, Tiny Tim, led me to Mike's house. We talked for a few minutes. I was hoping he'd contacted you by now."

Jamming another marshmallow onto her stick, Moxie pursed her lips and shook her head. "Nope. Haven't heard from him."

"He stopped by Spa and Paw, you know," I said quietly. Giving up on open-fire cooking, I poked at the logs. "He didn't want you to get an 'unpleasant surprise' — his words — in public." Moxie didn't say anything, so I kept talking. "He still seems like a nice guy. One who regrets whatever happened years ago, and who wants to make it up to you. Even if that means implicating himself in a murder to take the focus off you."

Moxie jolted and faced me for a moment, her eyes wide. I'd surprised her. "He did that?"

"I think so. At least, that was his plan."

Moxie returned her attention to the fire. "What if he really committed the crime?" she noted in a whisper. "It's a possibility."

"Yes," I conceded. "But my gut tells me that's not the case. I could be wrong, but I don't think the guy who cares for the world's worst-behaved pug — and who still cares for you — murdered anyone." I recalled how Jonathan had described his discussion with Mike as more of a counseling session than an interrogation. "And I get the sense that Jonathan agrees, although he hasn't said that explicitly."

For once, Moxie's eyes didn't light up at the mention of Jonathan Black. I thought the fact that she was still focused on Mike was telling. "You really think he still cares about me?"

"Yes. I really do," I promised her. "And I think you two should at least talk."

239

I thought I spied a tear glistening in the corner of my best friend's eye, and her voice sounded choked. "I don't know, Daph. . . ."

"Mike told me that he didn't cheat on you," I added. "He said the old story is wrong."

Setting down her own stick, after her second marshmallow had dropped into the fire, Moxie shifted to face me again. "Then what *did* happen?"

Something worse.

That's what Mike had said. But I wasn't sure I believed him. And I had no details. So I simply told Moxie, "I think you should ask him yourself. Meet someplace neutral, like the Silver Moon, or the Lakeside, or Oh, Beans. . . ." I rattled off three of the best public meeting places in Sylvan Creek, because I wasn't 100 percent sure Mike hadn't committed murder. "And *finally* ask for the truth, which really might set you free." I loved that Moxie was stuck in the past, in many ways, but I believed that her heart needed to move forward. "Just reach out, okay? Obviously, I know where he lives, and I have his contact information. I can deliver a message, if you want."

"I'll think about it," Moxie promised, rising. Her eyes still looked watery, but she smiled and managed to tease me. "But only if you take one more turn around the ice."

"I'll skate — if you'll come to Bark the Halls," I countered. "Because it won't be the same without you. And you need to have some fun."

Moxie wrinkled her nose while she considered my bargain. Then she stuck out her hand. "Deal."

"Excellent!" We shook on our agreement, and I handed the paper bag, which was still nearly full, to some rosy-cheeked kids who were swooping in to claim our bench. While I was tottering away, they snatched up the sticks, too. I heard them calling "thank you" and laughing — probably at me — as I again stepped tentatively onto the slick surface. "This is seriously my last time out here," I added firmly. "I have had a long day, between wrecking a truck, getting threatened by Norm Alcorn — and stuffing myself with a half-dozen pancakes before turning down Jonathan's offer to take *me* to the ball."

Moxie might've been primarily focused on her lost love, but she still retained some interest in her law-enforcement crush. Completely ignoring the fact that I'd mentioned a car accident and a threat, she swooped around to face me, her mouth hanging open. "Did you just say Jonathan

Black asked you to Bark the Halls? And you *turned him down*?"

I nodded, my feet sliding in and out of their own accord. "Yes. That's what I said. I already promised Gabriel I'd go with him."

Moxie stood there in flabbergasted silence while a conga line of skaters and a pack of dogs tried to maneuver around us. Then Moxie Bloom, still stunned and speechless, completely wiped out, taking me down with her.

I thought I saw stars. But as I lay flat on my back, blinking up at the sky, I figured out that the flashing light came from a completely different, external source. I also realized that someone I hadn't even known was at Pinchwater Pond had likely overheard Moxie's and my conversation — which *wasn't* a good thing.

CHAPTER 28

"I hope none of my inevitable bruises show when I wear my gown — and that Gabriel isn't too unhappy, after he almost certainly overheard me talking with Moxie about Jonathan's invitation," I told Snowdrop, who was the only resident of Plum Cottage who seemed to care, in the least, that my ice skating misadventures might have negative ramifications at the upcoming ball.

Socrates, who had either mastered or overcome his ardor for Snowdrop, had shaken his head and wandered up to the loft at my first mentions of Gabriel and especially the dress, which I needed to pick up the next day. And Tinks, who had no interest in romantic affairs or social gatherings, let alone clothing, had slunk away when I'd tried to show him the picture Ivy had sent to my phone.

Snowdrop, however, was following me around the cottage, listening attentively as I

243

discussed my concerns about Bark the Halls.

"What are the odds Gabriel Graham would be snapping pictures at the pond?" I added, turning off the kitchen light for the night. It was almost time for bed. "I didn't want to mention Jonathan until I figured out what, if anything, I needed to say."

Snowdrop whined in a sympathetic way, as if she completely understood.

"And, as for the bruises, I swear, it's not like me to worry so much about my appearance," I noted, heading for the living room. "There's just something about this dress, you know?"

Close on my heels, Snowdrop yapped in agreement. She was a surprisingly good listener when the topic interested her.

"I realize you have a huge wardrobe of gorgeous clothes," I continued, padding into the living room, my big slippers slapping against the wooden floor. I was grateful to have wide soles under my feet, and, although I was usually open to all sorts of experiences, I couldn't understand why so many people wanted to put blades on the bottom of shoes. I tossed two logs on the fire, so we'd have heat for a while. "I'm sorry I couldn't bring anything back for you. I wasn't sure I should be in CeeCee's room, let alone take things."

In fact, I'd severely restricted my snooping, too. I'd seen several things, including some binders that I'd really wanted to check out. Especially one that was labeled *Product Designs — Toys, Apparel, Accessories.* As someone who dealt with a lot of pets, I was intrigued by what CeeCee might have in the works to sell at her franchises. I also wondered if the new products were in development because of the scandal I still needed to investigate. However, I'd refrained from touching anything, except some of Snowdrop's clothes.

"I did look at your outfits," I told the poodle, who continued to follow me, as I turned off a small lamp near the door. "You have some unique, beautiful things that must've cost a bundle!"

Snowdrop whined again, this time more softly. I wasn't sure if I'd made her sad by mentioning CeeCee, or if she was also sorry that I hadn't snagged a few of her designer duds back at the hotel.

Turning, I looked into her dark eyes, noting that her expression wasn't quite as haughty as before. Her fur was also flattened and her cashmere sweater was a mess.

"Not to pressure you," I ventured softly, hoping I wasn't about to break our fragile connection and send her scurrying back to her crate. "But do you want to change out of that dirty sweater? Because I have a hand-knit, free-range yak cardigan that I think might fit you."

I'd ordered a sweater for Artie from former murder suspect and holistic pet healer Arlo Finch, who also knit canine clothes, hoping to give the cardigan to the Chihuahua for Christmas. But I was pretty sure the red-and-green-striped sweater was too big. Plus, paisley bow tie aside, Jonathan never dressed up the little dog. I wasn't really sure what I'd been thinking when I'd contacted Arlo.

"Do you want to try on the sweater?" I asked again. "It's not cashmere, or haute couture, but it is one of a kind and pretty cute."

Snowdrop hesitated, dancing uncertainly on her paws. Then she sighed and growled, but not at me. The sound was clearly a grumble of concession, as if she were telling me, "Fine. I'll try your cheap clothes."

A little more gratitude would've been nice. But we were making headway.

"Come on," I said, leading the way up the spiral staircase. When we reached the loft, I dug around in my small closet until I found a bag from Arlo's new pet-therapy practice,

Peaceable Pets West in Sedona, Arizona. Pulling out the cardigan, I held it up for Snowdrop's approval. "What do you think?"

She couldn't help wrinkling her nose and whining with disappointment, which earned her a snuffle of rebuke from Socrates. I hadn't even realized he'd been watching us from his purple velvet pillow.

Snowdrop looked over at him, then her head drooped, as if she regretted acting snooty.

I couldn't help grinning. Socrates *was* still suffering from a case of unrequited puppy love, but he was clearly done fawning. In fact, I got the sense that the tables were starting to turn between the two dogs, and that Snowdrop was beginning to want Socrates's attention. She looked disappointed when he closed his eyes again, returning to his nightly meditation.

"You two will figure it out," I whispered to the poodle, kneeling down and helping her switch garments. As I'd expected, the red-and-green cardigan fit her perfectly and looked quite festive against her white coat. "You look adorable!" I assured her, standing up, the cashmere sweater in hand, so I could put it on a pile of my own clothes that needed laundered — only to realize that I probably shouldn't run the expensive garment through Piper's washing machine.

"Jeez, I hope this doesn't need to be dry cleaned," I said, checking for a tag, while Snowdrop, who seemed more pleased by her new outfit than she'd anticipated, walked too casually past Socrates.

I was about to tell her that he didn't like canine apparel, in general, so if she was trying to impress him, she was barking up the wrong tree. No pun intended.

However, before I could say anything, Socrates opened one eye, and I could tell that he thought she looked cute. His expression was quite transparent. At least to me, who knew him well.

"Why is romance always complicated?" I muttered, returning my attention to the sweater. Unfortunately, there were no instructions for laundering on the tag, which looked to be hand-embroidered in a distinctive, swooping font that spelled out *Park Avenue Pets.* I'd seen the label in other outfits in CeeCee's hotel room, too. The fabrics, to my admittedly untrained fingers, had felt sumptuous.

"I guess I'll call Mom for help," I said, placing the pretty pup garment into my wicker basket full of no-name jeans and shirts I'd picked up during my world travels. Then I set a pillow on the floor for Snowdrop, who didn't seem in any rush to retreat to her crate. On the contrary, ignoring the bed I'd made for her, she jumped up onto my mattress, where she sat down, watching me hopefully — when not shooting the lowly pillow disdainful looks.

I hesitated, weighing my options, because I usually had a rule about dogs sleeping in their own spaces. But Snowdrop was trying to fit in at Plum Cottage, and I doubted she'd ever slept on the floor in her former life, so I finally grumbled, "Fine. You can stay."

I climbed into bed, too. When I was settled under my comforter, I glanced at the basset hound who was already snoring on his humble cushion. Then I nudged Snowdrop, who'd curled into a ball, and whispered, "Do *you* want to go to Bark the Halls? I thought it might be beneath you. But you and Socrates might have fun."

Snowdrop raised her head, the tags on her diamond-studded collar jangling, and I swore I spied an eager gleam in her eyes.

I smiled. "I'll make an appointment with Moxie for you, and try to figure out what you can wear. If worse comes to worse, I can always contact Jonathan Black and admit that I know you have a whole wardrobe waiting in a hotel room."

Snowdrop wriggled happily, then curled up again and closed her eyes, while I reached for my cell phone, which I'd set in its usual spot on the nightstand, next to my old landline. I started to call my mother, to ask about washing fine fabrics, only to reconsider and check the Internet. A few minutes later, I was fairly convinced that handwashing would be okay.

As Snowdrop's snores joined Socrates's, and Tinks found his spot at the foot of the bed — after giving the poodle the stink eye — I next called up the Web site for the *Weekly Gazette,* to make sure Gabriel had made good on his promise to feature a photo of dogs and skating kids, as opposed to an image of me and Moxie sprawled on our backs.

Needless to say, I was pleased to see a picture of a lively game of crack-the-whip pop up, right on the home page, above the caption, *Old-fashioned fun keeps chills at bay at Pinchwater Pond, Sylvan Creek's skating destination for more years than even old-timers can recall.*

"So much for Norm Alcorn's overblown worries about Gabriel's digging up skeletons and exposing secrets," I whispered, thinking small-town life was softening up the hard-nosed reporter, just like it was doing for

Jonathan, who would never, ever have bent any rules during a homicide investigation when I'd first met him. "Before long, the *Weekly Gazette* will be full of reprinted school menus and articles about suppers at the Moose Lodge again."

Of course, I didn't really think Gabriel would ever carry things that far. And maybe he hadn't lost his edge at all, because when I scrolled down a little farther, the lead article, beneath the quaint feature photo, was headlined, MURDER WEAPON TIED TO LOCAL SALON.

I wasn't sure I wanted to read that story, but I knew that I would, just in case Gabriel, with his "sources," had included information I didn't know yet.

However, to be honest, I was more intrigued by the subhead: MEMORIAL SERVICE FOR FRENCH SCHEDULED FOR TOMORROW.

CHAPTER 29

"Honestly, Daphne, I'm not sure why you're going to this service," my mother complained, leading the way up the steps to Walzacker's Funeral Home, located in a lovely Greek revival building in an otherwise residential part of Sylvan Creek. The surrounding homes were all decorated for the holidays, smoke curled from most of the chimneys, and a snowman in a red scarf waved at us with twig arms from the house next door, so the setting wasn't as grim as one might've expected. Stepping onto the porch, Mom stomped snow off her low-heeled Stuart Weitzman boots — a slight downgrade in terms of height and brand, in recognition of the day's weather, which was blustery and prone to squalls. "Given that you and Celeste weren't exactly friends, your attendance is rather morbid, don't you think?"

"I feel a certain posthumous kinship with

CeeCee, since I found her body," I said, not bothering to remind Mom that she hadn't known Celeste French *at all.* I had no idea why she was stopping by the first of several services that would commemorate CeeCee's life. The others would be held in New York City, where CeeCee had had a penthouse, and in California, where her business was currently headquartered and where her ashes would eventually be interred, according to Gabriel's story in the *Gazette.* The Sylvan Creek event was just a gathering so local people could remember her and pay their respects to her family. Following my mother through tall double doors into a large foyer, I added, "And I am here on behalf of Snowdrop."

I hadn't exactly meant that I was representing the poodle — although I kind of felt that way. I'd mainly meant that I hoped to find someone who might know about her future, since Jeff Updegrove had seemingly disappeared.

Of course, my mother didn't wait for me to explain. She unfurled her favorite Burberry plaid scarf from around her neck while sighing profoundly. "You and those *dogs,* Daphne!"

Then she shrugged off her coat, shoved it into the arms of a man in a suit — who I didn't think worked at the funeral home, given his look of surprise — and sashayed off into a reception room that was filled with people and rows of folding chairs. If my hunch was correct, Mom planned to offer condolences and troll for news about the fate of the planned French's Poodles & More franchise, as related to local real estate.

Shooting the baffled bystander who continued to hold Mom's outerwear a look of apology, I followed her, passing a white-draped table that held cards and candles and dozens of photos of CeeCee.

Then I joined the milling crowd, immediately spotting Gabriel, who was speaking with people I didn't recognize. He hadn't whipped out his notebook, and he didn't have his camera, but I knew the event would yield a story.

I also spotted Jonathan, who nodded to me, but remained in conversation with Norm Alcorn. Judging from the way Maeve Templeton, Realtor, was hovering, vulture-like, I was pretty sure my mother would soon join that discussion or swoop in to monopolize Norm the moment the two men parted.

I, meanwhile, didn't know who to mingle with until the inevitable speeches started.

As suspects in CeeCee's murder, Moxie and Mike Cavanaugh certainly hadn't shown up, and the few former classmates I recognized were already in tight circles, forming the same cliques they'd belonged to in high school.

A few teachers had stopped by, too. They were also clustered together, chatting.

As I watched them, I noted that Bitsy Bickelheim, who'd had such a strange — and strong — reaction to the news about CeeCee's visit to Sylvan Creek, wasn't paying her respects. Then I also remembered the photo in the yearbook. The one in which Ms. Bickelheim had stood on the sidelines, between the cheerleaders and the football players.

"I need to look at that again," I muttered to myself, just as someone tapped my shoulder.

I half expected the stranger who'd accepted my mother's coat to shove it back at *me,* because I'd probably looked like Mom's assistant, the way she'd addressed me in the lobby. And when I turned around, someone was handing me something — but it wasn't an eight-hundred-dollar, double-breasted wool trench from Barney's.

It was a check with a similarly large sum on the line marked DOLLARS, and the phrase "For Care of Snowdrop" in the MEMO line.

I heard the surprise in my voice as my gaze darted between the signature and the face of the man who matched the name.

"Jeff Updegrove! You actually came back!"

"I really can't talk now," Jeff said, looking nervously around the room, where the only available activity was conversation. "I need to get going."

"The service hasn't even started yet," I reminded him. "And we need to talk."

Jeff was already walking away, and I followed him, the chatter in the main reception room fading and our footsteps muffled by heavy carpeting. The layout of the repurposed house was rather complicated, and he slipped around a corner.

I made the turn, too, and discovered that we'd reached the alcove where my mother should've left her coat, which I spied immediately. Obviously, the stranger in the suit had been kind enough to hang it up, while I still wore my jacket and was getting a little warm, chasing after a surprisingly speedy former parliamentarian and salutatorian.

"What is your big hurry?" I asked, blocking the exit, while Jeff rooted around for his coat. "We need to talk about Snowdrop —

and yearbooks, and keys!" I held up the check, which was still clutched in my hand. "And this payment . . . How long do you expect me to keep Snowdrop? Or are you taking her when you leave town? Or today?"

I'd asked a lot of questions and still hadn't covered everything I wanted and needed to know, and Jeff, who'd pulled a nondescript black overcoat from a sea of nondescript black overcoats, finally turned around. His cheeks were ruddy, and a few beads of sweat had formed on his forehead, just beneath a comb-over that made him look about ten years older than he really was.

I had a feeling that being part of CeeCee French's executive team had contributed to his premature aging.

"I answered most of those questions in the note I left you," he said, slipping on his coat. "I told you that I'll take the dog with me when I return to California on December 27th, after visiting my family."

"There was no note," I said. "And no way to contact you."

Jeff's brow furrowed. "I put a note in the envelope. On my company letterhead, with my cell phone number and direct line to my office. I told you to contact me if the arrangement didn't work and I needed to find someone else to care for the dog."

"I don't think you left any note, except for a brief one on the envelope," I said, stepping sideways to block him. He was trying to move past me. "Otherwise, there was just a key and a yearbook."

I suddenly recalled that Jeff had placed a tiny sticky note on the yearbook. But he wasn't talking about that.

"I . . . I don't believe that was the case," he countered. "And I really need to be going. Family obligations, you know. CeeCee French's death should make my holiday less stressful, not more! She can't compel me to spend my whole day here, from beyond the grave. She stopped being my boss when she died!"

That all came out in a burst, and he jerked his hand, as if to clap it over his mouth, while I wished Jonathan had been there to witness everything. I thought the comment, or at least the way Jeff had blown up at CeeCee, was somewhat incriminating. Plus, I would have liked to prove a statement I'd once made about the fact that people tended to open up to me.

"Sorry," Jeff said, his voice hoarse with regret and his eyes miserable. "I didn't mean . . . I've just been under a lot of pressure, and that detective is here. . . ."

"Yes, Jonathan Black can be intimidating,"

I agreed, stepping back so we could move away from the alcove and into a stiffly formal sitting area that was nice enough, but still clearly part of a funeral home. It was just the vibe in the whole place, and I could hardly blame Jeff for wanting to return to his family visit. Yet I still needed him to answer a few questions. "But you can't hide from Detective Black. If he has questions for you, he's going to find you and ask them. And in the meantime, I need you to tell me more about Snowdrop and the other objects you gave me."

Jeff regained some composure, although his gaze kept darting over my shoulder, as if he expected Jonathan to come charging into the room at any moment, handcuffs at the ready. "If you are amenable, and the check I wrote is sufficient, I would like you to keep Snowdrop for a few more days," he requested. "As you can imagine, CeeCee's estate is quite complicated, and we have yet to find any provision for the dog — who is of no interest to the trainer, unfortunately."

I suddenly felt sorry for Snowdrop, who had a wealth of material goods, but no one running to claim her. "Why not?"

"She's spoiled rotten and miserable to be around," Jeff said. "She literally bites every hand that feeds her, with the exception of

CeeCee's." He shrugged. "I can't imagine who we'll foist her upon."

Snowdrop and I had gotten off to a rocky start, but she wasn't a bad dog at heart, and his choice of words rankled me. "She just requires a little patience, and surely she doesn't need to be 'foisted' on anyone. Surely, someone will step forward and give her the loving home she deserves."

Jeff snorted a laugh. "Yeah, we'll see."

I'd started out feeling sorry for him, for being under CeeCee's thumb, and I still suspected that working for someone who'd treated him badly had hardened him. But that situation also could've made him more sympathetic. And he could've found another job, somewhere along the way. Either way, I suddenly found myself not caring that Jeff Updegrove had forgotten me.

"If you need help finding a *good* home for Snowdrop, please let me know," I said, keeping the edge of anger out of my voice. "I'm pretty good at matching people and pets."

"I'll call you if necessary," he said. "There still might be provision for her, somewhere."

I suddenly felt very concerned about Snowdrop's future. However, there wasn't anything else to say at that point, so I asked, "Why did you leave me the key?"

"It's in the note —"

"I didn't find a note," I repeated, hoping that I'd shaken the envelope hard enough. It would be embarrassing to go home and learn that all along there had been instructions. "So just tell me, please, okay?"

"CeeCee's room is filled with Snowdrop's designer clothes." Jeff rolled his eyes, and I couldn't imagine how he'd managed to win parliamentarian, even, if he'd had the same attitude in high school.

I also wondered why I'd told him I'd never forget him, when I didn't think I'd ever really known him. I could probably blame the same impulse that had compelled me to don the leg warmers I'd been wearing in a picture on page forty-two of the yearbook. As I'd told Mike Cavanaugh the other day, we'd all made youthful mistakes.

"So, it's okay if I take some outfits?" I asked, not confessing that I'd already visited the room. I could tell Jeff was getting anxious to leave again. He continued to look past me, on high alert for Jonathan.

"Yes. Yes, of course," he said. "The dog is always dressed, and she certainly won't wear the knock-offs we sell in our stores, or the higher quality clothes available at Fetch! even." I was surprised that he'd just denigrated his own products, but I didn't interrupt him. "I'd hate for you to get bitten, just because Snowdrop's fashion whims weren't indulged," he added. "Who'd watch her then?"

Jeff really hated the poor poodle, and I silently vowed to protect her if there was no provision in CeeCee's will, as Piper had feared. I was afraid Jeff would dump her off at a shelter, which would kill a pampered pooch like Snowdrop, as surely as someone had murdered her person.

I studied Jeff, questioning whether he might really have killed CeeCee. I was starting to think it was possible. Then I asked, "What's the deal with the yearbook — which *did* have a tiny note attached? Why did you give the book to me? And why do you think it might be 'helpful'?"

He didn't respond. He was looking over my shoulder again, and his face suddenly blanched, as if he'd seen a ghost. Then he backed up a few steps, retreating toward an archway that I thought led to the foyer. The place was something of a maze.

"My parents mentioned that you have a reputation for solving murders," he said, continuing to edge away. "I thought recalling details about CeeCee's past might be helpful, if you were looking into her death. It was probably a stupid idea!"

With that, Jeff Updegrove turned on his heel and hurried out the door, leaving me alone in a pretty and yet melancholy parlor, wondering why he'd just lied — and who he'd just seen walk behind us, because I was pretty sure that, if that person had been Jonathan, he would've made his presence known.

CHAPTER 30

"Your life is so thrilling." Fidelia Tutweiler sighed, shaking her head wistfully.

My part-time accountant had joined me and the dogs at Piper's farmhouse for a year-end review of my books. Given that Fidelia was still taking accounting classes to supplement her degree from an already-defunct online program, Piper — who was a meticulous business owner — thought perhaps she should supervise the meeting. Not that we'd mentioned that to Fidelia. She believed I'd chosen the farmhouse over my cottage because there was more room to spread out the receipts I was *trying* to keep organized. We sat across from each other at Piper's breakfast bar, while my sister popped more corn to string on her Christmas tree, since she and Roger had eaten most of an earlier batch, the day I'd talked to them on speakerphone.

"You're sitting for a famous dog," Fidelia

continued, listing the so-called exciting aspects of my life and glancing at Snowdrop, who sat next to Socrates on a braided throw rug near the oven.

I was trying not to make a big deal out of what appeared to be a growing friendship, nor the fact that Snowdrop was *on the floor,* like a normal dog, and still sporting her red-and-green, yak-hair sweater. In fact, she looked quite cozy.

"You also got threatened by the president of the chamber of commerce," Fidelia added, summarizing things I probably shouldn't have mentioned while she was supposed to be focused on bookkeeping. "Plus, former high school classmates leave you mysterious presents — and you got *my* part in *A Christmas Carol!*"

Piper was dumping steaming hot popcorn into two green bowls, and her hand jerked, so she spilled some fluffy kernels on the marble countertop. We exchanged shocked, puzzled glances. Socrates had jolted, too. The tags on his collar were still jingling when I turned back to Fidelia. "*You* auditioned for the role of the Ghost of Christmas Future?"

"Yes, and I was sure I'd get the part." Fidelia sighed again and picked up a yellow highlighter. Uncapping the pen, she swiped

265

it over some numbers on one of the receipts. I hoped *she* knew why she'd done that, because I had no idea. "I really went all out at the audition."

"How so?" Piper inquired, sounding as if she already knew the story was going to exasperate her. "I have *got* to hear how this all went wrong for *both* of you."

If Fidelia caught the sarcasm in Piper's voice, she didn't let on. "I've been trying to improve my social life, and I thought community theater really seemed like the way to go," she said, highlighting some more numbers on a different slip of paper. The action seemed random, and I wondered if I'd made a mistake by suggesting that we enjoy hot toddies to ward off the chill outside. "I went to the audition in a full costume, complete with a terrifying rubber mask that made it difficult to breathe," Fidelia continued. "And I didn't break character the whole time. I walked up onto the stage, pointed at a trash can that was filling in for Scrooge's grave until the set could be built, and then floated away out the door when Ms. Bickelheim yelled 'cut.' I thought the whole thing was rather impressive." She shot me an almost accusing look, to the degree that meek Fidelia could manage that. "Until I learned *you* got the part!"

Piper looked like she wanted to *thunk* her head against something, while Socrates lay down, whined, and placed his paws over his muzzle. Snowdrop, who was unfamiliar with Fidelia — but who had barked with disapproval at the accountant's droopy cardigan — appeared confused.

"So, you never said a word, even to give Ms. Bickelheim your name?" I asked, trying to lead Fidelia to her own revelation. "You didn't even let her hear your voice?"

"Of course not." Fidelia frowned at me and Piper, like *we* were clueless. "The ghost doesn't speak. And I thought it would be dramatic to just leave. . . ." All at once, a light went on behind her brown eyes, which matched her brown hair. "Oh . . . Ms. Bickelheim had no idea who I was, did she?"

"Nope, not a clue," Piper said, opening the fridge and grabbing some butter and parmesan cheese. I had a feeling the second batch of popcorn was about to go the way of the first. "And, for some reason, she thought Daphne had tried out," Piper added, dropping nearly an entire stick of butter into the still-warm pot before heading for her pantry, where she retrieved some dog biscuits, a shaker of garlic salt, and a mini jar of freshly chopped rosemary. She placed the biscuits into a waiting bowl on the way across the kitchen. I was happy to note that Socrates and Snowdrop sniffed the air, looked at each other, and crossed the floor in tandem. Then I returned my attention to Piper, who was telling us, "It's a classic, if completely ludicrous, case of mistaken identity."

"Oh, goodness!" Fidelia sat up straighter. "That explains why Ms. Bickelheim kept congratulating me for redeeming myself after my last 'horrid' performance, and telling me how brave I was to even dare approach the stage again!"

I was insulted, because I'd done my best to deliver my lines during a major equipment malfunction that had left me hanging upside down over the audience at one point. But, more than that, I was excited about the prospect of giving up my part to someone who really wanted it.

"This is great, Fidelia," I said, raising my toddy and toasting both of us. I took a sip of the warm bourbon, honey, and lemon, my mood improving even more. "You can take over for me. I haven't even rehearsed yet, so you're at least as prepared as I am!"

"Oh, no." Fidelia shook her head, dashing my hopes. "I'm afraid I've already decided that the acting lifestyle isn't for me. The fans, late hours, and wild parties . . . It would be too much."

"It's the *Sylvan Creek Players,*" Piper pointed out, drizzling butter into one of the bowls, then hitting the popcorn with a generous dose of garlic salt and parmesan cheese, followed by a pinch of the rosemary. The kitchen smelled amazing, and I wondered if my sister was starting to get some domestic tendencies since settling into a relationship with Roger. She set the bowl between me and Fidelia, pausing to give the highlighted receipts a funny look before sitting down next to me. "I don't think there's a lot of partying going on," she noted. "Some of the Players are in their eighties."

"Well, even so, I was nervous just to audition," Fidelia confided, while I began to gather the scattered receipts, pulling them into a pile in front of myself. I was starting to think bourbon and accounting didn't mix. Fidelia didn't seem to notice that I was ending the work portion of the day. "While a part of me was hurt, to be overlooked — again," she said, "I was also relieved when I heard you'd be playing the role, Daphne." Smiling, she raised her glass. "So, break a leg! I will be in the audience on opening — which is also closing — night, cheering you on!"

"Try not to break *anything,*" Piper suggested, grabbing a handful of popcorn. "Not legs, harnesses, or scenery."

"I don't think it's possible to mess up this role," I assured her, with a quick glance at Fidelia. "No offense."

She smiled. "None taken. Especially since I now know I aced my audition."

"Now that the play — and the die — are cast, what's this about you and Norm Alcorn, Daphne?" Piper inquired, while I checked the clock on her microwave. I needed to leave soon to rehearse *Fidelia's* part. "What did I miss?"

"You were busy lighting candles when I told that tale," I explained. Piper always placed real candles on the deep sills of the farmhouse's original, twelve-paned windows during the holidays. She'd lit them early that day, because the sky was a deep, wintry gray. "Basically, Norm told me that, if I didn't use my 'influence' on Gabriel to convince him to stop printing negative news about Sylvan Creek in the *Gazette,* Norm would turn the rest of the chamber against me and ruin my business."

Piper's eyes were wide behind her glasses. "That doesn't sound like Norm."

I grabbed some popcorn, too, and pushed the bowl closer to Fidelia. I sensed that she didn't drink alcohol very often and should probably get something into her stomach. "Trust me," I said, tossing a few kernels into my mouth. The rosemary was a fresh, seasonal counterpoint to the salty cheese and garlic. "Norm might've been wearing a Santa suit, but he was not feeling very jolly toward me that day. I am definitely on the naughty list, in spite of contributing nearly all of the dog treats for Bark the Halls."

"Oh, I wish I was going to that," Fidelia lamented.

"Then you should go," Piper said flatly. "You don't need to have a date. Lots of people go solo."

"Really?" Fidelia looked to me. "Are you going alone? Because I know Piper will go with Roger."

I hated to disappoint her, but I shook my head. "Sorry. Usually, I have gone by myself, which was always fine. There's no lack of people to talk to. But this year I'm attending with Gabriel."

All at once, I was struck by a thought, which I didn't voice yet, for fear of getting her hopes up. And Piper wasn't done discussing my strange encounter with Norm Alcorn.

"Maybe Norm is just stressed about everything that happened with CeeCee — both the murder and the continued uncertainty about whether we're really getting a local-business-crushing pet discount store," she suggested. "Plus, there's Dunston's recent illness. The poor dog is recovering, but it was very worrisome for a while."

"What was wrong with him?" I inquired, reaching for a shoebox near my elbow and shoving my pile of receipts back from whence they'd come. I was better about saving important papers, but still not exactly organized. "Did you ever figure it out?"

"I think he got into something," Piper guessed, sipping her toddy. I heard toenails clicking as Socrates and Snowdrop reclaimed their places on the rug. I didn't even look at them, for fear of drawing attention to the fact that they seemed to be joined at Socrates's dappled and Snowdrop's pompom-covered hip. "My best guess is that he ate something toxic, maybe over the course of several weeks. But Norm won't let me run any more tests. He says the dog has been poked and prodded enough."

"But if tests could help solve the mystery —" Fidelia, who already seemed to be shaking off the effects of her thimbleful of alcohol, started to voice an opinion I shared.

But Piper raised a hand and cut her off. "It's not my call. And I firmly believe that

Norm *loves* Dunston. I'm sure he's trying to make the best decisions possible. And the dog *is* doing better."

"Do you think it could've been Dunston's diet?" I asked. "I could volunteer to make him some homemade food."

"That's nice of you, but I kind of doubt it would help," Piper said. "Norm assured me that, as the biggest supporter of Sylvan Creek businesses, he buys all of Dunston's food from Fetch!, and Tessie Flinchbaugh only carries quality brands."

"True," I agreed, daring to peek at Socrates and Snowdrop, who weren't exactly curled up together on the rug. But there wasn't a lot of space between them, either. Snowdrop was dozing off, and, not realizing he was being observed by me, Socrates let down his guard and gazed at her fondly.

I could still hardly believe that my stoic sidekick had fallen for a snobby fashionista, but that seemed to be the case.

Piper had followed my gaze. "What's up with the poodle?" she asked. "Mom said Jeff Updegrove was at CeeCee's memorial service. Why isn't Snowdrop with him now? And why didn't he leave any instructions for her care, in the first place?"

I overlooked that last question, because, lo and behold, when I'd shaken the envelope

273

again, then dug inside with my hand, because the paper had been wedged tightly, I'd managed to find the note Jeff had referenced, on his company letterhead, as promised.

"I get the sense that Jeff's not exactly a dog lover and wants as little contact with Snowdrop as possible," I said, speaking very softly. I was afraid that, if Snowdrop was a light sleeper, she might overhear her name, and my negative tone of voice. Socrates was listening, though, and he growled softly on her behalf. I overlooked the rare show of anger, because I'd felt like growling at Jeff Updegrove, too, back at the funeral home. However, to be fair, I said, "Jeff did pay me quite well at the service to watch her for a few more days."

"I'm probably not going to like the answer, but I have to ask why you, of all people, attended CeeCee French's memorial," Piper asked, sounding like Mom. "And please tell me you're *not* trying to solve her murder."

I was about to admit that solving the case had been part of my motive for visiting the funeral home. But Fidelia spoke before I had a chance.

"I don't think you should discourage Daphne from investigating," she chimed in, hopping off her tall stool, as if she was preparing to leave. I suddenly realized it was growing even darker outside, the sun setting behind the clouds. "It sounds as if Moxie's in trouble. And if it weren't for Daphne's incessant meddling, and kind heart, you might've been convicted of murder," she reminded Piper. "And I might be in prison, if not for homicide, at least for attempted armed robbery, if your sister hadn't intervened."

Fidelia was not the most socially adept person, but I appreciated the sentiment. However, she was exaggerating how close she'd come to being incarcerated for robbery.

"You pointed a carrot at me, not a gun," I said, realizing, suddenly, that Fidelia had played a ghost on more than one occasion. On the night she was referencing, she'd shown up at my door wearing a white sheet and wielding a root vegetable, in hopes of obtaining a valuable painting. That performance had been so unconvincing that I'd welcomed her inside and offered her a snack. "Even if I'd called the police, you probably would've gotten community service, at most." I got down from my stool, too, and grinned at my sister. "Piper, however, should be grateful. She really might be serving time if I hadn't solved my *first* murder to save her."

"You also nearly got killed, Daphne," Piper noted, as Fidelia and I retrieved our coats from pegs near the door. Socrates nudged Snowdrop, who opened her eyes, yawned, and stood up too, shaking herself. "Why does that part always seem to be overlooked?"

"I feel like that's the part that's always *emphasized,*" I said, pulling on my barn jacket. Then I glanced at the clock again and realized I was running late for rehearsal. "Speaking of people who've tried to kill me, can I borrow Mr. Peachy's truck again?" I asked Piper. "The dogs and I walked here, because the access road is still pretty messy."

"Sure," Piper agreed, while Fidelia buttoned herself into a shapeless wool coat.

My barn jacket wasn't the height of fashion, but I couldn't help thinking that I'd have to help Fidelia step it up a notch, if my plans for Bark the Halls worked out.

"Thanks," I told Piper. "Are the keys still in the ignition?"

"Yes. And please don't wreck it again!"

Fidelia shook her head wistfully. "Your life is *so* exciting, Daphne."

Then my part-time accountant, the famous poodle nobody wanted, a lovestruck, taciturn basset hound, and I tromped out into the snow.

As Fidelia drove away, and I helped Snow-drop and Socrates into the truck on a dark and gloomy evening, I hoped that my *after-life* — at least as portrayed on a high school stage — would be downright dull.

Yet, deep in my heart, I doubted that would be the case.

CHAPTER 31

A light snow began to fall as I drove the truck, which lacked its wreath, to Sylvan Creek High, the clouds obscuring the moon and causing the winding road to be even trickier to navigate than usual. My alma mater had been built in the 1960s on donated farmland, which had saved taxpayers money and allowed for the construction of expansive athletic fields. But everyone — especially kids like me who'd gotten stuck riding the bus, even through senior year — always complained about the school's isolation.

"This really was a bad place to build a school," I told Socrates and Snowdrop, steering around a final curve in the road. The weak headlights illuminated a brick-and-concrete sign that read SYLVAN CREEK HIGH, with the tagline HOME OF THE FIGHTING SQUIRRELS! "I have to say, the choice of mascot leaves something to be

278

desired, too."

The dogs didn't make a peep in reply, so I checked the rearview mirror and — in spite of my promise to Piper — nearly drove into a ditch again. "Were you two . . . ?"

I started to ask if Socrates and Snowdrop had been about to bump their little noses together, canoodling in the back seat, like two high-school kids, themselves. Then I quickly caught myself, not wanting to mess up what appeared to be a budding canine romance.

Plus, I had made the final turn into the parking lot closest to the gymnasium and auditorium, the latter of which the Players always rented for their productions.

I'd expected to see at least a dozen vehicles in the dark lot. However, there was only one other car — a beat-up Prius — and the lights near the back entrance weren't lit, either.

"I know I have the right time," I told the dogs. Looking in the mirror again, I saw that they'd edged apart, and both seemed sheepish. I pretended like I didn't notice and pulled my phone from my pocket, checking Ms. Bickelheim's text. Then I pocketed the phone again. "This is definitely where we're supposed to be. And I recall using this entrance the last time I played a ghost. The rest of the school was always locked up."

Socrates made a low, grumbling sound, deep in his broad chest, and Snowdrop whined softly, as if she had a bad feeling about the empty lot. I was a bit concerned myself, but I opened my door, telling them, "Maybe everyone's just running late. It is the holiday season, and people have a lot going on. We'll at least try the door."

Hopping out of the truck, I helped the dogs exit, too. When all eight paws were on the ground, they both looked up at me and shook their heads.

"I'm pretty sure this is the last rehearsal," I said, overriding their objections and leading the way to a flat, metal door that almost disappeared against the school's brick wall. "If I don't do a run-through tonight, I'll have to play my part live, in front of a crowd, without one chance to practice." We'd reached the door, and I rested my hand on the handle. "I know the part isn't big, but I'd at least like to know when and where I should stand and point."

Socrates and Snowdrop exchanged glances that seemed skeptical, to me, but I pulled on the handle.

To my surprise, the door opened. The school seemed so deserted that I'd half-suspected Ms. Bickelheim had texted me the wrong information.

However, I found myself staring into a dimly lit corridor that smelled like a combination of disinfectant, musty paper, old sneakers, and cheap pizza sauce. Two dark windows, built into the walls, were labeled TICKET SALES.

Beyond those were doors, opposite each other, marked GYMNASIUM and AUDITORIUM.

"We've come this far," I told my canine companions. "Let's at least peek inside."

Socrates shot Snowdrop a look that I was 99 percent certain said, *This is happening, so we might as well play along.* Snowdrop's puffball tail drooped, but she followed me and Socrates inside.

The door clanged shut behind us, the sound ominous in the empty hallway. But when the echoes faded away, I heard something else in the distance.

"Christmas music!" I cried softly.

Of course, the dogs, whose ears were much keener than mine, heard it, too.

"Come on," I said, leading the way toward the auditorium — only to stop halfway down the corridor, in front of a glass case full of photos of athletes, as well as medals and trophies won by former Fighting Squirrels.

It only took me a moment to find a picture of a uniformed Brett Pinkney, who'd pitched Sylvan Creek's only no-hitter, his junior year. And the photo I'd seen in the yearbook, in which Brett and Mike Cavanaugh stood together as football team captains, fall of our senior year, was posted, too.

"I had completely forgotten we were state champions that year," I said, looking down at Socrates and Snowdrop. "Go, Squirrels, I guess!"

Both dogs rolled their eyes, so I resumed walking, my booted feet clomping and their toenails clicking on the old, but gleaming linoleum.

As we approached the double doors to the auditorium, the music grew slightly louder, while my heart began to race.

I was flashing back to my disastrous, previous performance and suffering a touch of stage fright regarding the upcoming show, too. And my fear only intensified when I opened one of the doors, revealing a deathly silent, empty theater — and something so scary, spotlighted on the otherwise dark stage, that I yelped, Socrates took two steps backward, and Snowdrop, to her credit, launched an all-out attack.

"I'm so sorry," I told Ms. Bickelheim, who had silenced the carols playing on her cell phone so she could concentrate on searching my costume for possible tears.

The black robe had been displayed center stage on a prop mannequin, the hand outstretched so the specter had appeared to be pointing at us. Ivy Dunleavy had done a great job. The sight was terrifying, and Snowdrop had charged the spirit, teeth bared, trying to pull it down until Ms. Bickelheim had risen from a dark row of seats — a somewhat alarming development, in and of itself — and cried out for the poodle to stop.

"The whole thing was just scary," I added, shooting Snowdrop a grateful glance. I was surprised and impressed by her effort to protect us all, while Socrates and I had recoiled. The normally unflappable basset hound appeared sheepish, although a rash charge, undertaken without careful consideration, would never have been his style. "Your reaction was completely appropriate," I told him softly, earning the slightest wag of his tail. Then, as the dogs wandered off to explore backstage, I turned back to Ms. Bickelheim, who continued to fuss with the garment. "Snowdrop didn't mean any harm."

"I suppose the sight was somewhat alarming," Ms. Bickelheim conceded, beginning to disrobe the mannequin. "I was merely worried because, as you are likely aware, the Sylvan Creek Players operate on a limited budget, and Ivy Dumphree's creations — while magnificent — are not cheap!"

I did know all those things, except for the name Ms. Bickelheim had used. "You mean *Dunleavy,* right?"

My former teacher, who was drowning under a sea of black fabric, hesitated, a look of confusion in her pale blue eyes. Then she managed to wave one hand dismissively. "Dumphree, Dunleavy . . . So many students passed through my classrooms, back in the day. I can't recall *anyone's* name anymore. They just slip right out of my mind!"

"Yes, I can imagine," I agreed, stepping forward to help her with the costume, which was huge. I was too late, though. By the time I'd crossed the stage, the mannequin was bare, and Ms. Bickelheim dumped the robe into my arms, while I looked out over the empty seats, getting a twinge of stage fright again. "Speaking of remembering things, do I have any lines?" I inquired, fumbling to hold the slippery cloak, which seemed almost animated and determined to slink away. "And where *is* everybody?"

Ms. Bickelheim, who wore a striped, flowing tunic over plaid leggings — the wild patterns a dramatic departure from the pencil skirt and silk blouse she'd worn in the yearbook photograph — blinked at me for a moment, as if she didn't understand my questions.

"The rest of the Players already had their dress rehearsal," she finally said. "I didn't want to make them watch while you learned your role, from square one, at the last minute. We've all been very confused about your failure to attend regular rehearsals, after your very committed and impressive audition. And you of all people should know that the third ghost has no lines. You performed the role beautifully, right on this stage, just a few weeks ago."

"That wasn't . . ." I started to explain the whole mix up with Fidelia Tutweiler, but quickly abandoned the idea. The evening seemed strange enough without adding another layer of confusion. Instead, I adjusted the costume in my arms, asking, "Do I need to put this on?"

"Yes, of course!"

Ms. Bickelheim was starting to sound exasperated with me, so I did my best to find the bottom of the cloak and slid the garment over my head, flailing around to find the sleeves. While I was completely in the dark — literally, as well as figuratively — I heard something scraping across the floorboards.

When my head miraculously emerged from the proper hole, I discovered that Ms. Bickelheim had dragged a tall stepladder to center stage. I eyed the object warily, and, although I already knew the answer to my question, because the costume was puddled around my feet, inquired, "What's that for?"

"When the stage is dark, before the climactic act, the prop master will place this ladder here and help you ascend, then arrange your cloak so it covers the apparatus." I presumed that meant rungs of the ladder. "After which," Ms. Bickelheim continued, "you will point at Scrooge's grave, stage left."

I turned in that direction, only to be corrected. "Other. Stage. Left."

"Oh. Okay."

"Well?"

I stood there stupidly, keenly aware that Socrates and Snowdrop were observing from what I now knew was stage right. "You want me to . . . ?"

Ms. Bickelheim thrust a finger into the air. "Ascend, oh spirit! Ascend!"

I took that to mean I should climb the ladder, which was an awkward journey, given the voluminous folds of the robe that tangled around my feet. I thought that bode poorly for opening — and closing — night, but I managed to rise to the top and stand upright. The position felt precarious, and I wobbled as Ms. Bickelheim adjusted the lower part of the cloak so the ladder was concealed.

Stepping back, she assessed the scene, then directed, "Don the hood!"

I suddenly felt like I was back in high school, taking orders as a student, and I did as I was told, slipping the hood up over my head. The cowl drooped over my eyes, blinding me, but Ms. Bickelheim seemed pleased by the effect.

"Terrifying!" she proclaimed.

Snowdrop agreed. She clearly knew that I was under the swath of black fabric, yet I heard her utter a low growl and quickly pulled off the hood before she charged again.

My decision to break character did not please my director. "Daphne, you can't do that during the actual performance, no matter what happens," she reminded me, shooting Snowdrop and Socrates dark looks, too. "And I'm not sure dogs should be in a high school, even in a pet-friendly town like Sylvan Creek. There are limits!"

I shifted to look down at Ms. Bickelheim and wobbled again. "Sorry," I said. "But I take Socrates everywhere. I didn't think about school rules, since it's been a while." I managed to offer the dogs an apologetic look, too, without tumbling to the floor. Socrates appeared insulted, and Snowdrop was still watching me with a hint of distrust in her dark eyes. I addressed Ms. Bickelheim again. "And please don't be too hard on Snowdrop. She's adjusting to a lot of new things in the wake of CeeCee's death."

All the color drained from Ms. Bickelheim's face, and she stammered. "That's . . . That's . . . *Celeste French's dog?*"

I looked between my former teacher and Snowdrop about ten times, trying to figure out why Ms. Bickelheim had such a strong reaction to a poodle in a red-and-green-striped sweater. My head swiveled so much that I almost did tumble from my perch. When I managed to get control of myself again, I looked down at Ms. Bickelheim once more, only to realize that she wasn't pale and trembling with fear. She was *angry*.

I took a moment to consider my circumstances, noting that I was in an unwieldy robe, in a nearly empty and isolated high school, with a woman who hadn't been happy to learn that CeeCee French had planned to visit Sylvan Creek. Then my curiosity got the best of me, and, ignoring Socrates's warning look, I dared to ask, "Why did you dump coffee all over Gabriel Graham when you heard that CeeCee was coming home? What happened, back at Oh, Beans?"

Ms. Bickelheim's cheeks went from alabaster to bright red in under three seconds, and she said, loudly enough to reach the back row of seats and dramatically enough to win a Tony, "It wasn't what happened at Oh, Beans, Daphne! It's what happened back when you and Celeste were in high school!"

My silence and the confusion on my face must've spoken volumes, because Ms. Bickelheim took a step closer, looking up at me. She seemed baffled, too. Then her voice grew softer, and she asked, with obvious disbelief, "You . . . You really don't know, do you?"

CHAPTER 32

"I thought everyone in Sylvan Creek knew my story, but pretended otherwise," Ms. Bickelheim said, after we'd managed to get me safely off the ladder and out of my costume.

We sat in the wings on props for the upcoming play, Ms. Bickelheim on the edge of a fake bed, where Scrooge — played by local historian Asa Whitaker — would sleep between his nocturnal visits. I'd taken Bob Cratchit's tall chair, from the counting house scenes. The seat was rickety, and I thought Tom Flinchbaugh, who would play the role, might be the show's first casualty, before I inevitably tumbled off the ladder.

Socrates and Snowdrop sat quietly together on a rug between us, as if they also wanted to hear whatever Ms. Bickelheim was about to say regarding her past.

Smoothing her wild, graying hair, she studied my face. "I was sure there must've been rumors when I disappeared from this school."

I shook my head. "Not really," I assured her. "At least, not in my class. Everybody was focused on graduation. We all just wanted to leave and explore the world or go to college. To the extent that we even thought about you teachers outside of school — no offense — we probably all just thought you'd made a smart decision, quitting."

Ms. Bickelheim knit her brows. "You . . . You really believed that I *quit*?"

"That's what we were told."

My former teacher took a long moment to think. Then she said, "That's the story the administration begged to tell, to prevent a scandal, back in the days when nobody really reported news in Sylvan Creek."

Obviously, Norm Alcorn *wasn't* the only one who'd noticed that Gabriel Graham had changed the town's ability to cover things up. I didn't comment, though. I stayed quiet, letting Ms. Bickelheim talk. I was practically on the edge of my shaky seat.

"I always thought the *worse* lie — the complete fabrication — would circulate, regardless," she continued. "I've lived for years wondering if people know that I was actually forced out. And if they secretly think I'm a monster."

That word, "monster," was ominous, and I glanced at Socrates and Snowdrop to see if they thought we should exit quickly, stage left. Or maybe right. But Snowdrop was listening, her head cocked, and Socrates also seemed wrapped up in the tale. His brown eyes were trained on Ms. Bickelheim, who was still speaking, but in a distracted way, delivering a quiet monologue to the empty seats.

"I suppose, against all odds, the person who caused my downfall managed to keep her mouth shut, probably because she knew that, if the claims she had made secretly, to the administration, were ever carefully investigated, her lies would be exposed, and her reputation besmirched, too — although not destroyed, like mine."

I already suspected who the villain in this mysterious tale was, but I asked anyway. I also needed to know the hidden plot twist that Ms. Bickelheim kept referencing, without providing details.

"Who was behind your . . . departure?" I asked. "And why do you say your reputation was ruined? Because I think most people in Sylvan Creek are very fond of you."

All at once, Bitsy Bickelheim's eyes, which

292

had been clouded with melancholy and regret, blazed to life with unadulterated hatred, and she glared at Snowdrop, as if the dog was a proxy for the person she'd despised.

"CeeCee French and her lies were the reason I was forced out," she said, spitting her former student's name.

Her tone was so vitriolic that Snowdrop stood up and backed nervously away on her delicate white paws. Socrates rose, too, stepping gallantly between the poodle and the woman who continued to glower at her.

"I was cheerleading adviser, and I refused to grant her every whim," Ms. Bickelheim continued. "She had to have her way!"

Although I'd seen Ms. Bickelheim in the photo with the pyramid of cheerleaders, I hadn't realized she'd been their adviser.

"And maybe my reputation is fine, according to most people around here," she added. "Although I know everyone thinks I'm a little unhinged. But it's awfully hard to keep one's chin up, let alone get a new teaching job, anywhere, when your private record says you were accused of having an affair with a student!"

Chapter 33

"Well, that was unexpected and intense," I told Socrates and Snowdrop, as we drove down Sylvan Creek's main street on our way home after rehearsal. Not that I felt prepared for the play. I never did learn if I needed to do more than climb a ladder and point. We'd beaten a pretty hasty retreat after Ms. Bickelheim's confession, which had left me with more questions than she'd answered.

I wasn't sure if *she* was telling the truth about the alleged romance, because it was possible that CeeCee's accusation had been warranted.

As I steered Mr. Peachy's old truck slowly past the town Christmas tree, being careful in a sudden squall, I attempted to block out the image of CeeCee's body, and instead tried to recall details from one of the non-sports yearbook photos. The one of Ms. Bickelheim in the classroom. When I'd seen the image, I'd noted that she'd been very young, and very pretty, and that boys had probably drooled over her.

"What if some high school guy made an advance, and Ms. Bickelheim was flattered and let things go too far?" I mused aloud. "And what if CeeCee actually saw something? Because there usually is a grain of truth behind rumors, as Moxie can attest."

Socrates, who seldom barked, uttered a sharp woof, reminding me that Ms. Bickelheim's past was none of my business.

Snowdrop, however, seemed to appreciate my defense of her deceased person, in the wake of Ms. Bickelheim's scathing accusations. Her soft yip was lighter and encouraging.

I hoped they weren't about to have their first spat on the eve of Bark the Halls, and I decided to change the subject. Or, more accurately, I pulled over, right next to the Pinkney's Pines temporary Christmas tree lot, underneath the town clock.

It was getting late, and the lot was empty, all the trees baled and stacked in Brett's pickup. But there was a light on in the hut, and colorful lights still glowed on a temporary picket fence that defined the sales area, so I opened my door, telling the dogs, "I'll be right back. I want to toss a replacement tree in the back of the truck and get a wreath, too, if Brett has any."

Slamming the door, I trudged through the snow to the hut, where I knocked on the half-open door, although clearly no one was inside the small shelter. And, while I'd expected someone to be around, because of the lights, I nevertheless jumped when Brett Pinkney stepped up behind me. I had no idea where he'd been standing, or how long he'd been watching me.

"Hey, Brett." He'd spooked me, but I greeted him with a smile — which wasn't returned. He stood silently before me, a knit cap on his head, a heavy orange-and-brown flannel jacket on his body, and a stern expression on his face. Not sure what I'd done to earn the chilly reception, I forged ahead. "I was just hoping to get a tree and a wreath for my sister's truck, if you don't mind helping me out."

Clearly, he did mind. "Sorry," he said, in a clipped tone. "Lot's closed for the night."

I looked at the colorful lights and an open cash box that I could see inside the shelter. Then I smiled more broadly at the one-time quarterback. "It'll only take a minute, and I have cash. I'd really like to replace my tree and get my sister a new wreath, since I sort of smooshed the previous one in a slow-motion car crash. Whatever you've got in the truck will be fine. My last tree was pretty humble."

I was talking too much, which was my usual reaction when people stonewalled me, and I finally got myself under control, only to discover that my speech hadn't made a difference.

"Sorry," Brett repeated, walking away from me and unplugging the cheerful lights. "It's my last night here. Gotta move the inventory back to the farm. If you want a tree, go there tomorrow. More wreaths to pick from, too. Only got a few in the truck bed."

"I . . . I . . ." I was trying to understand why he wouldn't let me lighten his burden by taking a tree, right then and there. It would be one less thing for him to unload.

But Brett wasn't going to listen to logic. Stepping into the shed, he snapped off that light, too, and I heard the cash box scrape against wood as he picked it up. And when he emerged into the snowy night, I saw that he'd also grabbed something else. An object that dangled from his left hand, while his right hand balanced the box.

Scissors.

A big, sharp pair, made for cutting the twine used to bale the pines.

As I stood there, mute and staring too hard, my reclusive former classmate went to his truck, opened the door, tossed the box and scissors inside, then climbed in, himself, and drove away.

I continued to linger, watching as Brett drove off, the taillights on his vehicle mingling with the pretty lights in all the shop windows and the Bijoux's glowing marquee.

I was taking a moment to consider my second strange encounter of the evening — and waiting for someone whom I'd seen crossing the street, heading in my direction.

I assumed that Gabriel wanted to discuss plans for the dance, and I should've been better prepared to talk with him, because I felt like we needed to discuss our relationship, in the wake of my revelation about my feelings for Jonathan. Whether or not those feelings were reciprocated, I probably owed it to Gabriel to make sure that, at the very least, we were on the same page about keeping things light and commitment-free.

However, Gabriel didn't mention the ball right away, let alone greet me. He had a big grin on his face — a reporter-with-a-scoop expression — and his eyes twinkled when he asked me a question that sounded very reminiscent of a traditional Christmas carol. "Did you see what I saw?"

CHAPTER 34

"I'd offer you some coffee, but the pot has been brewing all day, and it's pretty much dark glue at this point," Gabriel said, while I shrugged out of my coat and took one of the seats near his desk.

As usual, Gabriel dropped down onto the old chair behind his piled-high desk and propped his feet on a blotter from years gone by, while Socrates proceeded to give Snowdrop a tour of the *Gazette*'s stuck-in-time headquarters.

I took a moment to look around, too, and was surprised to discover that Gabriel had placed a small, artificial tree on a teetering pile of newspapers dating back to goodness knew when, next to a table that held a black Remington typewriter I suspected he still used now and then. The wobbling fake pine was smothered under a lumpy wad of shiny silver garland and cheap glass balls, but it was nonetheless a surprising nod to the

300

holidays.

"I like the décor," I teased. "I'm glad you're in the spirit."

"Speaking of spirits!" Gabriel swung his feet off the desk and rooted around until he found a sheet of paper, which he held up, grinning from ear to ear. "I received this snail-mailed press release yesterday."

For a guy who had a printer's tray full of block letters, inches from his elbow, he was awfully amused by a traditional form of correspondence, but I was too intrigued, and slightly worried, to interrupt and point that out.

"The missive is from Bitsy Bickelheim," he continued, "who, as I assume you know, is president of the Sylvan Creek Players. And she lists you as one of the 'local luminaries' who will be onstage during a 'spectacular' production of Dickens's *A Christmas Carol.* Specifically as a 'dreadful specter who portends the future.' "

I groaned. "I actually *can* 'portend' what's to come, and it involves me falling off a ladder while wearing a cloak."

"Sounds exciting." Gabriel set the news release down, where I assumed it would disappear into the mess on his desk. Yet, he never missed an event, as far as I could tell. And, not surprisingly, he promised, "I will

301

definitely be there to review the performances."

"Please, don't be too harsh," I requested. "I didn't even get a chance to rehearse my part, because Ms. Bickelheim saw Snowdrop and went into a tailspin."

The dogs had rejoined us, and Snowdrop yipped disapprovingly about the incident. Socrates stood stiffly, too.

"What happened?" Gabriel inquired, one eyebrow arched. He obviously sniffed a story, which I didn't intend to share. At least, not in its entirety. However, I did tell him, "Ms. Bickelheim used to be a teacher at Sylvan Creek High. She had some run-ins with CeeCee French, years ago, and apparently they still rankle. Seeing Snowdrop triggered a negative response."

The posh poodle yipped again. I had to admit, I was starting to appreciate how she stood up for herself, now that she'd toned down the arrogance.

"Wow." Gabriel kicked up his feet again and laced his hands behind his head. "Sounds like Bitsy has a powerful aversion to CeeCee French — as evidenced by your experience, and the fact that I still have a coffee stain on my pants, from the day we surprised her by mentioning that Ms. French was returning to Sylvan Creek. So, what's the story?"

"I don't think it's for me to tell," I said, glancing at Socrates, who gave me a look of approval. I met Gabriel's gaze again. "But, let's face it, we're both wondering if that aversion was strong enough to compel her to commit murder." Before Gabriel could start theorizing, I added, "But we have no idea if Ms. Bickelheim had an alibi, or access to a weapon . . . nothing like that. We — or more accurately I — have only identified motive, at this point."

Gabriel slid his feet off the desk again and leaned forward, crossing his arms on the old blotter. His dark goatee made the spark in his eyes all the more devilish. "You know who did have a potential weapon in his hands, this very evening?"

"Yes, I noted that, too." I didn't look at Socrates, who would disapprove of the turn the conversation had taken. I was glad that he couldn't report to Piper, who would agree that I shouldn't be speculating. However, if I could find an alternate weapon for Jonathan to consider, that might help Moxie. "Those were very sharp-looking scissors in Brett Pinkney's hand."

"So, now we have a potential weapon, but no motive." Gabriel watched me closely. "Unless there's something more you can

303

share about Pinkney, who I know was yet another of your high school classmates. Does he, perhaps, have some intriguing connection to CeeCee French, like the incident with Moxie Bloom and the punch bowl?"

I shook my head. "I don't know, Gabriel. CeeCee and Brett dated, off and on, but for all I know, it was just the stereotypical, superficial pairing of the school's head cheerleader and top jock. I don't even know how much they really cared about each other."

"What if it was a lot — at least on one side?" Gabriel mused. "You never know what lurks in the hearts of teenagers. And, by all accounts, Pinkney went from being a star athlete to a tree-farming hermit. There has to be a story there."

"Maybe," I conceded, rising to leave. The snow was falling more heavily past the *Gazette*'s windows, making picturesque little drifts on the twelve panes. "But maybe not."

"Daphne . . ." Gabriel rose, too, and I pulled on my coat while he stepped around from behind the desk. "We're still on for the ball, right?"

We met each other's eyes for a long time, while I figured out how to respond. I hadn't said much back at the skating pond, when Gabriel had almost certainly been within earshot, but there must've been a twinge of disappointment in my voice when I'd mentioned turning down Jonathan's invitation. I could tell, right then, that Gabriel knew I was having doubts about our relationship, casual as it was. And, most important, I didn't want to be unfair to him.

"I really want to attend the dance with you," I finally said, "as long as you are honestly good with the way things stand between us." I held his gaze steadily. "Because I like getting coffee or dinner now and then, and solving the occasional murder with you. But I'm not looking for more at this point. I have some conflicting feelings going on."

He nodded. "I understand, and we're on the same page. I'm not much for commitment right now, myself." He gestured around the office. "I'm basically married to this place."

"Then we're good for the ball," I said, feeling as if a weight had been lifted from my shoulders. "Will I just see you there? Because, traditionally, I get ready at Moxie's apartment, with her and sometimes Piper. It's right across the street from the hotel, so you don't really need to come get me."

"That sounds good," Gabriel agreed. "I need to arrive early to shoot some photos when Elyse Hunter-Black's secret décor is finally revealed, so your plan makes sense."

"Great." I moved to the door and rested one hand on the knob, while the dogs crowded me, clearly ready to head home. But I paused and turned back. "Gabriel, could you do me a favor?"

He jammed his hands into the pockets of his jeans. "What's that?"

"I know you're going to dig into Bitsy Bickelheim's story," I said. "But please — please — don't print anything that you aren't *positive* is true." I didn't mean to sound like Norm Alcorn, who wanted everything sanitized. But I didn't want some old rumors that had ruined Ms. Bickelheim's life to be printed, either, unless there was proof they were true. And even if there was a grain of truth at the heart of CeeCee's accusation, so much time had passed that I didn't believe the scandal was worth rehashing in public. "Or, better yet, don't print anything at all."

"Assuming there's even a newsworthy story there —"

"And I don't think there is," I interrupted.

"But if there is something worth printing, I'll triple-check my facts," Gabriel promised.

"Thanks," I said, hoping that was a promise he'd keep. Then I opened the door for the dogs, and we all hurried to the truck.

The whole ride home, I found myself pondering questions I hadn't discussed with Gabriel. Because, the more I thought about it — mulling over images in the yearbook Jeff Updegrove had left me for *some specific purpose* he wouldn't own up to — the more I believed that Brett Pinkney might have had not just a weapon, but a motive, too.

CHAPTER 35

That same night was truly silent at Plum Cottage, as snow continued to blanket the woods surrounding my little home. Socrates and Snowdrop quickly fell asleep by the fire after sharing some chicken and rice. I was tired, too, but starving, and I puttered around the kitchen in my oversized flannel robe, leggings, and big fluffy socks, heating up some homemade curried corn chowder. I also wanted to spend some time with Tinkleston, since I'd be out late the next evening, too, at the ball. Not that Tinks, who was enjoying a snack in his favorite spot amid the herbs on the windowsill, minded being left alone. In fact, I thought he preferred solitude most of the time.

"You like your independence, don't you?" I asked him, daring to stroke his back while I gazed out the window. The snow was falling more steadily, so Sylvan Creek would be a winter wonderland for Bark the Halls.

I smiled down at Tinks, who'd finished his treat and was gazing up at me with his intelligent orange eyes. "Too bad there's no Meows and Mistletoe dance for cats."

Tinks shook his head quickly in response, and I gathered from his expression that he wasn't interested in donning an outfit and mingling with other felines.

Then again, his smooshed-in face, with its severely downturned mouth, always made him appear to be grouchy.

"I know you're happy sometimes," I told him, moving to the stove. The soup, which I'd made using corn I'd frozen during the summer, was bubbling away, and I ladled some into a small earthenware crock. Grabbing a spoon from a drawer, I sat down at the table, where I'd left Jeff Updegrove's old yearbook.

Tinks hopped off the windowsill and jumped up onto the icebox behind me, the better to peer over my shoulder as I flipped a few pages, still trying to figure out why Jeff had given me the annual.

"Maybe if I go through all the senior portraits, I'll spot something or someone," I mused, taking a big bite of the creamy chowder, which gained extra depth and warmth from the pinch of curry powder I'd added. Then I located the senior portraits and began to scan the faces, some of which were familiar and some, to my surprise, I'd forgotten until their features and names triggered memories.

A few minutes later, my crock of soup was empty — and I'd gained nothing except regret over wearing earrings that looked like two dream catchers for a portrait that would define my late teen years for generations to come.

"I don't think those earrings were *ever* in style," I told Tinks, who stood up, arched his back, and yawned.

Closing the yearbook, I also yawned, rose, and stretched before taking my crock to the sink and washing it out, along with the dirty pot. I next stoked the fire, being careful not to wake Socrates and Snowdrop. Then I grabbed my cell phone from my coat pocket and climbed the spiral staircase to the loft, where I burrowed under the down comforter. A moment later, Tinks joined me at the foot of the bed.

I was about to place my phone in its usual spot on the table next to the old landline. However, at the last moment, I changed my mind and sent a text to Jonathan.

Is it okay to enter CeeCee's room at the hotel and get some outfits for Snowdrop?

And would you do me a favor?

Jonathan replied promptly.

Personally, I'd rather you didn't take any outfits — because dogs shouldn't wear novelty clothes. As a detective, though, I have no objections, assuming you can gain entry.

"Shouldn't be a problem," I noted quietly, as a second text popped up.

As for the favor — I need to know what it is before making any promises. I'm sure you can understand why I'm wary.

"Yes, I suppose I can," I admitted, texting a thank you for the permission to pick up some clothes and outlining the favor, too.

Jonathan's reply was immediate. A strange request, but, yes, of course.

"Great!" I said loudly, disturbing Tinkleston. His head popped up from the nest he'd made on the comforter, and he shot me a dark look. "Sorry," I apologized. When he disappeared again, I sent back, Thanks! Will make someone very happy!

Then I moved to put away the phone for the night, only to stop myself again, as I finally made a decision on a topic I'd been thinking about all day.

Sending one more message to a person whose contact information I'd never used before, I snuggled deep under my blankets, hoping I'd done the right thing. Because, if my instincts were *wrong,* I'd probably just set Moxie Bloom up for a Bark the Halls disaster.

CHAPTER 36

"Thanks so much for grooming Snowdrop and for my updo," I noted, as Moxie, Socrates, Snowdrop, and I prepared for the dance, all of us gathered at Moxie's apartment, which I swore was strung with even more colorful lights. She'd completed her gingerbread version of Sylvan Creek, and the miniature village took up the whole table she'd used as a workspace. The surface was dusted with sugar "snow," while the real thing continued to fall softly outside.

The heart of the storm had passed overnight, leaving Sylvan Creek glittering like a town in a softly swirling snow globe, and I went to the French doors to look down at Market Street, where icicles dripped like jewels from the storefronts and the Bijoux's marquee was glowing. Across a side street, people and pets — all attired in holiday finery — were already entering the Sylvan Creek Hotel for the ball. Then I noticed something odd, and I turned back to Moxie and the dogs. "Why is Market Street plowed, but Linden Lane is covered in snow and blocked off with pine roping, all the way to the corner by the hotel?"

Moxie, who didn't have much preparation to complete, since she'd donned her vintage, emerald-green satin gown around noon, shrugged. "I have no idea," she said absently, turning pages of the yearbook I'd brought along, in hopes that she might spot some clue I was missing. She sat in one of her two rockers, Sebastian on her lap. The white rat wore a bow tie, although Moxie said he wasn't attending the dance. He was just "in a party mood," according to my best friend, who added, "The garland was in place when I woke up this morning, and no one's disturbed the snow since. I had to add half a bag of sugar to *my* Linden Lane to maintain accuracy!"

I expected Socrates, who had mixed feelings about edible artwork, to groan at Moxie's insistence upon replicating the community down to its last gumdrop detail. However, for once, the normally curious basset hound wasn't listening to the human conversation. His gaze was fixed on Snowdrop, who was already attired for the evening's event.

I'd stopped by the hotel earlier that day to select a few outfits and had brought them to Moxie's garret. We'd laid them out on the floor, on a throw, and Snowdrop had selected a red velvet, gold-beaded "gown" that went beautifully with her pure white fur, which Moxie had poofed and shaped into perfect snowballs on her head, feet and hips. The doggie dress, from Park Avenue Pets — the same company that had created Snowdrop's cashmere sweater — must've cost a bundle, but she looked quite fetching.

Socrates clearly agreed. He wasn't even fussing with his bow tie.

Moxie remained distracted, too, by the yearbook, which I was starting to regret sharing with her. She was almost too absorbed in the photos, a look of solemn concentration on her face as she slowly turned pages.

"Moxie," I said softly, sitting down across from her. "Maybe you should stop looking at that. It doesn't seem very helpful."

Moxie ignored my advice and flipped another page, apologizing, "I'm sorry, Daphne." She stroked Sebastian with her free hand, until he hopped down, scurried across the floor, and shimmied up onto the table, where he stole a bite of the Pettigrew

Park gazebo, compromising Moxie's attempt at authenticity. She didn't seem to care. Her gaze remained fixed on the images from our senior year. "I didn't notice anything that seems like a clue to solve a murder," she added. "Although CeeCee's picture shows up on nearly every page."

"Yes, so why don't you —"

I reached out to claim the yearbook, which Moxie was turning, so I could see the open pages. To my surprise, she was showing me the pyramid of cheerleaders. "I do have to say this strikes me as odd," she said, raising my hopes that she'd found a clue — only to dash them when she explained, "Usually the tiniest girl gets the top spot. CeeCee was slim, but tall."

I'd noted that anomaly, too, but I didn't think it would help to solve the murder. However, I again noticed Ms. Bickelheim in the background, and I pointed to her. "Did *you* know that Bitsy Bickelheim was the squad's adviser? Because I had no idea, until she told me last night, during our private rehearsal."

Socrates and Snowdrop must've started listening at some point, because both dogs growled in harmony.

Moxie gave them a curious glance, then answered my question. "I'm afraid I had no

316

idea." She shrugged. "I had a lot of pep, and always support rodents . . ." She next shot Sebastian an indulgent look, while he continued to consume the gazebo. "But I had no interest in pompoms and megaphones or the Fighting Squirrels."

"You didn't hear any rumors about Ms. Bickelheim during our senior year, did you?" I asked, keeping the question vague. I didn't want to impugn our former teacher's reputation — I'd already speculated too much with Gabriel — but Moxie had always known all the local gossip, even back in high school. I was curious to know if she'd ever heard tales of a liaison between Ms. Bickelheim and a student. "Anything about why she left Sylvan Creek High?"

"No, not a thing," Moxie said, turning to another page.

I suddenly wished I'd insisted upon reclaiming the yearbook, because she'd stumbled across the photos of the boys' sports teams. She must've immediately spied Mike Cavanaugh, standing with his arm around football co-captain Brett Pinkney, or the shot of Mike in his baseball uniform, without Brett, because I heard her suck in a sharp, but quiet, breath. Then she muttered, "Oh, goodness."

"I know Mike's in there a lot, too," I noted

quietly. I wanted to ask her about Brett's absence from the spring shot, but I was more worried about my friend's state of mind than about solving the murder, right then. "You're not upset, are you?"

Sighing, Moxie finally closed the book and set it on her coffee table. "No, I'm not upset. To be honest, I just wish I would run into him and get it over with."

I'd been worried all evening, but I felt a surge of hope. "Really?"

"Yes." Moxie nodded. "I'm tired of looking for him every time I leave my home."

"You . . . you know there's a chance he might come to Bark the Halls, right?" I ventured nervously. Then I blurted the truth. "Because I texted Mike and urged him to come, and bring Tiny Tim."

Moxie's green eyes got huge, and for a moment I worried that I'd messed up not just her evening, but one of the most important relationships in my life. Then she took a deep breath and said, "It's okay, Daphne. I've been thinking about what you said back at the pond." Her cheeks flushed, and I thought she meant the part about how Mike still cared for her. "I was sort of hoping he might show up. It would be like a reunion from a movie, you know? Two old flames, parted at a high school holiday dance, only to meet again as adults at a Christmas ball."

"Moxie . . ." I didn't want her to think something magical was going to happen. "I only invited him because he seems so isolated, missing out on everything. And Tiny Tim deserves to go, too. I don't want you to get your hopes up."

Moxie reached out and squeezed my hand, a wistful smile on her lips, which were a bold shade of crimson. "I don't really expect him to explain everything, then sweep me away on a white horse. I'm just ready for some closure."

"Okay." I was relieved that her expectations were realistic, by Moxie's standards. In truth, I was probably more hopeful than my best friend. I secretly wanted them to at least dance once, if Mike showed up. I was increasingly convinced that Mike hadn't killed CeeCee, in part because I kept recalling his haunted look when he'd discussed combat. He hadn't relished hurting people. He'd also seemed genuinely surprised when I'd mentioned the weapon. And I knew there was still something between him and Moxie.

Of course, I didn't say that. I stood up, wiping my hands on the jeans I was still wearing. My palms had gotten a little sweaty when Moxie had given me that wide-eyed look. Then I glanced at Socrates and Snow-drop, who were waiting patiently in their varying degrees of finery.

In truth, Socrates probably wished we could all just hang out in the garret, *sans* ties, ribbons, and bows, but I suggested to Moxie, "Why don't you take the dogs to the dance? I don't want to hold you up, since I'm running late."

"Yes, why aren't you dressed, Daphne?" Moxie inquired, looking around her apartment, as if my *missing* gown might material-ize. Then she looked me up and down. "You're not going to wear jeans, are you? Because *both* your dates will probably wear tuxes!"

Moxie hadn't given up hoping that I'd manage to pull off some sort of two-dates-at-once, movie-worthy caper, although I'd told her, dozens of times, that I didn't plan any shenanigans.

Well, I had schemed a little, but my plan was pretty much the opposite of Moxie's cinema-style fantasy — in which things always went wrong, as she, of all people, should know.

"I only have one date," I reminded her. "And I'm not wearing jeans . . ."

I was about to admit that I was getting a tiny bit worried about my gown, which Ivy

Dunleavy should've delivered by then, when all at once, Moxie's doorbell rang, and I grinned, telling her, ". . . because my gown is here now!"

CHAPTER 37

"Oh, Ivy, this is gorgeous," I said, pulling a garment bag off the gown she'd created for me. I wished that Moxie, Socrates, and Snowdrop could've been there to see the dress, but they'd headed across the street. I suspected that Moxie was eager to see if Mike had arrived, while Snowdrop was excited for the party — and Socrates probably wanted to get the whole thing over with and get out of his tie. I freed the gown from the last of the plastic and stood back. "It's just beautiful!"

"Thanks." Ivy smiled, but in a distracted way. She wasn't as captivated by her own creation as I was. She was gazing raptly around at Moxie's apartment. "This place is amazing!"

"Yes, Moxie goes all out for the holidays," I agreed, still focused on the dress. It was a deep pewter satin, and I knew from our fittings that when I put it on, the fabric would bring out the gray in my greenish-gray eyes. The design was off-the-shoulder, with a wave-like hook-and-eye lace pattern down the front that was like a nod to my usual bohemian style — only taken to a dramatic, glamorous place. All at once, I got cold feet and looked nervously to Ivy. "Do you think it's too much for me? I don't usually dress up. As Socrates — the philosopher, not the dog — once said, 'Beauty is a short-lived tyranny!' "

Ivy gave me a funny look. Then she assured me, "It's perfect, Daphne. And I don't think you'll suddenly become insufferably vain."

"I suppose not," I said, running my hand down the lace, while Ivy wandered over to the gingerbread re-creation of Sylvan Creek, where she bent down, peering closely. Some of her long, coppery hair slipped over her shoulder, and she quickly caught it, before it could sweep down mini-Market Street, Godzilla-style, and wreck the town. "Look!" Ivy gasped, oblivious to the near tragedy. She didn't seem to notice that Sebastian had wreaked havoc on the park before disappearing, either. She was too pleased to have spied a small storefront. "It's my shop! Even smaller than usual!"

I abandoned my dress for a moment to

join her, bending down, too. Our eyes met across the tiny street, and I saw that hers were twinkling. "There should be a light on in my window," she joked. "I feel like I'm always working lately." Ivy quickly amended, "Which is a good thing! At first, I was afraid I'd fail, although Norm Alcorn assured me that the chamber would have my back."

"Lucky you," I muttered, under my breath.

"What's that?"

"Nothing," I assured her. We both straightened. "You're going to the dance, right?" I asked, noting that she wore a hoodie and a pair of leggings. "You can get away for that, can't you?"

The light in her eyes dimmed. "No. Not this year. I need to make some last-minute alterations for Ms. Bickelheim, who requested changes to Scrooge's and Bob Cratchit's costumes. I'm going back to work."

"You'll attend the play, won't you?" I asked, worried that she had *no* social life. "You'll at least see your handiwork onstage, I hope!"

"Yes, I wouldn't miss that," Ivy promised. "But, for the most part, I keep my nose to the grindstone. My goal is to save my pennies and make the shop a success, so I'll have more free time next year." A shadow darkened her eyes. "It would be nice to visit my parents in Appleton, too, if I could swing a plane ticket."

"What's Appleton?"

"*My* Sylvan Creek," she explained. "A small town in Iowa where I grew up." She suddenly seemed wistful. "I always thought I'd go back there, after New York, but circumstances — like a reasonable lease on a small storefront in a tourist town — seem to keep me on the East Coast for now."

Her comment triggered a memory. Something Mike Cavanaugh had said about returning home. But I couldn't quite make the connection, and Ivy's attention was drawn elsewhere. She wandered over to the area that served as Moxie's living room, where she gave the yearbook a funny look. However, she was mainly interested in the dresses that Snowdrop hadn't chosen, which were still spread out on the throw.

"Oh, goodness!" Ivy gasped, giving me a questioning look. "These are fabulous. Do you mind . . . ?"

"No, please check them out," I said, moving closer as she knelt down. "They're all from a shop, or manufacturer, called Park Avenue Pets."

Ivy had picked up one of the little dresses

— a white silk confection with lots of tulle — and she was inspecting the stitching closely, but her head jerked when I said that. Her eyebrows shot up. "Really?"

"You've heard of it . . . them?"

She nodded. "When I attended F.I.T. — the Fashion Institute of Technology . . ." It must've been obvious that I'd forgotten her alma mater and didn't recognize the acronym. ". . . I walked past their storefront all the time. I used to think it was crazy that people would pay hundreds of dollars for dog clothes. But the quality and style always amazed me."

"Yes, well CeeCee French didn't lack for money," I said, as Ivy set down the dress and stood up.

She suddenly looked wary. "These were purchased by Celeste French?" Ivy took a step backward, toward the door. "The woman who was just murdered . . . ?"

All at once, I understood why she was edgy. She was alone in an apartment, above a closed bookstore, with a person who had a murder victim's expensive canine wardrobe in her possession. And she'd probably read that Moxie was a suspect.

"It's okay," I reassured her, as she continued to move toward the door. "I'm allowed to have the outfits, for CeeCee's dog. The detective in charge of the case knows I stopped by her room."

"Of course, he does," Ivy agreed, in a voice that said she wasn't sure she believed me. She'd reached the door and grasped the knob. "I really do have to get going now. Work, you know?"

With that, she slipped out into the stairwell. I heard her big, fleece-lined boots clomp down the steps, then the door at the bottom opening and closing.

Only then did I realize that I'd never paid her for my gown, and I ran to the French doors, throwing them open and hurrying onto the balcony, thinking I would call to her. But when I looked down, she was already across the street, heading toward her shop and out of earshot.

I watched until Ivy disappeared, my brain struggling again, because I had this feeling that at least one of the Iowa seamstress's inadvertent comments was key to solving a murder in my own hometown.

Soon, however, I started to shiver, and I turned to go back inside. But before I crossed the threshold, I heard a faint, distinctive sound, which made me forget homicide investigations, and the fact that I needed to stop by Ivy's shop as soon as possible, with a check in hand.

I was all alone, with the exception of Sebastian, who remained hidden, but I couldn't help noting with delight, "Sleigh bells!"

_____

CHAPTER 38

By the time I'd slipped into my gown and some shoes I'd borrowed from Moxie, and found a wrap in her closet to drape around my shoulders, I was eager to get to the dance. However, before I headed to the ballroom, I wanted to return Snowdrop's unworn dresses to CeeCee's room.

Heading upstairs, I discovered that the inn's upper stories were already deserted. Apparently, both locals and visitors were at Bark the Halls, dancing or enjoying rides in the sleigh I'd first seen at Jonathan's barn. I, myself, hoped to get a turn in the sleek, glossy vehicle, which was driven by a man in a livery and pulled by the gorgeous, high-stepping black Friesian horse on a route that ran down snowy Linden Lane and across fields that lay at the edge of Sylvan Creek.

But first, I needed to divest myself of some very expensive canine garb, and I made my way down an eerily dim corridor, the thick carpeting muffling my footsteps. Locating room 37, I inserted the key into the lock, turned the knob, and stepped inside, where I felt blindly along a wall until I located a switch. Flipping that, I blinked as the chamber was bathed in soft light from two old-fashioned-looking lamps on the dual nightstands.

The room was becoming somewhat familiar to me, and I took a moment to look around at CeeCee's possessions. A pair of sunglasses and some spare change remained on a dresser, near a television remote, and some human clothes were draped on an upholstered chair near the window. The closet, half open, was filled with CeeCee's clothes, and Snowdrop's apparel was arranged neatly in the dog's own large, open suitcase, which sat on top of a folding rack.

"Snowdrop came to Sylvan Creek with more clothes than I took for two months in India," I muttered, carefully arranging the fancy dog gowns on top of sweaters and jackets that looked more like "casual wear," but which still appeared pricey.

That task completed, I straightened, noting that CeeCee's temporary workstation, on a small desk, also seemed frozen in time. Her laptop was open, and some pens were scattered about the intriguing binders, including the one labeled *Product Designs — Toys, Apparel, Accessories.*

Moving closer, I saw that the binder appeared to be quite polished, as if the new items were close to being rolled out, as opposed to in the early stages of development. The cover featured color photographs and reminded me more of a catalog than a sketchbook.

As I scanned the collage of feathered cat toys, novelty dog bowls, and brightly colored collars, I couldn't help thinking that the designs didn't look very innovative.

And then something *completely* unoriginal caught my eye, and I sucked in a sharp breath. Forgetting that I didn't intend to touch anything but the dog clothes, I snatched up the binder and began paging through.

However, just as I found the correct section, someone stepped through the door, which I'd left open.

I dropped the binder, feeling guilty. But the person who'd joined me didn't seem to notice I'd been snooping. He grinned at me with appreciation and said, "Daphne Templeton, you clean up quite nicely!"

"I forgot I was dressed up," I told Gabriel,

who was moving around CeeCee's room, checking out her personal belongings with unabashed curiosity. As he tapped a few keys on her laptop, with no result, I returned his compliment. "You look pretty nice yourself!"

That was true. Gabriel had ditched his usual jeans and down vest in favor of a dark tuxedo with a burgundy bow tie. The suit fit him well, and he'd gotten a haircut, too. The sharp lines of his goatee suggested that Moxie had also given him a professional shave, although she hadn't mentioned that he'd stopped by.

"Thanks, Daphne," he said, pausing his perusal of the room to smile at me again. "So, given that you are all dressed up, why are you *investigating a murder,* instead of attending the big bash downstairs?"

Warmth spread from my cheeks to my ears. "I didn't come here to investigate. I was returning some of Snowdrop's clothes —"

Gabriel leaned forward and bent his ear with one hand. "Returning whose what?"

"I'm watching CeeCee French's poodle, Snowdrop, and I was told that I could borrow some outfits from her extensive wardrobe," I explained. "I was bringing some of the dresses back, because they are supposedly very expensive." I glanced at the binder, which had just made me doubt that statement. "At least, I believe that's the case. And I didn't want to be responsible for too many of her gowns, in case something happened, and one got ruined."

Gabriel laughed. "The dog has *gowns*?"

"Yes, and Ivy Dunleavy — the seamstress who made my dress — confirmed that they are quite pricey — if the labels are to be trusted."

My date peered closely — suspiciously — at me. "You're linking these crazy dog clothes to the murder, aren't you?"

"I . . . I'm not sure," I admitted, crossing my bare arms over my chest. I suddenly felt vulnerable, because he was scrutinizing me as a journalist, and I wasn't ready to confide the vague hunches that were swirling around in my head. As had happened in the past when I'd solved homicides, it was taking me a while to make connections between things I noticed and the person who'd committed the crime.

Moments captured — and omitted — in yearbooks.

Old tales with unexpected endings.

Teachers — and students — who disappear.

And people who come home to what's familiar . . .

"What are you thinking, Daphne?" Gabriel asked, his eyes narrowed. "What's going on in that formidable brain of yours?"

"Nothing worth mentioning yet," I told him. "Although, thanks for the compliment." Then I moved away from the desk, toward the door, and suggested, "We should get out of here. We're missing a party downstairs, and I don't think Jonathan would like us snooping around."

Gabriel, who'd followed me, halted and rubbed his goatee. "Ah, yes. *Jonathan.*"

I'd been about to take Gabriel's arm, but I drew back slightly. "What does that mean?"

He grinned again. "I don't think we ever have a conversation in which you *don't* mention Detective Black."

"Well, we usually do discuss murder," I pointed out. "And that *is* his stock-in-trade."

"Yes," Gabriel agreed. "And, as you mentioned, I also enjoy solving the occasional homicide with you." He stepped closer to me. "But, while I'm honestly not looking for a commitment, I think, if the right person came along, you're at a point where you might like that."

I opened my mouth to speak, but he held

up a hand, asking for permission to continue.

I nodded, and he said, "You're putting down roots, and I'm not sure that's the case with me. Sometimes — and this is probably apparent — I find myself missing my days as a hard-nosed city reporter." He smiled again. "Plus, Black keeps watching for you to join the party."

I licked my lips nervously, no doubt messing up Moxie's lipstick application. "You don't know that."

"Yeah, I'm pretty sure," Gabriel insisted. "He plays things close to the vest, but he's keeping an eye on the door, even though all the usual suspects — including his ex, Elyse; Moxie Bloom; Piper and her boyfriend; too many dogs to count; and your terrifying mother —"

"You think she's scary, too?"

Gabriel ignored the question. "The whole town is assembled. Including murder suspect Jeff Updegrove. Yet, Black's got one eye on the door."

"I think that's just how SEALs act," I pointed out. "He's probably conditioned to be alert in a crowd." I noted that Gabriel hadn't mentioned Mike Cavanaugh. "Or there's a suspect who hasn't arrived yet."

"Maybe," Gabriel conceded. "But I'm

pretty sure Black's not sniffing out killers tonight. I'm almost certain he's a guy waiting for a girl." I started to stammer more objections, but Gabriel winked and nudged me with his elbow. "Go on, Daphne. Have a nice evening with the date you should've been here with, all along."

I felt terrible and wanted to honor my promise to him, and I tried to protest again. "But . . ."

"Honestly, Daph, I'll be fine," he assured me, his eyes twinkling. "I'm lining up a few dances with Ms. Hunter-Black. I hear she's currently unattached."

I still wasn't convinced we should cancel our plans, but I said, "Don't forget Fidelia Tutweiler. She's here, too."

Gabriel furrowed his brow. "Okay . . . I will consider Fidelia as a potential partner."

I lowered my eyes. "I still feel strangely about this." Then I met his gaze again. "I agreed — happily — to go with you, and we would have fun."

"I won't take yes for an answer this time," he teased, nodding toward the door. "Now, go on."

I hesitated. "You aren't coming?"

Gabriel Graham flashed me his most devilish grin ever, and I knew that he really was fine with ending this particular date before it began.

"I'm not going anywhere," he told me, "until I figure out what you saw in this room that put that strange *I'm close to solving a murder* look in your eyes." He raised both hands. "However, I will promise not to take anything, and to leave everything just as I found it, in a room that *isn't* a crime scene."

In spite of those reassurances, I didn't want to leave him alone in CeeCee's room. However, I knew the look of determination in *his* eyes, and I reluctantly moved toward the door.

"Daphne?"

I turned to see that Gabriel hadn't resumed his search for a clue that I wasn't even sure existed. I honestly didn't know if what I'd spied had any relevance to the crime. In fact, I doubted that was the case. Regardless, Gabriel was watching me with a funny look on his face, and I ventured, "Yes?"

"*I* strongly suspect that somebody at this dance has blood on his or her hands," he said cryptically. I also wasn't sure if he meant CeeCee's killer was in attendance, or if he was referring to someone else. And, although I knew that I'd be safe in a ballroom full of friends and neighbors, I felt a

shiver run down my spine when he urged,
"Be careful, okay?"

CHAPTER 39

The Sylvan Creek Hotel dated back to the Civil War, and over the years it had become a charming architectural anomaly, with quirky staircases and corridors that led to seemingly random rooms. Because I knew the building pretty well, I was able to follow the third floor hallway to a pair of French doors that opened onto a balcony overlooking the ballroom.

And when I stepped onto that overlook, I understood why Elyse Hunter-Black had wanted to keep her masterpiece under wraps.

"Oh, wow," I said, resting one hand against my chest. "That is just . . . wow."

The expansive room below had been transformed into a dark and snowy forest, complete with at least fifteen evergreens and one gnarled, pure white *oak tree,* which stood in the center of the floor, its branches hung with white lanterns, each holding a flickering candle. More candles glowed in dozens of frosted-glass globes, which appeared to be suspended in midair above the dancers. And gorgeous banks of white poinsettias ringed the walls, making it seem as if the room were surrounded by deep snow. In one corner, a string quartet played softly, filling the air with delicate, haunting music.

I took a moment to enjoy the scene, which was sparkling, yet warm with firelight and the comforting scents of vanilla and sugar, and quickly spotted lots of people and pets I knew — including a "couple" who made me break into a big grin.

"Thank you, Jonathan," I said softly, watching him dance with Fidelia Tutweiler, who wore a very unusual and conservative brown dress, as well as a dreamy smile that stretched from ear to ear. I'd never seen her look so happy, and I was glad that I'd texted Jonathan, asking him to dance with her if she appeared lost in the crowd. He likely would've done that anyway, without my prompting. Jonathan — whose suit was obscured by Fidelia, who clung to him, as if for dear life — had a tough, reserved exterior, but he had a soft spot, too, for wallflowers, misfits, and those who felt abandoned. I doubted he would've let a woebegone ac-

340

countant linger alone by the sumptuous buffet tables.

Still smiling, I next located Piper and Roger, who were with a group of friends, chatting. My sister looked lovely in an understated black dress, while Roger wore a classic tux.

Of course, my mother was there, the bodice of her white gown covered by an icy cascade of gems that matched the décor. I imagined she'd harangued Elyse Hunter-Black, with whom she was speaking, into revealing the ball's color scheme, if not the actual design.

Elyse also wore white, but her dress was simple and form-fitting, clinging to every delicate, perfect curve. She didn't seem to wear any jewelry, but her two greyhounds, Paris and Milan, sported glittering, three-inch-wide collars studded with crystals, reminiscent of Snowdrop's diamond collar.

As I watched, Gabriel, who had apparently given up searching for clues and taken the traditional route to the ballroom, approached the two women. A moment later, grinning his most appealing grin, he extended his hand. Elyse smiled, bowed her head slightly, and accepted the offer to dance.

"They would actually make a decent

couple," I whispered to myself, surprised by the revelation. I should've realized, months ago, that they were each accomplished, intelligent, and driven, and had one foot in city life. Plus, Gabriel's dark good looks were the perfect counterpoint to Elyse's fair beauty. As my former date took Jonathan's ex into his arms, I nodded. "Not a bad pair!"

Then, while Gabriel and Elyse began to turn slow circles, I scanned the room again, locating Socrates and Snowdrop, who were *definitely* canoodling. The two dogs stood near the oak tree, bumping noses and exchanging sniffs, their romance thwarted somewhat by Artie, who, as promised, wore a dashing aquamarine paisley bow tie and cummerbund. The hyperactive Chihuahua was spinning circles fueled by holiday excitement, while his lab "big brother," Axis, in a more subdued black tie, flattened his ears, as if he disapproved of his canine sibling's lack of decorum.

I found Artie's behavior quite acceptable. It *was* a party. And I wanted to be happy for Socrates, who wasn't ignoring his best buddy, but who was clearly focused on his "date." However, I couldn't help worrying that he was being set up for disappointment, since Snowdrop was likely destined to leave

Sylvan Creek soon.

In fact, at that very moment, Jeff Updegrove — whose tux didn't fit as well as one might expect for a high-ranking executive — was eyeing the poodle with a strange, unpleasant look on his face. Then Jeff's scowl deepened when Norm Alcorn approached him, lightly tapping his arm. Jeff didn't seem pleased to be bothered, and, in spite of the fact that his hotel was hosting what seemed to be an incredibly successful event, Norm was clearly agitated, too. As I observed, he grabbed Jeff's wrist, the same, impulsive way he'd recently snared mine. A sharp look from Jeff caused Norm to pull back, but didn't end the conversation. The two men resumed conferring, then — perhaps realizing the ballroom wasn't the proper spot for a serious discussion — they walked off together and disappeared through the double doors that led to the lobby.

"I don't trust Jeff," I muttered, my fingers tightening around a wooden railing that separated me from a bad fall. "And I'm not so sure about Norm right now, either."

All at once, I recalled Gabriel's warning about someone at Bark the Halls who likely had blood on his or her hands.

I doubted that Norm was guilty of more

than trying to bully me, and he wouldn't be on Gabriel's radar. But did Gabriel believe *Jeff* might be guilty of CeeCee's murder? Because my former classmate was definitely a suspect, in my opinion. Along with obviously resenting — maybe despising — his former employer, Jeff had been in possession of CeeCee's room key after her death, a circumstance that continued to strike me as strange.

I was still pondering that when, seemingly out of nowhere, a tiny pug, wearing one of his many red "bah, hum-pug" sweaters, dashed across the dance floor, weaving himself in and out of legs and generally tripping up everyone in his path.

"Tiny Tim!" I cried softly, happy to see the mischievous pup. Then my smile quickly faded when I realized the pug's presence likely meant Mike Cavanaugh was in attendance, too.

I'd wanted that — *suggested* that — but my heart still hitched in a funny way as I leaned over the railing, searching for Mike — and Moxie. And I nearly tumbled forward when I saw them talking in a dimly lit corner, next to one of the pine trees.

It was impossible to read their expressions from my awkward position, and a moment later, my attention was drawn to movement *behind* the tree.

"Brett Pinkney?" I whispered, in disbelief.

I couldn't ever recall Brett attending Bark the Halls. And he wasn't dressed for a ball that evening. He sported one of his usual flannel shirts, and, as I watched, he moved quickly to cut some netting from the evergreen.

Apparently, the winter wonderland hadn't quite been finished in time.

Balling up the netting, Brett shoved a pair of scissors into his back pocket, then quickly and unobtrusively exited through one of several doors that were camouflaged by paneling.

I returned my attention to Moxie and Mike, not sure if their reunion was going well. Moxie's back was to me, and Mike appeared tense. Then he reached out and touched her elbow. I saw Moxie nod, and they walked toward the main double doors, perhaps also heading to the lobby, where it would be quieter and easier to talk.

When they'd exited the ballroom, Mike's arm still lightly on Moxie's elbow, I exhaled with a *whoosh*. I hadn't even realized I'd been taking shallow, nervous breaths the whole time I'd been watching them.

"At least the punchbowl's still standing," I whispered. "Although, there's still a chance I've made a mistake, urging Mike to come."

"You? Make a mistake by meddling?"

The deep, teasing voice, which came from behind me, caused me to spin around, so I nearly got tangled in my gown. The move was appropriately clumsy, given my history with the man who'd joined me, and who was extending his hand and asking, "Would you care to dance, Daphne?"

CHAPTER 40

I didn't know a thing about ballroom dancing, and I couldn't help feeling nervous as Jonathan slipped one practiced arm around my back and took my right hand into his left.

Okay, fear of stepping on his feet wasn't the only reason butterflies were fluttering around my stomach.

It felt strange, and wonderful, and terrifying to be so close to the detective who had at first aggravated me with his attempt to put my sister in jail, then frustrated me by refusing to admit that I was as much a help as a hindrance when it came to solving crimes, only to ultimately earn my respect and affection with his intelligence, humor, depth — and genuine compassion, although he tried to downplay that side of himself.

And, let's face it, I'd always been drawn to Jonathan's good looks, which were enhanced that night by a classic, perfectly tailored black tux with an understated black tie and a white shirt that complemented his smile.

Apparently, he was pleased with my appearance, too.

"You look gorgeous," he said, for at least the tenth time, his voice low with genuine appreciation. "That dress is —"

"The biggest splurge of my life."

"And well, *well* worth every penny."

I waited for a follow-up reference to my guacamole-stained cowgirl boots, but the joke never came. Looking up at him, I realized that he didn't plan to tease me. At least, I didn't think so, as I studied his dark blue eyes by the dim, flickering light of the lanterns suspended in the branches that twisted above us, creating a private, quiet space amid the crowd.

"Jonathan . . ."

I had no idea what I wanted to say. And I wasn't sure how he'd pulled me a little closer. All at once, my hands were resting on his broad shoulders.

"You were late," he noted softly, taking my right hand again. Distancing us, just a tiny bit. "I thought you might not show up at all."

Warmth crept into my cheeks. "I was

upstairs in CeeCee's room. Talking with Gabriel."

Jonathan raised an eyebrow. "Talking? Or investigating?"

"Both," I admitted, the butterflies swirling when his hand brushed upward on my spine, just an inch. "Actually talking, investigating . . . and breaking up. To the extent that we were ever together, really."

Jonathan Black was a smooth dancer. I somehow hadn't tromped on his feet once in the crowded room, but he stopped us for just a moment. "I didn't come between you, did I? Perhaps I shouldn't have asked you to the ball, when I knew you two were —"

"No, it's not your fault," I interrupted him, as we resumed gently swaying. I glanced to my left, where Gabriel was dancing with Fidelia Tutweiler. I swore, as she spun in the arms of yet another handsome man, she was getting a sparkle in her eyes, some color on her cheeks and — although it probably wasn't possible — some gloss to her hair. Gabriel's grin seemed genuine, too, and I returned my attention to my partner. "Gabriel and I just seem to be heading in different directions. And that's okay." I smiled. "He *did* think you were watching the door for me, though. But I guessed you were on the lookout for suspects."

Jonathan broke our gaze to look around, and I saw a muscle in his clean-shaven jaw twitch. I'd summoned the detective. "Yes. There are quite a few assembled here." Then he looked down at me again. "And I'm sure you won't focus on our dance until we discuss the whole roster."

"Not the *whole* roster," I said, because part of me wished we hadn't started talking about the murder at all. But now that we'd begun, I noted, "However, I was surprised that Jeff Updegrove came back to town." My stomach tickled again with the excitement of piecing together a puzzle, and of being so close to a man who'd intrigued me since the day we'd met. I tried to focus on the case for one more moment. "But I'm not convinced that means Jeff's innocent."

"I am," Jonathan informed me, to my surprise. The song ended, and we stepped apart, but we didn't leave the dance floor. "I tracked down the people who were in the room next to Updegrove's on the night of French's murder," he explained. "They confirmed that he was holding loud phone conversations all evening. And housekeeping restocked his minibar twice — without earning tips. It seems that he has an alibi.

Although he doesn't come across as a pleasant person."

"No, I don't think so, either," I agreed, somewhat disappointed that Jonathan had ruled out a prime suspect before I'd done so. That feeling was tempered by happiness when the quartet began to play another soft melody, and, without asking, Jonathan reached for my hand again and wrapped his arm around me. It felt more natural, this time, to be so close to him. "I wish I'd never signed Jeff's yearbook at all," I noted, settling into the new rhythm. "And I'm pretty sure I voted for him to be class parliamentarian, too."

Jonathan grinned down at me. "I can only imagine you in high school, Daphne. I'd like to see that yearbook."

I pictured the photo of me in my leg warmers. "I don't think you need to . . ." I started to tell him that he wouldn't want to peruse my annual when all at once, I realized that he probably should. "Actually, you might want to check out a yearbook that Jeff left me. I think there might be a clue in there."

Jonathan frowned. "Have you been keeping something from me, Daphne?"

I didn't want to debate investigative protocols during our dance, so I asked,

"Can we discuss it later?"

"Yes, I suppose so." Jonathan's hand rested more firmly on my back, and shadows darkened his eyes. "You know that Mike Cavanaugh and Moxie aren't cleared yet," he said quietly. "And there's still no explanation for the disappearance of the scissors from Spa and Paw."

I understood what he was doing: reminding me that murder investigations in Sylvan Creek, where I knew everyone, had a way of creating rifts between him and me. Whatever was happening between us wouldn't change the fact that he had a job to do, while I would protect my friends.

"The truth will resolve everything," I assured him. Somehow, my hand had crept back to his shoulder, and I inhaled his familiar, spicy cologne, a masculine note against the sugary-sweet air in the ballroom. For a moment, my head swam. Then I got control of myself and said, "I'm sure you're following every lead, and Moxie and Mike will be fine."

At least, I hoped that was the case, and not just in relation to CeeCee French's murder. I was still concerned about Moxie and Mike's disappearance together. Especially since I hadn't seen them return.

I glanced around the room, spying Socrates, Snowdrop, Axis, and Artie, who were getting acquainted with Tiny Tim. The pug and the Chihuahua looked especially compatible, their matching, bulging eyes alight as they faced off, happily stamping their paws as prelude to a friendly tussle. I suspected something would be broken, or a table overturned, by the end of the night.

Meanwhile, my sister and Roger Berendt had started dancing at some point. Piper had as close to a dreamy look on her face as I ever expected to see, and Roger looked blissful, too. Like a man who might have plans to hand out at least one gold ring that holiday season.

At the edge of the dance floor, my mother was haranguing a couple I believed to be tourists, no doubt trying to convince them to set down roots, and pick up some property, in Sylvan Creek.

But I still didn't see Moxie and Mike — nor Jeff Updegrove and Norm Alcorn.

"Speaking of leads . . ." Jonathan's deep voice snapped me back to reality, and, when I raised my eyes to look up at him, I saw that he was laughing, for some reason. "You could follow mine, you know."

I hadn't even realized I'd taken control of the dance, and I laughed, too. "I'm afraid I'm not a very good dancer," I said, letting him guide me again. "I didn't attend finishing schools, like you."

Jonathan's eyes twinkled with amusement. "They were boarding schools. Not finishing schools."

The tiny revelation about his past was, like all the other hints, intriguing. But all at once, I suffered a chill in my core, as if the icy scene around us had come to life. He seemed to sense the change in mood, too, and our dance slowed to a near standstill while I searched his eyes.

"Jonathan . . . What happened this year? What did you mean in the park, when you said it's been 'interesting'?"

He didn't answer right away, and my heart sank lower, because I was afraid I already knew the answer. Moxie had tried to drop hints, too. She'd either heard rumors, or worried and reached out when Jonathan had stopped getting his hair cut during chemotherapy. He wouldn't have been her first client to disappear for a while, and he would've pledged her to silence if she'd discovered the truth. So I wasn't surprised, only heartsick, when he finally admitted, quietly, "Remember that illness I mentioned, once?"

I nodded, recalling our conversation in Pettigrew Park on a chilly fall evening, when Jonathan had explained why he'd left the

354

Navy. He hadn't wanted to be a burden to his team, or put them at risk by dropping in and out of service while undergoing treatment.

"You should've called me," I said, my voice tight. "I could've been there for you."

"I considered it," he said, surprising me again — and pulling me even closer. We were standing completely still at that point, lost in our conversation and oblivious to everyone around us. "I spent a lot of time debating whether to contact you. But I was afraid that wouldn't be fair."

"I . . ." I tried to protest, but he shrugged, adding, "Maybe I wasn't fair to shut you out."

My fingers tensed on his shoulders. "And now?"

"I'm in remission, with a good prognosis." Jonathan's body felt warm and strong against mine, even as he reminded me, "But nothing is guaranteed."

He was offering me a way out before we became more entangled in each other's lives, but I wasn't interested. "Nothing is ever guaranteed, for anyone," I said. "That doesn't mean we should keep each other at arm's length. It's really a reason for people to pull each other closer, don't you think?"

Jonathan smiled, and there was a warmth

in his expression that I'd never seen before. "I anticipated that, as a student of philosophy, you'd say something to that effect."

We grew quiet then, and I felt like I could've stayed that way, just resting against him, for the entire evening. And yet the moment, perfect as it was, didn't last. Someone was stepping up to us, clearing his throat, and clapping a hand on Jonathan's back.

Pulling reluctantly away, I discovered that Gabriel Graham had joined us, a grim expression on his face.

For a moment, I thought he hadn't been completely honest with me about his feelings, back in CeeCee's room. Then I quickly realized that Gabriel wasn't angry or jealous. He was just deadly serious.

"What's wrong?" I asked, withdrawing another step from both men.

Gabriel's gaze darted between the two of us. Then he lowered his voice, so he wouldn't panic anyone when he said to Jonathan, "Sorry to interrupt, Black. But Jeff Updegrove was just found in a frozen heap next to the sleigh outside."

CHAPTER 41

"Honestly, Daphne, another murder!" Mom complained, stalking around the Sylvan Creek Hotel lobby, where she, Piper, Roger, and I had convened after Jonathan had been called away. Socrates, who'd somehow ditched his bow tie, was, of course, there, too, along with Snowdrop, who continued to look resplendent, even as she snored by the fireplace, tuckered out from the party. Axis and Artie had also stuck with us, as if they understood that I was their default caretaker when their regular person was busy. Axis sat patiently by the front desk, while Artie trotted around, showing off his fancy attire and perhaps looking for his new playmate, who, in typical Tiny Tim fashion, had disappeared. "First, you monopolize poor Jonathan Black," Mom added, tsk-tsking. "Then you ruin the biggest event of the year. I'd nearly sold a young couple on, at the very least, a vacation rental on the shores of Lake Wallapawakee!"

Of course, Mom was blaming Jeff Updegrove's homicide on me, although I had a rock-solid alibi with the lead investigator on the case. And, as expected, my mother had somehow reduced the situation to a real estate crisis. Finally, I was not surprised that she'd pinned the abrupt end of Bark the Halls on me.

Needless to say, the event had wrapped up quickly with the arrival of ambulances and squad cars. Most guests were being dismissed, but those of us who'd had a connection to Jeff — including me — had been asked to stick around for a while.

My family members and Roger were probably free to go, but they'd stayed for moral support. Or, in my mother's case, a chance to express her frustration with me, related to a murder I'd had nothing to do with. I hadn't even found the body this time.

"Could we, just once, have a nice evening that doesn't end in a hail of bullets, Daphne?" Mom continued, pacing and waving her hands, while her face remained remarkably placid. Moxie guessed Botox deserved the credit — or blame. "I swear, whenever you attend a soiree, people get gunned down in the streets!"

Moving closer to the fire and pulling

Moxie's wrap more tightly around myself, because uniformed officers kept opening the front door, I debated whether to inform Mom that no one — except me — had been shot at, recently. I also considered reminding her that I'd helped to clear *her* of the last, and to my knowledge only, "soiree"-related murder in Sylvan Creek.

However, before I could say anything, Roger Berendt, of all people, spoke up on my behalf.

"Now, Maeve," he said calmly, from his perch on one of the lobby's settees. Piper sat next to him, her hand resting on his arm — which she squeezed as he dared to contradict a woman who did not appreciate contradiction. I saw my sister's knuckles whiten, but Roger forged ahead. "You have to admit that Daphne has helped you and Piper by solving murders. I think she has a gift, as opposed to a curse."

Judging from the fact that everyone seemed to accept that word — "curse" — as related to me, I got the sense that it had been used behind my back before. Probably more than once.

My mother certainly didn't seem surprised by the term, probably because she was the one who'd bandied it about. She stopped pacing and gave Roger a dead-level, withering gaze, which he endured without flinching. In fact, he didn't seem to notice that a Realtor with a capital *R* was about to pounce on him, like a tiger in a Chanel gown.

Then, all at once, Mom's shoulders slumped, just slightly, and she sighed. "Perhaps I am placing a tiny bit too much blame on Daphne," she agreed, shocking me, while Roger gave me a small, surreptitious smile and a wink. He definitely had a strategy for dealing with my mother and wasn't quite as mild-mannered as I'd thought. I heartily approved, and appreciated his attempt to stand up for me. I smiled back as Mom added, "It's just quite disappointing, to have such a lovely event interrupted by another homicide — next to Elyse Hunter-Black's gorgeously restored sleigh, no less. It was such a nice surprise for the whole community!"

My mother's comments were insensitive, to say the least — Socrates made a loud grumbling noise — but I had to admit that I'd suffered a twinge of disappointment, myself, to have missed the opportunity for a ride I'd secretly been hoping to take, ever since I'd seen the sleigh parked at Jonathan's barn. Then I immediately felt guilty for wanting something so frivolous when one of my former classmates had lost his life.

"Why didn't anyone notice the crime happening?" Piper mused, with a glance out the windows that faced Linden Lane, where the ambulance was parked, its red lights flashing. My sister disapproved of my amateur crime-fighting efforts, but she loved solving puzzles. "There was a line for the sleigh rides."

"From what I understand, the driver was on a break," Mom said. "He'd requested a half hour to get a warm drink since — of course — Elyse had insisted that he wear a fitted coat, top hat, and driving gloves, as opposed to the down parka and insulated cap he'd tried to wear. An outfit that would have destroyed the ambiance, as surely as Daphne's latest murder destroyed the ball."

Well, Roger had tried, on my behalf. I met his apologetic gaze and shrugged, silently telling him that he was fighting a losing battle, but that I was still grateful for his support. Then I addressed Mom, who finally sat down on a suitably throne-like wingback chair. "How do you know all that?"

"I ran into Norman" — that was what Mom always called Norm Alcorn — "a few minutes ago, when I excused myself to use

361

the facilities near the staff offices." Mom lifted her chin, letting us know that she was normally above using what everyone else called the bathroom.

Socrates made another rumbling sound, and I looked down to see that Artie had joined him and Snowdrop by the fire. The Chihuahua had also conked out, his vest askew and his tongue hanging out of his mouth while he dreamed. Axis remained by the front desk, and, growing too warm, I wandered over to give him a pat.

"Norman happened to be exiting his office," Mom added, "and he shared everything that he'd been told by the police." My mother rested a hand on her cascade of jewels. "He seemed quite shaken!"

Bending down to pet Axis, who wagged his tail, I recalled that I'd last seen Norm leaving the ballroom with Jeff. Neither man had looked too happy.

And I'd forgotten that the hotel even had offices. But, of course, it was a fairly big operation, employing a full-time event planner, as well as a general manager and someone who coordinated housekeeping. As the inn's owner, Norm would have a work space, and there were likely more employees with offices, too. Private spaces at the rear of the hotel, where a person could probably slip in and out of a back door, unnoticed, and maybe even hide bloodstained clothes until they could be disposed of permanently, after the police were gone.

Straightening, I was about to ask Mom what Norm had been wearing when she'd bumped into him, because I'd last seen him in a jacket and tie. If the jacket was missing, or he'd changed his shirt, that could be telling.

Then I hesitated, because I had no real reason to suspect Norm of murder. Just because he'd pressured me to speak with Gabriel about toning down negative coverage of local events didn't make Norm a killer.

Plus, I was assuming that Jeff had been stabbed, like CeeCee. But the fact that the homicides were almost certainly related didn't mean the weapons were the same or similar. For all I knew, Jeff had been poisoned, bludgeoned, or gunned down, as per my mother's worst fears.

"This second crime has to be tied to CeeCee's death, don't you think?" Piper noted, making the same connection I'd just made.

However, I was only half-listening to my sister and Roger, who was expressing agreement, while my mother again bemoaned the fact that murder was bad for business. My attention was mainly on the front desk, as I replayed the conversation Norm and I had recently shared, standing in that same spot.

I'd set my boxes of dog cookies on the gleaming counter, pushing aside the few objects that were always there. One of which was now missing . . .

"Oh, gosh," I muttered under my breath, my gaze sweeping the blotter and the omnipresent stack of mail. "Where's the . . . ?"

Behind me, I heard Mom chastise me for being rude. "If you're going to converse, Daphne, please speak up. We can't hear you when you mumble!"

Then *her* voice was drowned out by a rush of cold air when the door opened again. I assumed that yet another police officer had entered the hotel, until something crashed into my knees, nearly knocking me over.

I didn't need to glance down to know who'd arrived on the scene, but I looked, anyway, because there's nothing cuter than a pug in a knit sweater with a grumpy catchphrase.

"Hey, Tiny Tim," I greeted the dog who was turning quick circles on the carpet. Skidding to a halt, he yipped twice, then trotted toward the door, where he stopped and looked back at me before barking again.

"What is he *doing*?"

Roger sounded confused, and Piper and my mother also seemed baffled. Or, more accurately, Mom appeared appalled by the ill-mannered canine who'd lacked the decency to wear formal attire to the ball, like his counterparts.

Only I grasped what the precocious pug was trying to convey, and — suddenly realizing that I hadn't ever seen Moxie and Mike rejoin the party after their disappearance — I groaned and said, reluctantly, "Lead the way, Timmy. I'm coming!"

CHAPTER 42

Stepping outside the hotel, I glanced quickly to my left, where squad cars were parked at the intersection of Market Street and Linden Lane. I couldn't see the sleigh, but someone was leading the gorgeous Friesian horse, now blanketed, to a waiting trailer. And amid the flashing lights, I spotted Jonathan, who was conferring with Detective Doebler and Vonda Shakes, their heads bent together and Jonathan's back to me.

I wanted to tell him that I was leaving — and where I thought I was going — but he was so deep in conversation that I wasn't sure if I should bother him with what was probably pointless information. Moreover, Tiny Tim was growing impatient. He yapped again, and I turned to see him trotting off down the street, heading in the direction I'd expected.

With one last, uncertain glance at Jonathan, I followed the pug past Spa and Paw, toward Flour Power. We didn't make it as far as my bakery, though. All at once, Timmy darted between two buildings, leading me down a narrow walkway to the alley that ran behind the storefronts.

As I'd anticipated, we were heading back to Mike's apartment. My canine guide didn't move quickly, but I struggled to keep up in Moxie's heels. And I was shivering in her wrap, which had been fine for crossing the single street that separated Moxie's apartment from the hotel, but which wasn't meant for longer treks on frigid evenings.

"Wait up," I called to Tiny Tim, who'd turned the final corner, onto the dead-end lane lined with pretty Victorian houses in pastel hues. "Wait . . ."

I didn't need to keep calling. When I rounded the corner, too, I discovered that Tiny Tim had stopped halfway down the block. But he didn't stand at his front door. He'd paused before a neighboring pale-pink confection of a house that was surrounded by gumdrop-shaped shrubs.

As I approached, confused, he barked so shrilly that his entire body jerked on his stiff legs.

"What is this about?" I asked softly, walking closer and crouching down, to the degree that I could do that in a custom-fitted gown. Reaching out, I stroked Tiny Tim's soft, wrinkled head while I peered into the shrubbery. Then my hand froze in place, and my blood ran even colder, when I spied what the little pug had wanted me to see.

A pearl-handled letter opener, which was *almost* concealed by one of the bushes, and which had tinged the snow red.

To my admittedly untrained eye, it appeared that the sharp-looking object, which I'd last seen at the Sylvan Creek Hotel, had been tossed hastily. Perhaps by someone fleeing to a different house, down the block.

I couldn't seem to move, even when I heard footsteps approaching from the same direction Tiny Tim and I had just come. I was completely locked in place until Jonathan bent down and grasped my arm.

He locked up, too, just for a moment, when he saw the object that had put me in a deep freeze.

Then he helped me to my feet and pulled his cell phone from the pocket of his overcoat. Shrugging out of the coat, he wrapped it around my shoulders, telling me, gently but firmly, "You should go home now, Daphne. It's going to be a long night for some of your friends, and they might want you there in the morning."

CHAPTER 43

Recalling how quickly I'd recovered from my minor truck accident with the help of a stack of pancakes, I decided to pull out the big guns for Moxie Bloom, who had texted me no fewer than twenty frowny faces, somewhere around midnight. I'd still been awake, trying to get Axis, Artie, Snowdrop, and Socrates settled into my tiny cottage, while Tinkleston had loudly expressed his displeasure with the temporary living situation. It had been a long night for me, and as Jonathan had predicted, for Moxie, too, so I didn't make reservations at the area's fanciest brunch spot, Magee Mansion, until 11 a.m.

Even so, sitting across from me at a table in the sunny atrium, Moxie appeared tired and a bit drawn. That was worrisome, because she normally bubbled over on the occasions we'd splurged and visited the Magee, which was housed in a renovated

Georgian Colonial estate in the adorable, nearby village of Zephyr Hollow.

The restaurant was only open for brunch and packed during the holidays. Fortunately, I often watched the head chef and owner's three Chow Chows — Ina, Bobby, and Alex — and she'd finagled me a spot in Moxie's favorite room, which overlooked a pretty, now snow-covered, garden with a glittering pond and icicle-hung gazebo.

Moxie's face was turned toward the lovely landscape, where brilliant red cardinals flitted among crimson berries on the branches of winterberry trees, but her gaze was focused inward, and her mouth drawn down.

"Are you okay?" I asked, reaching across the table to give her wrist a squeeze. My timing was bad — she was holding a forkful of the mansion's legendary cinnamon roll French toast bake — and I quickly withdrew my hand as the gooey, icing-covered bite fell back into a delicate white casserole dish. "Tell me what happened."

Facing me, Moxie set down her fork without taking a bite. Instead, she nibbled her lip. "It should've been a dream come true," she noted, speaking more softly than was probably necessary. All of the mansion's dining rooms were filled with chattering parties, made up of both locals and visitors to Sylvan Creek, Zephyr Hollow, and nearby ski lodges. A holiday brunch at the Magee was a tradition for many families. "Not only was Jonathan Black wearing a suit when he questioned me," Moxie continued, "he was in an *Armani tuxedo,* with black satin peak lapels and a classic one-button closure!"

"Um, how do you know the brand, let alone those details?" I asked, digging into my own mini baking dish, which held the day's special, a cheese-and-croissant breakfast casserole, with fluffy eggs, nutty Gruyère, and sweet croissant bread crumbs. I was sympathetic to Moxie, but starving. And, although I'd thought Jonathan had looked a cut above most of the other party goers, I added, "All tuxes look basically the same to me."

Moxie shook her head, already regaining some color in her cheeks and some spark in her eyes as she warmed to the topic of fashion. "Oh, no!" she objected, picking up her fork again. "Tuxedos are all about the details. The slant of a pocket, the cut of the shoulders, the quality of the fabric . . . Each little feature can make or break the suit. And Jonathan Black's was just *perfect.*"

Grabbing a carafe, I poured some heavy cream into my bone china mug of house-blend coffee. "So, you could tell it was Armani, just by the details?"

"Goodness, no!" Moxie dabbed at her lips with a cloth napkin. I was glad she'd started to eat. "At a certain point, he took off the jacket, so he could roll up his sleeves. And when he left the room to question *Mike,* I checked the label."

"Moxie . . ." I hated to shift the topic away from tuxes, given how she'd perked up. Yet, I still felt I should offer, one more time, "If you want to talk about last night — either what happened at the police station or with Mike — I'm all ears. But I understand if you'd rather just enjoy brunch."

The light in Moxie's eyes dimmed, but, as Jonathan had anticipated, she wanted to unburden herself. "There's really not much to say about the murder, except that I feel terrible for poor Jeff Updegrove. But I have no idea why there was a bloody letter opener near Mike's house."

"Was it the murder weapon?" I inquired, as Moxie and I switched dishes on some wordless cue. That was our tradition. "Has that been determined yet?"

"Not that I know of." Moxie took a bite of the casserole and gave me a thumbs up while she chewed. Swallowing, she noted, "I don't think there was time to run whatever tests need to be run, but it seems kind of likely, don't you think?"

"Yes, I actually thought that when I noticed the opener was missing from the hotel's front desk." I'd tried the French toast, and, although an opinion wasn't really needed — the dish was consistently flawless, like an Armani tux, only with icing — I flashed a thumbs up, too. "I felt like it was always there, holding down stacks of mail."

Moxie and I sat back so a server in a crisp, white dress shirt could set down two small bowls of winter fruit salad we'd ordered to finish off our meals on a bright, citrusy note. When the young man stepped away, Moxie said, "At least neither Detective Black nor Detective Doebler could find a motive for me to kill poor Jeff, unlike with CeeCee. I could barely recall anything about him, except that he'd been a truly outstanding parliamentarian. Way better than most. And exceptional parliamentary service is hardly a reason to kill someone!"

I wanted to ask Moxie what the heck that particular school officer even did, but I had a more pressing question. "What about an alibi, Moxie? You had one, right?"

"Yes," she assured me, pushing aside the empty casserole dish and drawing the bowl of fruit closer. "Only it's really flimsy, and backed up only by Mike, who, in turn, only has *me* to vouch for him."

"If you don't mind my asking, where were you both?" I'd scraped the last drizzle of icing from the casserole dish and reluctantly set down my fork. If I'd been at home, I probably would've licked the plate, but even I had some decorum, and I set the plate at the edge of the table. "What happened between you two last night?"

In spite of Mike's ominous pronouncement at his apartment — his warning that whatever had happened in high school had been worse than what anyone believed — I'd secretly hoped that he was exaggerating, and that he and Moxie would rekindle their old spark. However, Moxie slouched down, seeming tired again.

"It was very strange to see him, at first," she confided. "Like being kicked in the stomach, while my heart started racing in a way that might've been good — or bad. Neither one of us seemed to know what to say, so we just stood there in the busy ballroom, trying to find the right words. Then we realized Brett Pinkney was hiding behind some pine trees, for some reason —"

"I think Elyse's ambitious décor wasn't done in time for the ball," I interrupted. "I saw him cutting away some netting at the last minute, before sneaking away."

I'd actually forgotten that Brett had been at the ball — with a pair of scissors in hand — and that he'd disappeared out a side door, close to the time Norm and Jeff had left, too. I socked that detail away for future consideration, while Moxie continued her story.

"Mike and I decided we needed someplace more private to talk, so we went to the library, which was empty."

The hotel had a lovely, but little used, reading room, where guests could choose from shelves full of ancient, leather-bound classic novels, or play old board games or do puzzles, if they didn't mind a few missing pieces. However, the library was hidden away at the back of the inn. Plus, most people probably preferred to watch TV in the privacy of their rooms.

"So, nobody saw you?"

"I don't think so," Moxie said glumly, picking at her fruit. "We passed some people in the lobby —"

"Jeff? And — or — Norm Alcorn?"

Moxie shot me a funny look. "No. I don't think so. Why?"

"It's not important right now," I said, thinking the men's absence might actually be a vital detail. But it was one that I'd consider later. Taking a big bite of the sweet, tangy salad, I made a waving motion with my spoon, then covered my mouth and said, "Getting back to you and Mike . . ."

"Oh, yes." All at once, Moxie got a strange look in her eyes, something between bliss and wistfulness, and she spoke distractedly, her gaze fixed out the window again. "Once the awkwardness passed, we talked a lot about the recent past, and the present. What we've been doing in the last few years, and how Mike ended up in Sylvan Creek again." Two pink spots formed on Moxie's cheeks. A happy flush. "For a while, it was like nothing bad had ever happened between us. I felt . . ."

She couldn't seem to articulate her emotions, but I could guess. "You felt what you used to feel for him."

Moxie finally turned back to me, nodding vigorously, her eyes alight. "Yes. Exactly. And I could tell he felt the same way. We talked about getting together again." She seemed to realize that sounded like they were rushing things, and she held up her hands. "Just for coffee. To talk some more, and maybe — just maybe — see what might happen."

I could tell the story didn't have a simple,

happy ending. "But . . . ?"

Her face fell. "Mike wouldn't tell me what really happened at the formal, when he and CeeCee disappeared." She pressed her bow-like lips together, steeling herself. "And I can't even *think* about seeing him again, if I can't trust him."

I'd hoped for some holiday magic at that particularly enchanted Bark the Halls Ball, but I knew Moxie was right. "I agree," I told her. "You can't be with someone you don't trust." I reached out and squeezed her wrist again. "I'm really sorry, Moxie. I hope someday he tells you the whole story, and that it's something you can both move past."

Withdrawing my hand, I recalled that Mike had mentioned that someone else — someone still living — knew the truth about that fateful school dance.

Was that person still *alive?*

Was silencing the witnesses part of the killer's plan?

Because Jeff had probably been at the formal, and he'd given me the yearbook, which HAD to hold some clue . . .

"Daphne?" Moxie's voice snapped me back to reality, and I tried to shake off my suspicions about Mike Cavanaugh. I didn't want to be wrong about his character. I didn't think I *was* wrong. But I had to admit that evidence seemed to be stacking up against him, and I was glad that he and Moxie hadn't gone anywhere more private than a library in a hotel.

"You're right to be cautious," I repeated. "Mike needs to be completely honest with you, if he even wants friendship."

Moxie cocked her head at me, while the server slipped the check onto our table. I grabbed the bill before Moxie could, because I'd promised that brunch would be my treat. Happily, she didn't argue. But I didn't like the new look in her eyes. The glimmer of curiosity.

"So," she said, a faint smile tugging at the corners of her mouth. "You've been awfully quiet about *your* night." Moxie leaned forward, propping her elbows on the table, lacing her fingers together and resting her chin on the bridge they made. "Did you have a nice time with Gabriel? And did you dance with anyone who wore Armani?"

I'd passed half of the previous, restless night trying to find a link between CeeCee French's murder and Jeff Updegrove's death. The remaining hours had been spent reliving my slow turn on the floor with Jonathan Black. Yet, for some reason, I wasn't quite ready to talk about the ball.

"That is a topic for another day," I said, placing more than enough money on the table to cover the check and provide our server with a hefty holiday tip. Then I checked the time on my phone and was shocked to discover how late it was. Pushing my chair back and grabbing my napkin off my lap, I stood up. "Right now, I have to go walk Norm Alcorn's dog. You don't mind if I rush off, do you?"

"No, of course not," Moxie agreed. "Give Dunston a hug for me, okay?"

"Will do," I promised, brushing crumbs off the long skirt of my intricately patterned maxi-dress. The outfit wasn't practical for dog walking, but everyone dressed up for brunch at the Magee. I tucked the napkin near my empty fruit bowl, telling Moxie, "I'll call you later, okay?"

"Daphne, wait."

I looked down at my best friend, who must've been worried about something all during our meal, and who still seemed unsure about whether she should mention whatever was bothering her. I could tell by the uncertainty in her eyes, and the way she was twisting her napkin around her hands.

"What's up?" I asked.

"You never asked how things ended, with me and Mike."

I was running late, but I had to know why she was bringing this up. I sank back down onto my chair. "What happened?"

"He said he understood why I wouldn't want to see him. Said it was probably for the best, actually."

I had no idea what that meant, but it didn't sound good. As much as my gut told me that Mike was a good guy, I suffered another twinge of doubt. "And . . . ?"

Moxie looked miserable. "We were both pretty upset when we parted ways."

My heart picked up its pace. "Where?"

Moxie looked half sick when she confided, "The lobby of the hotel. The last time I saw him, before I ran home in tears, Mike was standing right near the front desk. Alone."

CHAPTER 44

The bright sunlight that had made the atrium at Magee's so cheerful disappeared behind a layer of gray clouds as I drove to Norm Alcorn's house on the Rolling Green golf course. The upscale development was beloved by my mother, who tried to foist the large, low-maintenance homes — each with course access — onto all of her single, male clients, including Jonathan, whom I'd never heard talk about the sport.

Normally, the thought of Jonathan Black wearing plaid pants and chasing a ball around a manicured lawn would've amused me. However, I was still shaken by Moxie's admission that she'd last seen Mike Cavanaugh standing next to the counter that usually held the letter opener *I'd* last seen lying in a patch of red-stained snow.

"Maybe I'm letting nostalgia, or some romantic daydream I have on Moxie's behalf, stand in the way of accepting reality," I muttered, turning into the long driveway that led to Norm's attractive, two-story, stone-and-siding home, where a simple pine wreath hung on the door. "Maybe I'm refusing to face facts."

I told myself that, but as I hopped out of the truck — still lacking its wreath, which I fully intended to replace — my gut kept insisting that Mike would be proven innocent.

The key to both murders is somewhere in that yearbook, I thought, bending to find a different kind of key. A metal one, which Norm kept hidden under a rock that looked absurdly fake. He might as well have left his house unlocked, for all the good the hunk of gray plastic did.

A much better deterrent to crime was waiting inside the door. When I climbed the steps to the porch, I was greeted by a series of deep, resonant *woofs,* which echoed out across the empty golf course.

Anyone who didn't know that Dunston, who weighed about 150 pounds and stood nearly three feet tall, was a fuzzy, black love bug would almost certainly think twice about entering the house uninvited.

I, on the other hand, knew that the Newfoundland was a friendly, gentle spirit who only barked because he was happy for company.

Inserting the key into the lock, I spoke to him, certain that he could hear through the door. "Hey, buddy. I'm happy to see you, too. I hope you're . . ."

I was about to say "feeling okay," but when I swung the door open, the state of Dunston's health became quite apparent — even viewed from flat on my back, on the throw rug that lay just behind the door.

"You are definitely fit as a fiddle," I told Dunston, who had first knocked me down when I'd opened the door. Then, during our walk, he'd dragged me from the third to the seventh tee and back again, his massive paws kicking up snow. I'd flailed along behind him, holding his leash in one hand and the hem of my dress in the other. Pulling off my coat, I draped it around a chair that flanked Norm's granite-topped kitchen island, while Dunston trotted across the tile kitchen floor to get a big, sloppy drink. "*You* should've pulled the sleigh at Bark the Halls."

As soon as I made the joke, I wished I hadn't brought up the dance. I hadn't seen Jeff Updegrove's body, but I could imagine him slumped near the sleigh, which I could also picture vividly — probably because I'd just spied a photo of the vintage vehicle on a copy of the *Weekly Gazette.*

The paper lay on the island, next to a crumb-filled plate and a half-empty cup of cold coffee that told me Norm had rushed off that morning. He was normally fastidious.

Taking the plate and mug to the sink for him, I returned to the paper, glancing at the story, which was, of course, written by Gabriel.

". . . Updegrove, a former resident of Sylvan Creek . . . recently served as chief operations officer . . ."

"Another job, like parliamentarian, that no one can explain," I noted to Dunston, who was alternately sniffing his empty food bowl and shooting me plaintive glances.

Trying to ignore the dog's big, brown eyes, I returned my attention to the paper.

". . . died of a stab wound . . . bloody letter opener from the Sylvan Creek Hotel found blocks from the scene . . . Detective Jonathan Black declined comment . . ."

"Not surprising," I told Dunston, who was

nudging the bowl in my direction with his massive muzzle.

Although I often fed the blatantly begging pup, I didn't have specific instructions to do so that day, and I again averted my gaze, skimming the long article.

". . . speculation that Updegrove's death is linked to the recent, still unsolved murder of pet store magnate Celeste French . . ."

"Gabriel really needs to give me . . . I mean, Jonathan . . . time to solve that first crime," I complained, just as an empty bowl bumped into my foot.

Looking down — but not too far, given Dunston's height — I met a pair of *desperate* eyes, and I couldn't help melting. Especially since I feared that Norm might've forgotten the dog's breakfast, in his haste to leave the house.

"Fine," I grumbled, rumpling the Newfoundland's big, bushy head. "I'll give you one scoop, since I don't know when your person is supposed to return, and you seem pretty hungry."

Dunston barked loudly and happily, the sound filling the whole spacious kitchen.

"Just don't tell Norm," I requested, heading for a door that led to the garage. Opening that, I picked my way past two recycling bins to reach another large plastic container, where Norm, who was also very organized, stored Dunston's food.

However, when I opened the lid, I discovered that the bin was nearly empty, the red scoop lying next to just a few bits of kibble.

"Sorry, Dunston," I said, with a glance at the doorway, where the dog waited at the top of two steps. "There's hardly a full bite in here."

Dunston *woofed* again, then trotted down the steps and across the garage, his tail wagging when he reached a pallet covered by a dark tarp. The plastic obscured something big and lumpy, and, when I followed Dunston, who was nosing around the mound, I saw the corner of a bright blue bag peeking out.

"Is this a stash of food?" I asked, grinning at the clever dog. "Are you asking me to refill your bin?"

His tongue lolling out — a doggie smile — Dunston barked again.

"I suppose I'll be helping Norm," I noted, lifting the edge of the tarp. Then I froze in place when I read the brand name emblazoned in yellow letters across several thirty-pound bags, which lay atop a pile that was at least ten sacks deep. I looked at Dunston again, asking with disbelief, "Norm buys you *CeeCee French's discount food*?"

"Not anymore."

For a split second, I thought the dog had answered. Then I realized Norm Alcorn had arrived home at some point and was standing in the doorway, where Dunston had just been. But he didn't look as happy as the dog.

Nor did he sound pleased when he told me, in a low growl, "You really, *really* shouldn't have looked under that tarp, Daphne. That was quite a mistake on your part!"

CHAPTER 45

"Norm, why?" I asked, as he poured me a cup of coffee from a fresh pot he'd just brewed, after apologizing for scaring the bejeepers out of me in the garage, and for threatening me at the hotel the other day. Apparently, he'd been quite burdened by the fact that he was hiding *300 pounds of toxic, mail-order kibble* on his property, when all of Sylvan Creek believed him to be the uncontested champion of local merchants. I shot Dunston, who was chowing down on new food Norm had just picked up at Fetch!, a sympathetic look. "Why feed him something so awful?"

"I was just trying to save a little money," Norm admitted, setting the coffee before me and taking a seat across from me at his kitchen table. The table — adorned with a tiny Christmas tree — sat in a window-filled nook that overlooked the golf course, and he gazed outside at the expanse of snow, a look of regret in his blue eyes. "The hotel has required quite a bit of maintenance lately, including replacement of the entire heating system. Things are rather tight." Shifting in his chair, he shot *me* an irritated glance. "And I never should've let your mother talk me into buying this big place. I don't even like golf!"

I didn't know why I was being held responsible for my mother's admittedly strong powers of persuasion, but I found myself apologizing. "Sorry about that."

Norm shrugged. "It's not your fault. Really."

I didn't see how it was my fault at all, but I shifted the conversation back to his other bad decision, regarding the kibble. "So, getting back to the food . . ."

"Oh, yes." Norm tugged at his signature bow tie. Red and green polka dot, for the holidays. "I was looking to cut costs, and I saw a buy one, get one deal on Gourmet Grub on the French's Poodles & More Web site." His gaze flicked to the door leading to the garage, and he winced. "As you saw, under the tarp, I took advantage of the bargain, and a promotional code, quite a few times."

I put two and two together faster than Fidelia Tutweiler, which wasn't saying much for my accountant, because I was actually slow to reach a quite obvious conclusion. "So the food made Dunston sick? And he's recovered since you switched to a better brand?"

Norm nodded, a miserable expression on his face, while the dog in question padded over and rested his big head on his person's lap, as if to tell Norm that all was forgiven. Unfortunately, Norm hadn't forgiven *himself*.

"I thought all dog foods were basically the same," he explained, turning pleading eyes on me, as if he needed my absolution. "And I didn't realize what was happening until a few weeks ago, when the scandal about the arsenic in the food —"

I jerked back in my chair. "Arsenic?"

"Yes. The poison." Norm's thin hand absently stroked Dunston's broad head. "The food was . . . is . . . . manufactured overseas, with little or no regulatory control, and somehow excess levels of the toxin got into several large batches. It's not certain if it was an industrial accident, or if the cheap rice used in the kibble was grown in tainted water, perhaps near a mining operation, because rice *can* absorb harmful levels of arsenic." Norm frowned down at Dunston. "Either way, Dunston became very ill.

Could've *died.*"

I leaned forward, wrapping my fingers around my mug, which advertised Sylvan Creek's Tail Waggin' Winterfest. "Why didn't you let Piper do more bloodwork?"

Norm gave me a funny look, and I realized that I shouldn't know he'd refused the tests, so I quickly added, "When I told Piper I was walking Dunston this week, she said she hoped he was feeling better, since you had canceled some tests."

That sentence was technically true, and Norm seemed to accept my explanation. Plus, he was obviously eager to unburden himself. "By the time the blood tests were scheduled, I already knew what had gone wrong," he said. "And I'd done enough research to know that Dunston would recover once he stopped ingesting the chemical." Norm's pale cheeks flushed with shame, and Dunston looked up at him, whining softly, as if he understood the conversation. "I didn't want Piper — or anyone — to know I'd purchased the cheap food from a big chain." Norm lowered his eyes and his voice. "It was such a terrible mistake. A betrayal of Dunston — and Sylvan Creek."

Most people probably wouldn't have been so hard on themselves for trying to save some money, but those two things — Dunston and the town — were clearly everything to the bachelor who lived alone in an oversized house on a golf course.

"It's okay," I told him, while Dunston pulled away and lay down next to Norm's chair, yawning. "He's obviously doing well now. You should stop beating yourself up."

Norm shook his head. "I can't seem to let it go." Then he met my gaze again, and I saw a flash of anger in his eyes. "I even wrote a message to CeeCee French, telling her she nearly killed Dunston!"

"Really?" I forced myself to sound almost disinterested, although the comment nearly made me jump in my seat again. "You did that?"

Norm nodded, one sharp jerk of his graying head. "Yes. She'd been e-mailing me, *threatening* to bring her 'flagship store' here, and I let her know that I would fight her franchise plan even harder than before, since she and her products had nearly *taken my best friend's life.* In fact, I threatened to sue her, outside of the class action suit that was already looming."

Norm's eyes glistened, as if he was close to tears, and I had to restrain myself from reaching out to pat his hand. I didn't think he'd appreciate the gesture. Instead, I asked two questions that were competing for precedence in my mind. "So, you've known for a while that CeeCee wanted to locate a big French's Poodles & More store here? And how did she respond to your threat about the lawsuit?"

"She laughed at the prospect of the litigation — and I did know about her plans," Norm said, hunching his shoulders. Neither one of us had touched our coffee. "I'd been keeping things quiet, not wanting to panic the local merchants until I could meet with CeeCee, personally, when she came to town for the holidays. I'd hoped that, in spite of the dismissive tone of her e-mails, I could talk some sense into her, face-to-face. Convince her that she'd be killing Sylvan Creek, as surely as she'd nearly killed Dunston, if she located a store here!"

I leaned forward, studying Norm more closely, while my pulse picked up a few beats. I was honestly starting to wonder if he'd murdered the woman who'd threatened the two things he loved most in the world. It was beginning to seem possible, and I wished Socrates and Snowdrop had come along with me. It would've been nice to have backup on that lonely golf course, but, of course, only service dogs were allowed at the Magee, and the unlikely canine

couple had spent the day at Piper's farmhouse, where Jonathan was also picking up
Axis and Artie, at some point. I doubted
that Dunston, who was dozing, would rise
to my defense, if things went wrong between
me and his beloved person, but I nevertheless inquired, as nonchalantly as possible,
"What happened when CeeCee arrived in
town? Did you get a chance to meet with
her?"

Norm snorted. "Yes. And she told me that
I had no power to stop her. That she had
every right to purchase property here —"

"She didn't have a location yet?" I interrupted him, because I was hopeful that, if
the project was still in the early stages of
development, maybe it wouldn't go forward
without CeeCee's backing. I was also curious on behalf of my mother, who would
want to know if a real estate deal might still
be on the table. Then I immediately felt
guilty for seeing anything potentially positive related to a classmate's death, and for
wondering about an opportunity for my
mother, too. "Sorry," I muttered.

Norm had no idea why I was apologizing,
and he didn't really care. He was caught up
in his own story, which must've been weighing heavily upon his mind. "There was no
location for the store," he confirmed. Then

his voice took on a bitter edge. "But that wasn't about to stop Celeste French from hijacking the chamber's annual showing of *It's a Wonderful Life* and making her big announcement, although I'd begged her to keep quiet until I could break the news to chamber members, myself, in a more private setting. One where Gabriel Graham wouldn't be snapping pictures and sensationalizing everything. Especially since CeeCee — who knew I'd purchased some of her food — had threatened to tell everyone in town that I *endorsed her products*!"

So that's why Norm had looked so horrified when CeeCee had mounted the theater's steps, Snowdrop in her arms. He'd wanted to continue keeping the franchise plan under wraps — and he'd been terrified that CeeCee was about to tell everyone how he'd betrayed Sylvan Creek's merchants.

I, meanwhile, was getting nervous. Norm was agitated, and while he'd apologized for trying to intimidate me the other day, I knew that he could be threatening when backed into a corner. I stood up, getting ready to go, even as I tried to get more information. "Why do you still have all the food?" I asked. "Why not get rid of it?"

"There's *so much.*" Norm rose, too, carefully stepping around Dunston, who continued to sleep. "And I don't know how toxic it is. I have no idea how to safely dispose of it, without the whole world knowing that I bought it. So, for now, I've hidden it away." He stepped closer to me. "At least, it was hidden, until you found it."

Norm Alcorn's kitchen was sunny and warm — Mom often mentioned the development's reliable heat pumps as selling points for those who "appreciate maintenance-free living" — but in an instant, it felt like the temperature dropped ten degrees. I could only attribute the cold snap to the icy, warning stare Norm was suddenly giving me.

"I won't tell a soul about the food," I assured him, taking a step backward and reaching blindly for my coat, which was still draped over the chair at the island. "It's really nobody's business."

"No, it's really not. And I certainly don't need word leaking out to your friend at the *Gazette*."

Norm was making me uneasy again. Yet, part of me felt sorry for him. In a way, he was the most connected man in town. But he lived alone in a huge house, and his position with the chamber seemed to mean so much to him that he was — in my opinion — getting a little paranoid.

"I promise, I won't tell Gabriel about the kibble," I said. "To be honest, I really don't think he'd consider it news worth sharing in the paper."

As I said that, I suddenly wondered why CeeCee hadn't made good on her threat to mention Norm's purchase when she'd commandeered the Bijoux's lobby.

Had she simply changed her mind about publicizing Norm's "endorsement" of her shoddy product? Or had something — or someone — else compelled her to keep that mean-spirited tidbit to herself?

Unfortunately, I didn't feel like I could ask Norm what had happened, and I turned the conversation back to CeeCee's plans for Sylvan Creek as I moved toward the foyer.

"So, what do you think will happen now, with the store?" I ventured, sort of sidestepping, so I could keep Norm in view. "I saw you at Bark the Halls, talking to Jeff. Is the franchise still in the works?"

I'd asked that question in hopes of shifting Norm's focus away from me, but my query had quite the opposite effect. Norm, who was close on my heels, abruptly stopped, the better to study me with narrowed, suspicious eyes. "What do you *think* you observed at the dance, Daphne?" he asked, his voice soft, yet very serious.

"Because I'm not sure you saw things correctly."

I met his gaze for a long moment, trying to decide if he was close to threatening me again. Then, although I was sure we *both* knew that I had seen him talking to Jeff before they'd disappeared together, I said, "Maybe you're right. It was a chaotic night."

"Yes," Norm agreed, as I took the last few steps to the front door. "A very *unfortunate* and chaotic night. One never expects to be so close to a horrific crime. But these things do happen — to people who bring trouble upon themselves, in my opinion."

I didn't think CeeCee and Jeff should be blamed for their own deaths, so I didn't reply. Something about that comment also struck me as ominous, and, thinking it was high time for me to leave, I reached for the doorknob — only to have Norm reach past me, blocking the door with his arm and trapping me inside.

CHAPTER 46

"Thank goodness Norm just wanted to pay me," I told Socrates and Snowdrop, who were hiking with me down the short, tree-lined lane that connected Piper's farmhouse to my cottage. I'd parked the truck in the barn and picked up the dogs, who trotted along side by side, Snowdrop's red-and-green sweater a bright spot against the snow. I thought Socrates had a restrained spring to his step, while Snowdrop fairly pranced. Piper had also informed me that the duo had been inseparable all day. Knowing that Socrates, at least, wouldn't want me to make a big deal out of the budding romance, I continued telling them about my adventure at the Rolling Green development. "I thought Norm was going to kill me when he blocked the door. But he really just needed to write a check."

Socrates raised his muzzle to look up at me, and I saw relief mingled with censure in his brown eyes. I probably shouldn't have confided that some of my questions had provoked Dunston's person.

Snowdrop, meanwhile, beamed at Socrates, as if she approved of his disapproval.

"Don't forget that I took a class in Krav Maga," I reminded Socrates. "I was fully ready to break out some of my old moves."

Socrates rolled his eyes, the same way Jonathan had done when I'd told him about my weekend course at an Israeli senior center, while I stepped sideways to avoid a deep tire track that ran through the snow.

All at once, I realized that the tracks, which I'd been side-stepping the whole way from the farmhouse, shouldn't have been there. My van was still snowbound, although I suspected that the day's sunshine had probably made the lane passable even for an old VW with bald tires. Yet I hadn't attempted to drive the road yet.

"Who do you think is visiting?" I asked the dogs, just as we rounded a final bend in the road, and the question became moot.

I immediately recognized the shiny, black truck that was parked next to my van.

And, of course, I knew the tall, handsome detective who'd cleared the snow off my VW, and who was leaning against his pickup, his arms crossed over his chest.

Last, but not least, the dogs and I were quite familiar with the chocolate Lab who was loping to greet us, and the one-eared, drooling Chihuahua who was racing excited circles in the snow — and who wore the tiny, free-range-yak-hair sweater I'd purchased for him the previous winter.

I broke into a grin and was about to tease Jonathan for finally giving in and dressing up Artie.

Then I saw the expression on his face, and I thought the better of joking when he said, "Let's see that yearbook, Daphne."

"I must be missing something, too, or lack context to draw conclusions," Jonathan said, shutting Jeff Updegrove's yearbook and handing it to me. We sat side by side on my front steps, enjoying the sunshine, and I placed the annual on my lap, while Jonathan shifted to look at me. "I didn't see anything out of the ordinary — aside from a kid in a rabid-looking squirrel costume, who appears on quite a few pages."

I couldn't believe he was overlooking my leg warmers, and I didn't intend to point that out. In fact, I moved the yearbook to my side, out of his reach, while the dogs ran by the cottage, playing in the snow.

Glancing behind myself, I saw Tinks sitting near the window, glaring at Jonathan, who'd bested him once in a brief tussle.

"Why do you think Updegrove gave you the book?" Jonathan inquired, drawing my attention back to our conversation. The corners of his mouth lifted slightly. "Was it just to remind you about the promise you made, in your inscription?"

"I suppose there's nothing embarrassing in your old yearbooks," I said, leaning forward, the better to catch the sunlight and see his face. I doubted that Jonathan had ever made fashion mistakes, and he'd probably been a star athlete and prom king, too, but I added, "I guess *you* never had an awkward phase."

His eyes glimmered with amusement, and I knew he was picturing me falling down a hill at Lake Wallapawakee, tumbling into the creek at Pettigrew Park, and thudding down a staircase at Flynt Mansion. I spoke first, before he had a chance. "Do *not* ask when mine is going to end!"

Jonathan grinned. "I was debating whether to make that joke."

"You could've gone for it," I told him, with a glance at the yearbook full of incriminating pictures. "I don't *usually* have trouble laughing at myself."

"Yes, I know," Jonathan said, still smiling.

"It's one of the things I like about you."

My cheeks got warm. We hadn't discussed our moment at Bark the Halls, and I wasn't sure if we would or should. Reaching out, I tapped the yearbook, focusing us on the murder investigation again. "To answer your question about why Jeff might've left me the annual, I *did* see some interesting photos, but nothing that I would call clues."

Jonathan rested back on his hands. "Tell me about the 'interesting' shots, please. It can't hurt."

I hesitated. "First, about the letter opener . . ."

Jonathan didn't speak for a moment, and I thought he wasn't going to share anything. Then he said, "I can't tell you much, aside from the fact that it's almost certainly the murder weapon — which is public knowledge." He paused as the dogs darted past, with Snowdrop in the lead, before adding, "Beyond that, the *handle* was wiped clean. No prints at all."

"Why just wipe the handle?" I asked, thinking that seemed strange. "Why not wipe the blood off, too?"

"I've been wondering that myself," Jonathan noted. "And I keep coming back to the possibility that the blood was meant to be a dramatic touch. Because the whole placement of the letter opener, just visible in the snow near Cavanaugh's house, seems a little too staged."

"You mean, you think the weapon might've been *planted* near Mike's apartment?" I started to get excited on Mike's behalf. "That someone might've been trying to frame him?"

Jonathan's expression tamped down my optimism. "Daphne, the two recent murders are almost certainly related," he reminded me. "And Moxie's scissors are still considered the most likely weapon in French's homicide. Meanwhile, Mike and Moxie had left the dance shortly before Updegrove's death."

My heart sank. "The placement of the letter opener doesn't help Moxie at all, does it?"

There was genuine regret in Jonathan's blue eyes. "Sorry, but no. And my theory about the scene being staged is just that. A theory."

"It doesn't help that Mike and Moxie don't have strong alibis, either, does it?"

Jonathan spoke softly. "No. It doesn't."

I took a moment to think, my brain circling back to Jonathan's use of the words "dramatic" and "staged."

"Jonathan?" I ventured uncertainly. "I

don't want to get anyone else in trouble. . . ."

"But you know something."

I hesitated, then nodded. "It's about Bitsy Bickelheim. Who loves drama — and creates stage sets."

Jonathan leaned forward again, resting his arms on his knees and watching my eyes. "I'm listening."

Reluctantly picking up the yearbook, I located the pages with the cheerleaders and the most prominent sports. Holding the annual closer to Jonathan, I pointed to the picture of the human pyramid, with Bitsy Bickelheim in the background.

"Ms. Bickelheim was the adviser to the cheerleading squad, back when CeeCee was the student in charge." I paused, then asked, "Do you know about Ms. Bickelheim's past with CeeCee? The enmity between them?"

"No, I don't," Jonathan admitted. "I think this is one of those times that your status as a lifelong resident of Sylvan Creek trumps my police academy training."

"Yes, I think so," I agreed, shivering a little when the sun ducked behind a cloud. "Because something strange happened, senior year. An incident that there's no way you could know about."

Jonathan frowned. "Something beyond the

holiday dance, where Mike Cavanaugh ran off with French and broke Moxie Bloom's heart?"

Closing the yearbook, I set it aside again. "Yes. Something even bigger than that."

"Go on."

I tucked some curls behind my ear, suddenly getting cold feet — figuratively and literally. "I don't know if I should share the whole story."

"Daphne, your best friend is still my prime suspect," Jonathan reminded me. "I suggest that you fill me in, so I can decide whether I need to contact Ms. Bickelheim myself."

I nodded again. "Okay. And I didn't promise not to say anything, so I suppose it's all right to tell you that Ms. Bickelheim left Sylvan Creek High midway through my senior year. I'd always assumed that she quit, but it turns out she was forced out."

Jonathan arched an eyebrow. "Because . . . ?"

"CeeCee French accused Ms. Bickelheim of having an affair with a student. Ms. Bickelheim says CeeCee was motivated by anger, because the two clashed over issues related to cheerleading. But I honestly don't know."

Jonathan continued to watch me closely.

"You think there might be a grain of truth to the accusation?"

"I have no idea." I glanced at the dogs, who were rolling around in the snow. Even Socrates was on his back, his big paws flapping in the air. Then I returned my attention to Jonathan. "All I know is, Bitsy Bickelheim hated CeeCee French. Enough that she can't even stand to be in Snowdrop's presence."

At the sound of her name, Snowdrop, who had been wriggling around, too, rolled swiftly to her feet and barked sharply. It almost seemed like she'd understood the comment.

Jonathan glanced at the indignant poodle, then addressed me again. "How do you know that?"

"Ms. Bickelheim had a very strong reaction to Snowdrop during a private dress rehearsal for my role as the Ghost of Christmas Future —"

"I'm looking forward to that production," Jonathan interrupted, fighting back a grin. "I've preordered a front-row seat."

I hoped he was joking about attending the play and overlooked the comment. "Ms. Bickelheim took one look at Snowdrop and spilled her whole story."

Jonathan must've seen me starting to

shiver, because he stood up and extended his hand to me. "So, who was the student in question?"

"I have no idea," I admitted, accepting his offer of help. My legs were stiff, and when he released my chilly hands, I used them to dust off my butt. "Ms. Bickelheim didn't volunteer the student's name," I added. "And I don't know if it's important."

"Perhaps not," Jonathan conceded, bending to pick up the yearbook. "At the very least, I'll talk to Bitsy Bickelheim." He handed the book to me. "Anything else?"

"Just the fact that Brett Pinkney is missing from the spring sports."

"Yes, Pinkney." I could tell from the tone of his voice that Jonathan knew more about Brett's relationship with CeeCee than he had about Ms. Bickelheim's past with the victim. "French's high school boyfriend — before the incident with Mike Cavanaugh."

"I recall them being on again, off again," I said, as the dogs trotted over to join us. They all seemed tired, but happy, and I suffered a twinge of concern, to think that the poodle would likely be leaving us soon.

Or what would happen to Snowdrop, now that Jeff was gone, too . . . ?

"Daphne?" Jonathan's voice brought me back to reality. "Who was more invested in the relationship? Pinkney? Or French? Because, if two people keep getting back together, one of them is probably desperate to be with the other."

That was an interesting observation, and I suspected that he was correct. "If I had to guess, I'd say Brett was more smitten with CeeCee," I said, wrapping my arms around myself and pressing the yearbook to my chest. "Everybody assumed Brett would take over his family's tree farm, while CeeCee always made it clear that she was destined for bigger and better things."

"Yet, we don't always fall for people who fit easily into our lives," Jonathan noted.

That was true of humans — and, it seemed, dogs. The basset hound and the poodle who were nudging each other with their muzzles were definitely a strange pair. Still, I told Jonathan, "I don't know. It's hard for me to imagine CeeCee French being desperate for anyone's affection. Plus, she ran off with Mike at the dance."

Jonathan looked to the west, where the sun was setting, painting the sky a beautiful shade of orange. "Maybe French wanted to make Pinkney jealous?" he suggested, slipping his hands into the pockets of his black down jacket. "Or maybe we don't know the real story about what happened the night of the formal."

The comment surprised me. "Did Mike tell you anything, that day he confided in you about guilt that he carried?" I asked. "Because he said something to me that indicated the rumors about the formal weren't true. And that something even worse than a fling between two teenagers happened that night."

Jonathan shook his head. "Sorry, Daphne. Anything Cavanaugh said to me was shared with a promise of complete confidence. I can't tell you more."

"But —"

Pulling his hands from his pockets, he raised one, cutting me off. "Remember how you once told me 'girl code' trumps legal code?"

Regrettably, I had said that, during a previous investigation.

"Well, I have to maintain honor among soldiers," Jonathan continued, without waiting for me to respond. "I made a promise, related to some of the personal things Mike told me."

I continued searching Jonathan's eyes, which were already softening up. "Just tell me if it's okay for Moxie to see him again," I said. "Do you think she'd be safe? Or is

410

Mike Cavanaugh a killer with a secret, dark past?"

Jonathan winced and rubbed the back of his neck. "I can't make that call right now, Daphne. I just can't. Not in the middle of an investigation, when Cavanaugh is a legitimate suspect."

"But your gut feeling, as a person, not a detective —"

"Sorry, Daphne," he repeated. "I'd rather not say more."

"I understand," I said, but with clear disappointment. Then I led the way to Jonathan's truck, because I thought he was getting ready to leave.

However, before I'd taken two steps, he grabbed my arm. "Daphne. Wait." I turned back, and he released me. "I put a dog in a sweater, because he shakes so much in the cold, and dressed him up in a paisley vest and bow tie, for no other reason than to indulge his fashion whims. I never thought I'd cater to a Chihuahua like that. Living here, and being around you, is changing me. But I'm not great at sharing information. At least, not yet."

That admission, itself, was encouraging, because I knew I couldn't have any kind of relationship, beyond a superficial friendship, with someone who wouldn't confide in me.

We would need to reach a point where he gave me more than vague references to his childhood overseas, his time in the military, and the illness he'd recently battled again. However, I was also well aware that I continued to be Jonathan's polar opposite, and that I would need to meet him halfway on some issues, too.

"It's okay," I assured him. "I still don't lock my doors — yet. And I was pretty sure Norm Alcorn was going to kill me today, for snooping into his personal business, while I admittedly try to solve CeeCee and Jeff's deaths, if only to make sure my best friend doesn't go to jail."

I didn't think Jonathan even heard the last rambling part. "What happened with Alcorn?" he asked sharply. He didn't seem frustrated with me. Okay, maybe a little bit. However, he was mainly unhappy about the idea of Norm's threatening me. "What did he do?"

"Ultimately, nothing," I assured him, as the dogs all gathered around the pickup. "But Norm was very agitated when he talked about how CeeCee announced her plans for the franchise at the Bijoux." I recalled the pile of dog food in Norm's garage — and my own promise to stay quiet about the stash. I didn't want to break that vow, but I felt I should tell Jonathan. "If you haven't questioned him, you might want to consider it. Because not only did Norm hate CeeCee for threatening his town, but he also blames her for nearly killing his beloved dog, Dunston, too." My words came out in a rush. "I also saw him leave Bark the Halls with Jeff Updegrove, while you were very kindly dancing with Fidelia Tutweiler."

"I observed Updegrove and Alcorn, too," Jonathan informed me, opening the passenger side door, so Axis could jump into the back seat. Then Jonathan bent to pick up Artie and helped the Chihuahua into the truck — after deftly deflecting an attempted sloppy kiss. "I saw them leave together."

I should've known that Jonathan had seen the two men walk off, even as he'd twirled my starry-eyed accountant.

"And I'm familiar with Alcorn's recent history with CeeCee French," he added, slamming the door. "But he has a solid alibi for the night of her death — a speech to the local Lions Club. However, I might talk with him again. Especially since I feel like there's something *you're* not telling *me.*"

"Maybe," I conceded, glancing at Socrates and Snowdrop, who stood together in the snow, looking for all the world like an old married couple, sending off friends for the evening. I couldn't resist bending to give the poodle an affectionate pat.

When I straightened, I saw that Jonathan was frowning at the nearly bare pine tree I'd dragged to the edge of the woods. He gave me a quizzical look. "Is *that* your Christmas tree?"

Snowdrop whined and dropped to the ground, covering her muzzle with her paws, while Tinkleston, who must've had incredibly keen ears, yowled loudly inside the house.

"That was our tree, before we had an *issue* with it," I said obliquely, not wanting to pile onto the poodle's guilt. She was doing her best to fit in and get along with Tinks. "Unfortunately, something bad happened."

Jonathan broke into a huge grin. "It always does, doesn't it?"

I sighed, following him around to the truck's driver's side. "I suppose so."

He reached for the door handle, then turned back. "Dinner, later this week?"

I squeezed the yearbook more tightly to myself and cocked my head. "Are you buying?"

"I would expect to, even if you promised otherwise, in advance. However, I never said we're going to a restaurant."

414

"I'm intrigued," I admitted, wondering if Jonathan planned to cook. If he *could* cook. I'd never eaten anything but cheese at his house. "What's the plan?"

"You like mysteries," he said, with a glimmer of mischief in his eyes. "I'll text you when I get the details worked out."

"I can hardly wait." That was true. Then I suddenly remembered something and held out the annual. "Do you want to borrow the yearbook?"

"No, that's okay." He opened the door. "I plan to send Doebler to the high school tomorrow to pore over all four volumes, covering the years you and French were part of the elite 'Fighting Squirrels.' I don't think there's anything special in the copy you have — discounting your inscription."

"No, I suppose not," I agreed, glancing at *Magical Memories.* I was secretly happy not to hand over a book that I still believed contained some sort of clue. "I'll hold on to this for now."

Jonathan climbed behind the wheel, while Snowdrop barked to bid farewell to her new friends. Axis and Artie barked and yipped in response, and Socrates offered a quiet *woof.*

Then I led the way to the house, while Jonathan closed his door and started the truck's engine. But as I stepped up onto the porch, the driver's side window slid down, and he called to me. "Daphne?"

I turned to see Jonathan grinning at me. "What?"

"Really?" he asked. *Leg warmers?*

CHAPTER 47

"Well, I guess Jonathan did notice some of my fashion choices," I told Socrates, Snowdrop, and Tinks when it was just the four of us again, inside the cottage, which seemed almost too quiet.

Moving about restlessly, I tossed a few logs on the fire, warding off the chill as night fell. The dogs seemed antsy, too, and Tinks ran up and down the spiral staircase, burning off energy.

Heading to the kitchen, I switched on the old Bakelite radio, which had sat on the same shelf since I'd moved into my home.

I'd never touched most of the knobs, but the radio always seemed tuned to the right station for the occasion — and tuned into the past. The soft, scratchy sounds of an old version of "Silent Night" filled the cottage, and I found myself humming along, my mind flitting between the upcoming play, my pending date with Jonathan — and the two murders that had me completely stumped.

Jeff Updegrove, dumped near a sleigh, like a sack of toys forgotten by Santa.

Moxie's scissors, Brett Pinkney cutting netting — and a bloody letter opener, displayed in a way that seemed "staged."

CeeCee French left "like the world's worst present" under the town's biggest tree . . .

The quoted word and phrase, uttered by Jonathan and Moxie, ran through my head, along with an image of the massive pine in Pettigrew Park, while the radio suddenly seemed tuned in to *me* and my thoughts.

". . . lot in town is closed for the season, but there's still a big selection of fresh cut evergreens at the Pinkney's Pines farm, Sylvan Creek's family-run purveyor of Christmas trees since 1949. A local tradition, open until 6:30 p.m. each day, now through Christmas Eve . . ."

I first checked the antique clock that sat next to the radio. Then I turned to Snowdrop and Socrates, who seemed to anticipate that we were going somewhere. They stood near the door, Snowdrop shifting on her fluffy white paws, with an eager gleam in her dark eyes. Socrates didn't appear as excited for an outing, but he clearly wasn't going to let me and Snowdrop wander off

418

without someone to serve as the voice of reason.

"Honestly, Socrates," I told him, grabbing my coat. "You've really got to stop worrying. How much trouble can we get in, *buying a Christmas tree?*"

'Twas still a few nights before Christmas, but apparently most people in Sylvan Creek had already purchased their trees. Or maybe we were just cutting it a little close to Pinkney's Pines' closing time, because the few cars we'd passed on the way to the farm had been headed down the rutted, dark lane in the opposite direction, bouncing pines already tied to their roofs.

Jonathan had been kind enough to clear off my van, but I'd borrowed the old truck one last time, because it would be easy to toss a small tree in the bed. Plus, I wanted to surprise Piper by adding a new wreath to the grill.

"I hope we're not too late," I told Socrates and Snowdrop, who were strapped into the front seat together. Giving them a quick, sidelong glance, I noted that Socrates, who wasn't normally good about sharing his personal space, wasn't fighting the arrangement. Then I returned my attention to the road, which wound through a forest of mature pines that stood like snow-covered walls, their branches interlaced. "I haven't seen *any* cars headed in either direction in the last few minutes."

Socrates, who'd endured a terrifying incident with me in a lonely apple orchard, snuffled softly.

"This is a *Christmas tree farm*," I reminded him, as we emerged from the trees and Pinkney's Pines' big, red barn came into view. Split-rail fencing was hung with pine roping, a small bonfire burned in a circle of stones, and strings of lights crisscrossed the lot where precut trees were available for customers who didn't want to wander the grounds and cut down the evergreen of their choice. The scene conjured childhood memories, when my father would take Piper and me to pick a tree, and, as I steered the truck into the empty parking lot, I smiled at the dogs. "This is one of the happiest places in the world!"

I believed that, until I faced forward again and saw Brett Pinkney standing right in front of the truck, with a less-than-festive scowl on his face — and a very sharp-looking axe in his hands.

CHAPTER 48

"Are we too late?" I asked Brett, looking nervously around the farm as I helped Socrates and Snowdrop down from the truck. I wasn't sure why I'd even opened the door for the dogs. I was starting to think we should probably head home. I turned back to the Fighting Squirrels' former quarterback, who was tapping the axe handle lightly against one hand, as if testing the tool's heft. "We can turn right around and come back tomorrow."

"No, we're still technically open," Brett assured me, sounding far from enthusiastic. He squinted past me down the lane. "Although, it seems like business has died down for the night. I let the other guys go home already."

I didn't even look down at Socrates, who whined softly to hear that news. I was pretty sure he was picturing both of us cowering in a shed at the Twisted Branch orchard, waiting for a killer to break down the flimsy door.

"Well, we'll just grab a tree, and maybe a wreath, and be on our way," I said, clapping my mitten-clad hands together. Then, while Socrates and Snowdrop observed warily from their low vantage points, I gestured to the lot of precut pines. "If you could just show us something small, please, because we live in a very tiny cottage."

"Yes, I know where you live," Brett said flatly. The comment alarmed me, until I remembered that we both lived in Sylvan Creek. Everybody knew where *everybody* lived. At least, I hoped that was the case. "And I don't have anything under six-foot, precut," he added. "Most people don't want those little scraggly things, like the one you took from the burn pile."

My *cheeks* caught on fire. "Oh. You saw that?"

Socrates snuffled, while Snowdrop sneezed. The sounds were very reminiscent of snickers.

Brett took a moment to observe the poodle, who seemed to puzzle, or displease, him. And while Brett was distracted, I studied *him.* He still had an athletic build, with a lean, muscular frame, probably honed by farm work as opposed to time in a gym. He'd retained his good looks, too, but there were lines around his eyes and mouth, and I would've guessed that he was older than me, if we hadn't graduated together. Thick, dark-brown curls peeked out from under his knit cap, hinting at a full head of hair. In most ways, he seemed like the guy I'd known in high school — except for the expression in his eyes. The closed-off, angry-at-the-world look was very different from the carefree grin he sported in the yearbook football team photo, where he had his arm draped around Mike Cavanaugh's shoulder. . . .

"Come on," Brett said gruffly, as if he realized I'd been scrutinizing him. He swung the axe up over his shoulder. "Let's go."

I shot the dogs an uncertain glance. Snowdrop licked her muzzle, a nervous gesture, while Socrates shook his head, his ears swinging. He was clearly telling me that we shouldn't follow Brett Pinkney anywhere.

Socrates might've been right, but I didn't want to jump in the truck and drive off in a panic. For all I knew, we were overreacting to a very innocent situation at a place I'd just called one of the happiest on earth. And we certainly shouldn't have been surprised to encounter someone with an axe at a tree farm, so I asked, "Where, exactly, are we going?"

Brett was already walking away, and I took a few tentative steps after him. "We're going to get you the right-sized tree," he said. "I know the perfect one, where the new pines grow."

My feet kept moving, as if of their own accord, and the dogs were right beside me, Socrates huffing with disapproval. "Um, where, exactly, is that?" I asked Brett.

He turned back, finally smiling, but in a way that told me he thought the question was stupid. "At the far end of the property, near the edge of the forest, of course!"

The night was so cold, under a clear, moonlit sky, that the snow crunched and squeaked under our feet and paws as we made our way through rows and rows of pine trees. Brett led the way, his heavy boots blazing the trail for me and the dogs.

I was torn between enjoying the stillness of the evening and the smell of fresh pine in the frosty air, and fearing for all our lives. Yet, with each wordless step we took, I relaxed a little more, thinking that, if Brett planned to kill us, he probably would've done the deed at least an acre back, because, as it turned out, the untamed forest — a mix of pines and oaks and elms — was never too far off. He could've easily grabbed my arm and hauled me into the woods at any point. As far as I could tell, from the way we zigged and zagged through the cultivated trees, he had an actual evergreen in mind for me.

Snowdrop and even Socrates seemed to be warming to the adventure, too. The dogs never strayed far, but Snowdrop, in particular, hopped out of the tracks now and then to bound through the deeper snow.

I was just about to ask how much farther we'd have to hike, because I feared the formerly pampered poodle might wear herself out, when all at once, Brett stopped short.

I nearly bumped into his broad back, and he sidestepped, so I could see around him.

"There she is," he told me, pointing to a small tree with the blade end of his axe. "Can't be more than three feet tall. But shaped just perfect — skinny, not squat — for a small house."

"That is a nice tree," I agreed with a rush of relief, to realize I'd been right. Brett hadn't planned to lure us to our demise. He just wanted to make a sale. And he seemed to have a surprisingly genuine interest in matching person to pine.

I was just about to shoot Socrates an *I knew we'd be fine* look when Brett caught me completely off guard by saying, "But before I cut this thing down for you, I suppose you want to know whether I murdered CeeCee French, right?"

CHAPTER 49

"I don't need to know anything about your involvement — or lack thereof — in Cee-Cee's murder," I assured Brett, tripping over my words and stumbling back a step. Snowdrop and Socrates backed up, too. "You don't need to tell me anything."

"Daphne, you're always in the *Gazette,* solving crimes with the *real* detective . . ." I tried not to be insulted by that comment, because Brett was right. I wasn't an authorized sleuth. ". . . and you didn't come out here just to get a tree. You already have one, from the burn pile!"

"Actually, that tree got destroyed," I informed him. "So, I do need a new tree."

Brett crossed his arms, resting the axe on his shoulder. "And you had no intention of nosing around? Asking me questions about me and CeeCee's past? Because everybody — including the *real* detective, Black — knows that it didn't end well."

The second emphasized reference to Jonathan as the legitimate chief investigator on the case was probably superfluous, but I wasn't inclined to argue with a man who held an object that could fell mighty trees. In fact, I decided honesty might be the best policy.

"Okay, maybe I do have a few questions," I confessed, with a guilty glance at Socrates, who'd known all along that I'd intended to snoop. He hung and shook his head, while Snowdrop yapped loudly. I took that as support for my efforts to find her person's killer. "I'm mainly trying to find out what happened years ago, at the senior holiday formal, when CeeCee and Mike Cavanaugh disappeared." I hesitated, then added, "And I'm curious about why you're missing from the spring sports yearbook photos, too."

Brett furrowed his brow. "You're looking at old yearbooks? And you noticed *that*?"

I couldn't think of one good explanation for why I was nosing through our old yearbook, so I stayed the course with the truth. "Jeff Updegrove left his copy of *Magical Memories* with me, when he dropped off Snowdrop. I feel like he wanted me to find something in the pages, but, of course, I can't ask him now." I shrugged under my heavy coat. "I've been studying some of the pictures."

Brett's voice was low and wary. "And what've you found?"

"Nothing," I admitted, wishing we'd had our conversation by the bonfire. I was getting cold now that we were standing still. "Nothing that will help clear Moxie — or Mike — of either murder."

Brett was silent for a long time. Then he said, "I honestly don't know what happened the night of the formal. Mike and I were pretty good buddies, but he never talked about it."

I didn't want to press my luck, but Brett seemed more thoughtful than agitated, like he wanted to help his old friend, too, so I dared to ask, "What about CeeCee? She was probably your date for the dance, right? You must've been upset, too. Didn't you ever talk about it?"

Brett snorted, his breath coming out like steam from a racehorse's nostrils. "No, CeeCee actually had the nerve to ask me to the formal, despite all she'd done, but I turned her down. We were *over,* by then. I didn't care what she did at that point."

I had no idea what he was talking about. "What do you mean?"

"She'd messed up my life, but good. We

were finally through, forever. And good riddance!"

I looked down at Socrates, who was backing up again on his big paws and pushing Snowdrop back, too. I tried to ask, nonverbally, for a few more minutes. My basset hound protector didn't seem pleased, but I turned back to Brett. "I'm sorry. I still don't understand what happened between you and CeeCee."

"CeeCee French was desperately in love with me," Brett explained, spelling things out slowly, as if I were a child. "I'd push her away, but she'd never accept that I didn't care about her, the way she did about me. She thought she could force everyone to do anything she wanted — even *love* her."

I sucked in a quick breath, realizing that Jonathan had been right. CeeCee was the one whose love had been unrequited. And she'd apparently found that unacceptable.

"When I finally told her it was never happening, fall of our senior year, she went all out to get revenge," he said, his voice low and angry. He uncrossed his arms, so the axe swung to his side, and, although he wasn't mad at me, I stepped back, too. "CeeCee figured out who I was *really* in love with and — although this person didn't love me back — CeeCee had her banished

430

from the school. And, when it was over, I couldn't even function. Not in school. Not on the field." Balling his fist, Brett dug the palm of his free hand into his eye, as if he might be *crying*. "I took my place here, where I belong, and I've stayed here since."

I was almost positive that I'd already identified his "true love." She'd stood in the shadow of a tower of cheerleaders dominated by CeeCee French, staring sadly at Sylvan Creek High's playing fields, where a misguided student who'd probably declared his affection for her — maybe more than once — was practicing football.

"Brett, who was it?" I asked, certain that he'd confirm my hunch. "Who were you in love with?"

"Bitsy Bickelheim," he said softly, his voice choked with emotion. "And she never did anything wrong — except cross CeeCee, too, by trying to be a responsible adviser to the cheerleading squad. One who didn't always let CeeCee get her way."

There didn't seem to be anything more to say, and Brett quickly pulled himself together, hoisting the axe and stomping toward the little tree. "Enough with the past," he said brusquely. "That's over and done with. Certainly not something I'd kill over. I'm not one to destroy, or take, lives."

I didn't know Brett well, but I was inclined to believe him, at least when it came to human lives. He obviously had no qualms about putting an end to evergreens. As Socrates, Snowdrop, and I tensed, he hauled back the axe, prepared to fell my perfect Christmas tree. The one I'd dragged him across several acres, after regular business hours, specifically to chop down.

I probably should've worried about upsetting him again over the loss of a sale and the waste of his time, but, just as the axe reached the apex of its backswing, I heard myself calling out, "Brett! Wait!"

CHAPTER 50

"You really couldn't bear to chop down a tree at a *tree farm*?" Piper asked, scooping leftover chestnut-potato puree into a plastic container. We were in the kitchen at the farmhouse, cleaning up after my sister's annual attempt at cooking a holiday dinner that was usually attended by Mom, Socrates, Moxie, and me. While the menu remained comfortingly constant — the creamy puree, a festive salad with deep red beets and bright greens, and a glazed ham for the meat eaters — the guest list had been slightly different that year, since Moxie had decided to stay home. New attendees included Snowdrop, as well as Roger Berendt and Fidelia Tutweiler, who were in the living room, enjoying some afterdinner Cognac punch by the fire. Piper snapped the lid onto the container and handed me the serving bowl and spoon, so I could wash them in the deep, apron-front sink. "You know those trees are grown to be harvested, right?" she asked. "And they aren't sentient!"

"Yes, I think you went overboard, in terms of compassion," my mother observed dryly from her perch on one of the stools at the breakfast bar. In spite of having donned an apron to protect her "winter white" cashmere sweater and wool pants ensemble, she wasn't making herself useful. Like the non-family guests, who'd been forbidden to chip in, she also nursed a cocktail.

I wouldn't have minded a drink, myself, given that I needed to take the stage at the high school in less than three hours, but I didn't think drinking and climbing ladders in oversized cloaks was a good mix. Instead, I gave myself a consolation prize, licking the spoon before I dunked it into the sudsy water. My sister didn't cook often, but when she did, she applied her usual perfectionism. The puree was delicious.

"A tree is not like one of your *many* stray dogs and cats," Mom observed, with a wave of her drink and a pointed look at the dogs, neither of whom had ever been strays. Socrates ignored my mother, like he always did, but Snowdrop growled at the perceived insult. Then both dogs shambled off to the living room, while Mom gestured with her punch again. Another sip, and she might actually exhibit a facial expression. "One need not feel sorry for an evergreen!"

"I know you're probably right," I agreed, rinsing the serving spoon and handing it to Piper, who'd grabbed a plaid dish towel. "It just looked so happy, out in the snow. And there was a perfectly good alternative in the burn pile. Scrappy seems happy to be dressed up in lights and ornaments."

Slipping the spoon into a drawer, Piper shot me a skeptical glance. "You named a tree you got —"

"From Brett Pinkney's discard, scrap wood pile," I said, refusing to feel silly.

"Why in the world did you drag that poor man across his whole property — valued at nearly one million dollars for the land alone, not that he'll consider selling — if you had no intention of purchasing a tree?"

Of course, my mother had to put a price tag on a generations-old family business. And my sister didn't give me a chance to answer. "Your younger child was snooping into CeeCee French's and Jeff Updegrove's murders," Piper said, accepting the clean, rinsed bowl from me. "Weren't you, Daphne?"

I fished around in the sink, locating silverware — and avoiding my sibling's critical gaze. I had a basset hound who gave me enough disapproving looks. "I might've asked a few questions, in the interest of helping Moxie," I admitted. "But Brett couldn't tell me much."

"He told you something, though," Mom noted shrewdly. Maybe she hadn't downed as much punch as I'd believed. Or maybe the strong drink was heightening her always keen powers of perception. "What was it?"

"I don't feel like I should share details, but Brett admitted that CeeCee French used to be desperately in love with him." I scrubbed some forks with a sponge. "And when he wouldn't reciprocate, she found a way to punish him, and bring down the person he really cared for, too."

"Ouch." Piper, currently in love herself, winced and glanced in the direction of the living room, where Roger, who wore a bright green sweater vest, was deep in conversation with Fidelia.

My accountant's cheeks had a pretty flush, and she'd donned a red, silky blouse that featured a dowdy bow, but was nonetheless quite bold by Fidelia's standards. I really believed that a few dances with two of Sylvan Creek's most handsome men had boosted her confidence.

"Well, it's settled," Mom said, slapping

her free hand against the granite countertop and drawing Piper's and my attention back to the kitchen.

"What's that?" Piper asked, tossing the towel over her shoulder and moving quickly across the room to remove the tumbler of punch from Mom's possession. Our mother looked confused, and perhaps disappointed, until Piper distracted her with another question. "What's settled?"

"The murder," Mom announced. "Brett Pinkney did it."

Piper and I exchanged glances that said we agreed our mother was a bit tipsy. Then I spoke over my shoulder, addressing Mom, while I searched for the last few spoons in the warm water. "How do you figure?"

I could practically hear the dismissive wave of her hand. "It's *always* the strong, silent type."

That was not necessarily the case. In fact, one of the killers I'd caught had been quite gregarious. It was difficult enough arguing with my mother when she was stone-cold sober, though, and I had no intention of debating her after one — or perhaps two — drinks.

"I've got to leave soon and head straight to the high school, or I'd drive her home," I told Piper in a whisper, handing her the last clean utensils. "You are going to brew some coffee, right?"

"I heard that!" Mom said. "And I do not need a ride — or coffee!"

Her protests barely registered with me. My right hand, still soapy and wet, was darting out to grab my sister's left wrist, causing her to drop forks all over the floor.

"What the . . . ?" I gasped, staring at the big gem that glittered on Piper's ring finger, while Roger, Fidelia, and the dogs, roused by the commotion, joined us in the kitchen. My gaze darted from Roger, who looked as pleased as the punch we'd taken away from my baffled mother, back to my sister, whose eyes were twinkling like her *gorgeous, diamond engagement ring.* "Have you been wearing that the whole time?"

My newly engaged sibling grinned ear to ear. "Yes, Daphne. And I have to say, for a sleuth, you're not very observant!"

CHAPTER 51

"Piper was not wearing that ring the whole evening," I told Socrates and Snowdrop, who were strapped in the front seat of my van — which now sported a wreath on the grill, like the old truck.

I'd felt so badly about not buying the little tree, and taking a freebie, that I'd ended up purchasing no fewer than six wreaths from Pinkney's Pines. I wasn't sure what to do with them all, and I'd tossed one in the back seat for Bitsy Bickelheim, thinking I'd give it to her after the performance, instead of the more traditional gift of flowers. At least, I thought actors gave their directors some token of appreciation.

"Did you see a ring on Piper's finger?" I asked the dogs. Socrates was keenly obser-vant, and Snowdrop was no stranger to bling. I dared to glance at both canines as I steered down the road to the school. "I'm not sure how Mom would've overlooked that big rock, too — not to mention Fidelia."

It was dark in the VW, but I was pretty sure I saw a twinkle in Socrates's eyes, like he agreed that my sister had pulled a fast one on us, hiding the ring until she was ready to announce her engagement.

There was also a chance that my normally aloof basset hound best friend was suddenly approving of love.

"Regardless, it was nice to get some good news tonight," I added, pulling into the parking lot, which was already filled with cars. We were rather late, after spending quite a bit of time congratulating Piper and Roger; calming down a very excited Fidelia, who had a latent romantic side; and trying to convince my mother that Winding Hill was a perfectly wonderful place to raise children, and that the happy couple wouldn't have to buy "new construction" in a cul-de-sac any time soon, if ever.

Finding an empty spot, I parked and got out of the van, then helped Socrates and Snowdrop to the pavement. "Why aren't all these cars reassuring?" I asked, heading for the metal doors we'd used before, as fat snowflakes began to fall from the sky. "I feel more nervous now than when the place was abandoned!"

Socrates clearly disagreed — because he didn't have to go onstage. He and Snowdrop would watch from the wings, just like I would do until the next-to-last scene.

Opening the door, I let the dogs trot past me, then took the lead, showing them the way to a back entrance to the auditorium. I could hear muffled voices coming from the stage, because the play was already under-way, and I didn't want to walk through the main doors and past the audience.

"This way," I whispered, turning down a narrow corridor that would take us directly backstage. "And be quiet, okay?"

I wasn't sure why I said that. No one could hear us, and, not counting Elyse Hunter-Black's ghostly greyhounds, Socra-tes was the most reticent dog I'd ever met. Snowdrop wasn't noisy, either.

Needless to say, the dogs didn't respond, and a few seconds later, we reached the stage entrance and slipped inside, mounting a musty staircase and joining the rest of the cast, whose waiting members were huddled stage right — or stage left — just beyond a heavy velvet curtain.

I took my place there, too, trying to see past a bunch of people in Dickensian cos-tumes, so I could check out Asa Whitaker's portrayal of Scrooge.

I couldn't see much, but Asa's attempt at a British accent made me glad Fidelia hadn't auditioned us both for a speaking role. I wasn't sure I could've done much better than Asa, although I probably couldn't have done worse. Then someone standing in front of me — I was pretty sure it was Bob Cratchit — moved a little bit sideways, and I spied a character onstage who wore a green velvet costume, a bushy beard, and a laurel wreath upon his head.

My stomach churned, and I looked down at Socrates and Snowdrop, who probably couldn't see a thing through a forest of legs and skirts with huge bustles. "I'm pretty sure that's the Ghost of Christmas Present," I whispered. "I'll be on in the next scene!"

Someone tapped my shoulder and said, "Yes, you will be, and you are tardy!"

Turning, I saw Ms. Bickelheim standing right behind me — holding my cloak, wadded up in her arms, and scowling like Death herself.

"Unfortunately, the Kinnaman twins, who comprised our entire stage crew, drank some bad eggnog," Ms. Bickelheim explained quietly, leading me and the dogs behind the backdrop to the other side of the stage, where there was nothing but semidarkness and a waiting ladder. "It's up to the actors to do everything tonight. You'll be on your own."

I shot Socrates and Snowdrop a panicked look. "But —"

Before I could protest that I would appreciate some help from one of my fellow thespians — there were a bunch of them, standing right across the stage — Ms. Bickelheim added, in a hurried but hushed tone, "Put on your costume, and when the lights dim, carry your ladder center stage, climb up, and prepare to point at the tombstone *stage right*! Just like in rehearsal!"

First of all, I could've sworn that the tombstone had originally been stage left. Not that I knew which direction was which. And, second of all, we'd never completed my rehearsal.

There was no time to quibble. I could hear Scrooge begging the current ghost — who seemed to be knocking it out of the park — to tell him what would happen next to his stingy self, which I took to mean the scene was wrapping up. In a few minutes, the present set would disappear, replaced by a single tombstone.

All at once, Jonathan's words echoed in my mind.

443

". . . the blood was meant to be a dramatic touch . . . the whole placement of the letter opener . . . a little too staged . . ."

There wasn't much time to start a new conversation with Ms. Bickelheim, but the clock was running out on my effort to clear Moxie's — and hopefully Mike's — names, too, and I said, quietly, "I spoke to Brett Pinkney, and he told me everything. I'm so sorry, Ms. Bickelheim. It sounds like the whole thing was a mess, and you really did *nothing* wrong. The 'affair' was fabricated entirely by CeeCee to punish you — and Brett."

Bitsy Bickelheim stared at me for a long time, blinking behind eccentric, leopard-print cat-eye glasses until I started to get uncomfortable. Then, she finally said, in a low, icy tone, "Is this part of some private investigation, Ms. Templeton? Are you trying to lead me to say something? Because I know for a fact that you're attempting to solve CeeCee French's murder — and we both know I had motive."

Snowdrop growled at Ms. Bickelheim's mention of her deceased person, while Socrates made a grumbling sound, reminding me that he was available if I needed backup. He was also complaining about the fact that I'd just poked a hornet's nest.

444

"I am trying to solve the crime," I admitted, with a glance past Ms. Bickelheim to the stage, where the lights were dimming. Realizing that I still hadn't donned my costume, I shook out the robe and began to struggle into the fabric, pulling the cloak over my head and snagging my hand in the cowl. The garment was so large and shapeless that the only thing marking the neck hole was a label. A little, pink piece of fabric that gave me pause, for a moment, as I tried to sort myself out. Then I twisted the robe around, so the tag was in the back, and pulled the whole thing over my body. When my head emerged, I resumed addressing Ms. Bickelheim, who — in spite of being angry — adjusted my hem. "I'm not accusing you of anything," I promised her. "I just want to find the truth, on behalf of my best friend, so if you know anything, we could meet later. . . ."

Ms. Bickelheim didn't take me up on that offer. She compressed her mouth into a thin, angry line. And by the time she spoke, Scrooge and the Ghost of Christmas Present had exited the stage to a rousing round of applause, and the entire theater was plunged into darkness — which only made her warning more ominous.

"Be careful on the ladder, Daphne," she

said, her voice strangely deep and even. "The expression might be 'break a leg.' But it's your neck you really have to watch."

CHAPTER 52

"Here goes," I muttered to Socrates and Snowdrop, awkwardly hoisting the ladder and shuffling, to the best of my ability, to the center of the stage, while the heavy velvet curtain was drawn shut.

I couldn't see a thing, because the theater was still dark, and Ms. Bickelheim had yanked the hood over my head, covering my eyes, before she'd disappeared into the wings. I couldn't hear much, either, beyond the shuffling feet of some actors who quickly removed the previous ghost's armchair throne. I was pretty sure another cast member had rushed out to put Scrooge's Styrofoam tombstone in place, too, while I struggled not to stumble over the massive hem of my cloak, which I kept stepping on.

I wasn't even sure how I'd know when I reached the proper mark, so I guessed, to the best of my ability, and thumped the ladder down on the floorboards.

The auditorium seemed impossibly silent as I grabbed the ladder with one hand and tried to lift up the bottom of my robe with the other.

"Careful," I muttered, ascending the metal rungs — and trying not to be angry with Fidelia Tutweiler, who really should've broken character long enough to speak up at the audition.

Reaching the top, my breath ragged with nerves, I crouched and did my best to arrange the fabric so it covered the "apparatus," to use Ms. Bickelheim's word. Then, taking a deep breath and pretending I was on a yoga mat, I straightened and tried to balance, just as the curtain slowly parted. I could hear the pulleys squeaking, and people shifting in their seats, as the sound-muffling barrier between me and the audience was removed.

"Don't fall, don't fall," I whispered to myself, as a spotlight slowly dawned upon me. I could feel the warmth and vaguely discern the glow through the fabric of my hood. And, I had to say, I was somewhat gratified by the faint gasps I heard from a few of the more easily spooked patrons.

Then footsteps echoed across the floorboards before coming to a halt, not far from me.

"Oh, spirit most terrible," Asa Whitaker moaned in feigned fear, his accent veering between bad British and spot-on Jamaican. "What have *you* come to show me?"

I took that as my cue and slowly raised my hand, my finger shaking in suitably spectral fashion — although I wasn't acting. I was genuinely wobbly, head to toe.

Judging by the eruption of laughter, I surmised that I'd pointed in the wrong direction. I blamed Ms. Bickelheim, in part, for what I still believed were conflicting instructions.

Shifting slowly, I moved my hand until the giggles stopped. I presumed that meant my finger was pointing in the general direction of the tombstone.

All I could do then was stand with my arm outstretched while Scrooge completed a long soliloquy that soon had my arm shaking with *fatigue.*

In an effort to distract myself from my precarious position, my aching muscles — and Asa's *really awful* accent — I let my thoughts wander to the recent homicides, and things that might or might not be clues, but which stuck in my mind.

A pair of scissors that couldn't *be the murder weapon.*

A suitcase full of designer canine clothes —

and a catalog for French's Poodles, featuring snazzy, but discount, dog duds.

". . . when options run out . . . we turn to the familiarity of home. . . ."

A window in Moxie's gingerbread village that shouldn't have been dark.

And distinctive handwriting — created without pen or pencil . . .

I wasn't supposed to have any lines, but all at once, forgetting where I was, I broke character — proving once again that Fidelia should've played the role — and cried out, "I've got it!"

450

CHAPTER 53

"Asa Whitaker saved the play," I told Socrates and Snowdrop, who ran with me through the high school, after I'd half-tumbled off the ladder, dragged it offstage, shed my robe, and ducked out of the auditorium. We were headed toward the school library, and I was distracted, but I had to give credit where credit was due. "Asa might be terrible at accents, but he's not bad at improvisation!"

Socrates, loping at my side, offered a rare, sharp bark, clearly disagreeing. And, in retrospect, perhaps Asa's on-the-spot response to my slip of the tongue — *"Yes, you've got me, spirit! I shall change forthwith!"* — wasn't *that* brilliant.

"Well, at least the laughter stopped," I reminded Socrates, as we all wheeled around a dimly lit corner, headed straight for glass double doors that I hoped wouldn't be locked.

Reaching the library, I grabbed one of the silver handles and pulled hard, nearly flying backward when the door swung wide open.

"Typical Sylvan Creek," I told the dogs, as we slipped inside the dark, musty room, which smelled of old paper and the SpaghettiOs that the librarian, Ms. Kindercart, apparently still packed for lunch each day. "*Nobody* locks up!"

Snowdrop seemed to be enjoying our adventure, but Socrates — a veteran of several sleuthing exploits gone awry — did not share in the excitement. He hung back until I said, "We'll just look at the yearbooks, quickly. And if my hunch is correct, I will text Jonathan. I promise."

That seemed to placate him, and I calmed down, too, getting a little spooked when we walked through the silent stacks toward a corner that used to hold generations' worth of annuals.

Sure enough, the yearbooks were still there, and I quickly spotted the volume from my senior year. It stuck out a few inches, probably because Detective Doebler had just looked at it, and hadn't reshelved it neatly.

"Ms. Kindercart would *not* appreciate that," I told the dogs softly, plucking *Magical Memories* from the shelves and quickly

452

flipping through the pages, looking for a section I hadn't bothered with before: the *junior* class.

My finger trembling again, this time with renewed excitement, I traced the rows of smiling portraits until I found the one I wanted.

"I was right," I said, smiling at Snowdrop.

Socrates was busy sniffing around the stacks. He didn't seem impressed with the battered volumes — nor with my investigation.

Slamming the book shut, I placed it back on the shelf, aligning it correctly out of respect for Ms. Kindercart. Then I pulled my cell phone from the back pocket of my jeans and texted Jonathan, as promised, before telling the dogs, "Let's go solve another murder — and quickly, before the play lets out and the killer leaves the school!"

CHAPTER 54

The Pocono Mountains' latest snowstorm was picking up steam as I pulled into a parking spot behind Ivy Dunleavy's little shop. As I'd expected, the front window had been dark when I'd driven past — just like the miniature window in Moxie's gingerbread village, created using photos Moxie had taken the night of CeeCee French's murder.

Hopping out of the van, I hurried to the passenger side and opened the door, releasing Socrates and Snowdrop from their harnesses. Snowdrop leaped to the ground — I was honestly starting to wonder if she knew we were trying to catch CeeCee's killer — but Socrates didn't move to get down, until I reminded him, "I texted Jonathan. I'm sure he's on his way."

I wasn't really certain of that, since I hadn't received a reply yet, but I was fairly confident. Unlike me, Jonathan Black kept his phone charged and at the ready.

Regardless, we probably had at least fifteen minutes before Ivy would even leave the theater. The final scene, about Scrooge's redemption, was fairly long, and I wasn't going to do more than peek inside the *rear* window of Ivy's shop.

"Ivy, herself, noted that the shop should've been lit up, in Moxie's version of Sylvan Creek," I told the dogs, stomping through the snow and using my mitten to rub a circle in a thin coating of ice that covered the glass. "She said she was *always* working. Which is, of course, an exaggeration. But when you put all the clues together . . ."

Snowdrop barked quietly but encouragingly, while Socrates continued to look skeptical.

"This will just take a moment," I assured him, pulling out my phone again and tapping the screen until I found the flashlight app. Then I stood on tiptoes and shined the beam into the shop. "I knew it," I told the dogs in a whisper, although we were alone in a dark, snowy alley. "Scissors, everywhere — of course. And designer pet outfits, too!"

All at once, Socrates barked loudly, and I thought he was *finally* congratulating me for likely solving two murders — until Ivy Dunleavy stepped from the shadows and offered us an invitation that was served with a chilly half-smile, and backed up with a very inhospitable *gun:* "We'd be warmer inside, don't you think?"

"You lost weight, changed your name and your look — and lied about your home-town," I told Ivy, who had me, Socrates, and Snowdrop trapped in her small work-room. The space aggravated my claustro-phobia, and the half-clothed, headless man-nequins lurking in the shadows were making me edgy, too. I was, however, grateful for the large table, strewn with half-finished, but already gorgeous, outfits for dogs, that stood between us. "Jeff recognized you, though, didn't he?"

Ivy nodded, and her flat-ironed, copper-colored hair — which had been deep black and wavy during her high school emo phase — swung by her shoulders. "Yes. He'd been an outcast, in his own way. We'd even gone out, once or twice, in high school. He knew me well enough to see through the changes I'd made."

"He suspected you of the murder, didn't he?" I asked, fighting back my fear and clinging to the fact that Jonathan, and hope-fully Detective Doebler, would arrive at any minute. I forced myself to meet Ivy's eyes, which I'd recently seen in a photo, where they'd been ringed by thick, raccoon-worthy black liner. "Jeff knew you hated CeeCee — probably for bullying you. And he also knew you well enough to understand what you were capable of. He left me the yearbook, hoping I'd recognize you and solve the case, because he was scared to confront you. Scared that you'd kill *him* — which you did, anyway."

Ivy scrunched up her brow. "Yearbook?"

"Yes," I said, with a glance down at Socrates and Snowdrop. I'd tried to keep the dogs from getting herded into the shop, but Ivy had forced them to accompany us. Snowdrop looked ready to attack, which was alarming, but Socrates's expression was, as always, reassuringly calm. Then I turned to Ivy again. "Jeff gave me a copy of our senior year annual, right after CeeCee's murder. And I knew there was a clue inside. But I was looking at the wrong pictures, focusing on the seniors."

Ivy smiled, a heartless grin. "I guess his attempt to save his skin was pointless. I knew, the moment he saw me at the Bijoux, that he recognized me. And when he came back to town, I confronted him outside the ball. He'd guessed *far* too much."

I was surprised Jeff had gone anywhere

alone with Ivy, given his suspicions. "How did you convince him to leave with you? To go outside?"

"I didn't." Ivy's eyes glittered. "I meant to confront Jeff in his room after the ball. But as I was sneaking upstairs, prepared to break into his room and wait for him, I saw him arguing with Norm Alcorn."

"About what?"

"Norm was trying to convince Jeff to call off the plans for the superstore, now that CeeCee was dead. Norm believed the store was a twisted joke on CeeCee's part, and that no one else at French's Poodles & More probably wanted to follow through."

I forgot for a moment that the dogs and I were in grave danger. I was genuinely hopeful that the plans might fall apart. "What did Jeff say?"

"That his hands were tied."

"Oh." That news was disappointing — but I needed to keep Ivy talking until reinforcements arrived. "So, what happened?"

"They kept raising their voices, until Norm suggested they take the argument outside." The gleam in Ivy's eyes grew deadly cold. "I grabbed the letter opener and followed. And when Norm finally stalked off —"

I wanted her to talk, but I didn't want to

hear more of the gruesome details, and I interrupted her, asking the first question that came to mind. "Why didn't you already have a weapon, if you went to the hotel to kill Jeff?"

Ivy frowned. "I took the letter opener on impulse, thinking I could add more suspects to the list by implicating Norm and framing Mike, too, by leaving the weapon near his house. But, of course, I had come to the hotel prepared." She lowered the gun, if only to gesture at the table, which held not only fabric, but the array of scissors I'd seen through the window. "I'd intended to kill him with the same scissors I used to kill CeeCee — right here."

My blood ran cold, to realize that Celeste French had been murdered close to, if not on the exact spot, where Socrates, Snowdrop, and I now stood, huddled close to one another.

"I killed her with the same scissors I used to make your dress," Ivy continued, seeming to take some pleasure from the way I'd blanched. Her smile seemed more genuine — and crueler. "Isn't it nice to know that your lovely gown was crafted with a *murder weapon*?"

Down by my shins, Socrates snorted, as if to say that he'd known succumbing to vanity was always a mistake.

I ignored the rebuke, keeping my attention trained on Ivy. "But what about *Moxie's* scissors . . . ?"

Like most killers, Ivy couldn't resist bragging about her cleverness. "I knew that Moxie Bloom hated CeeCee, and the old story about the Christmas formal was common knowledge. Everybody in town would suspect her of snapping, after years of holding a grudge. So, after I killed Celeste and dumped the body in the park — as a Christmas gift to *everyone* in this town — I sneaked into Spa and Paw." She rolled her eyes. "Which, like every place in this hick village, is hardly ever locked!"

A trickle of cold sweat slipped down my spine. Ivy must've left the door ajar when she'd sneaked away that night, and Socrates had alerted me to close it.

"I got the scissors, which I meant to leave near the body," Ivy added, her cheeks flushing with sudden anger. "But this little pug, in a stupid sweater, knocked me over and stole the weapon I hoped to plant."

"Tiny Tim!" I cried, wondering if the pug had sensed something was wrong and interfered, or if he'd just been causing trouble. I decided to believe he was motivated by a desire to help, because he was a sweet dog at heart. "I hadn't been able to figure out how he got the scissors!"

Ivy glowered at me. "You know the dog?"

"Yes," I said. "He was adopted by Mike Cavanaugh, right before Mike returned to Sylvan Creek."

That revelation seemed to please Ivy, in a weird way. She laughed, a sharp, mirthless sound. "It's lovely, how things all tie together, isn't it? Mike's dog causes trouble for me; I cause trouble for Mike."

I didn't really find that amusing, and Ivy grew more serious again, too. "You know, the night I killed Jeff, I saw Mike leave the hotel and limp down the alley," she said, looking away for a moment, out the window at the falling snow. "He was right ahead of me, but never even noticed me following him."

Because he was suffering fresh heartbreak after seeing Moxie again.

Shaking off her momentary reverie, Ivy edged to the corner of her work table. Moving closer to me. "I was so surprised he'd returned to Sylvan Creek," she added. "Because you know what really happened, the night of the formal, right?"

I shook my head. "No. I don't." I hesitated, confused. "Do *you*?"

"Yes, of course." The last traces of menac-

461

ing glitter in Ivy's eyes glimmered out, although I didn't think Snowdrop, Socrates, and I were safe. She was still armed and agitated, her voice taking on a different edge as she told me, "Mike saw CeeCee follow *me* out of the gymnasium. She'd been bullying me all night — like she did most days at school, too. Mocking my makeup, my hair, and the gorgeous, ebony silk gown I'd made with my own hands. It was like she was mad at the world that night, but taking it out on *me*!"

I was pretty sure I knew the root of CeeCee's anger: her failure to force Brett to love *her* by removing the object of his affection from the equation. CeeCee had invited Brett to the dance, and — dumbfounded by her audacity — he'd turned her down.

I didn't relate all that to Ivy, though. I let her continue her story, while Socrates listened patiently, too. I hoped he was devising a plan, because I really had nothing, at that point.

"I ran away crying, and CeeCee took off after me," Ivy related, her voice choked. She was enraged and suffering again as she relived the incident. "Mike must've seen us, and he followed." Ivy shrugged as she tried to piece together parts of the tale that she didn't know for sure. "I guess he didn't make a big deal out of it and tell Moxie he was going to play the hero." All at once, her expression softened. "I think he really was a nice guy, for a jock. Not all full of himself, you know?"

I suspected Mike was still nice. But I hadn't yet heard the rest of the story. The part that was supposedly worse than betrayal of a girlfriend. "What happened next?"

Ivy's eyes glistened again, rage and pain once more taking hold, and her hand, holding the gun, trembled in a somewhat alarming way. "CeeCee followed me to the courtyard, where she started pushing me. Grabbing my shoulders and shaking them!" A tear slipped from Ivy's eye, but she didn't wipe it away. "Mike found us, and when he tried to pull her off me, begging her to stop, CeeCee spun around and *slapped him.*" I winced, and cringed more when Ivy said, "She hit him with enough force to make his head snap sideways — then Mike grabbed CeeCee, roughly, and shoved her away from himself, so hard that she fell down."

There was an ounce of humanity left somewhere inside Ivy, because she grew quiet and got a distant, almost haunted, look in her eyes. "I'll never forget the expression on his face when he saw what he'd done. He looked horrified, staring down at his hands. Then he ran away."

I couldn't ever condone violence against women, and I could understand Mike's self-loathing, at having shoved CeeCee. But I wasn't sure if he should still be punishing himself for what sounded like a complicated spontaneous incident.

"How did you figure out I was the killer?" Ivy inquired, interrupting my thoughts — and taking another step in the dogs' and my direction. Her hand, holding the gun, shook, and, having just held a similar position while wearing one of her creations, I knew she must be getting tired.

I really hoped Jonathan had received my text and was on his way. In the meantime, I would do my best to stall her by explaining how I'd pieced the clues together.

"I saw the drawing for a dog outfit in your sketchbook, when you showed me and Moxie your designs at Oh, Beans," I said. "I didn't know what it was at first, and it didn't mean anything to me, anyhow — until I started caring for and dressing Snowdrop."

Ivy blinked at me, confused, because I wasn't telling my story very well. Her hand continued to shake, too.

"When Jeff dropped her off, Snowdrop wore a beautiful cashmere sweater, which I didn't know how to clean," I said, with a glance down at the poodle, whose lips were curled. I shook my head, just slightly, telling her to back down, and Socrates nudged her with his muzzle, too, presumably urging patience. Then I addressed Ivy again. "When I looked for directions, I noticed the hand-stitched Park Avenue Pets label."

"My *former* label," Ivy growled, her eyes narrowed. "Until CeeCee French — ever the bully — began to *knock off* all my designs, selling nearly identical clothes in her megastores, turning out her cheap merchandise so quickly that my snooty clients declared my designs 'irrelevant' and 'low class.' I had to close my Manhattan storefront and crawl back here, my tail between my legs!"

I'd seen the copies of Ivy's designs in the catalog I'd found in CeeCee's room. The one that introduced new products that would be available in CeeCee's stores. The canine clothes had been the same as the outfits in Snowdrop's wardrobe. I hadn't been sure if the poodle's garments were actually cheap — or if, as Ivy had just confirmed, CeeCee had been ripping off Park Avenue Pets' ideas.

All at once, I was struck by an important question. "Did CeeCee even know who you were when she was pirating your work? Was she bullying you again?"

"No," Ivy informed me, her voice dripping icicles, while, outside, the snow came down harder. Fat flakes were falling past the shop's rear window, and I wondered if the storm had delayed Jonathan, who should've arrived by then, even if he'd had to drive from his home in the country. "I had reinvented myself by the time CeeCee started *stealing from me,*" Ivy added. "In fact, I doubt she even knew the person behind Park Avenue Pets. She sent *minions* to the shop when she needed prototypes."

"Like . . . secret shoppers?"

Ivy nodded, her mouth a thin, white line. Then she said, "If she'd known my identity, I never could have lured her here."

My stomach clenched. "You . . . ?"

Ivy could tell that I was horrified to realize CeeCee's murder had been premeditated, and she laughed. "Yes. I pretended I was a naïve, up-and-coming designer who would create exquisite pet clothes that she'd be welcome to copy and sell for next to nothing, because I was desperate to launch my career." The flicker of amusement in Ivy's eyes guttered out. "Cheapskate that she was, CeeCee couldn't resist at least looking at my designs. Alone. Here."

466

I glanced at the glittering array of scissors and, feeling queasy, rested one hand on my stomach. Both dogs stood stock-still, too.

"How did you put everything together?" Ivy asked, drawing my attention back to her. "You couldn't have known about my New York store."

I cleared my throat, which felt dry, then explained. "I saw something in CeeCee's hotel room that made me suspect she was knocking off *someone's* designs. And when I donned my costume tonight, I also noticed the label, which was hand-stitched in the same distinctive script I'd seen in Snowdrop's sweater — and my gown. When I stood onstage, I started putting two and two together."

Ivy appeared wary. "How so?"

"You'd told me that you had lived in New York City," I reminded her. "And you couldn't resist handling Snowdrop's clothes — your own creations — when you dropped off my gown at Moxie's apartment. You had to compliment your own handiwork."

Ivy's cheeks flushed again, with embarrassment. "Any seamstress would've been drawn to the outfits. That's hardly proof —"

I spoke over her. "And when you saw Moxie's gingerbread re-creation of your shop, you joked that a light should've been burning, because you were always working. But I knew that Moxie was very careful about capturing Sylvan Creek just as she'd seen it the evening of CeeCee's murder. For once, you'd turned off the lights — so you could dispose of CeeCee's body, without risking that anyone would see." Ivy opened her mouth, perhaps to protest, but I didn't give her a chance. "I initially thought you'd shut off the lights because you'd gone somewhere to meet CeeCee — maybe an encounter that had gone wrong. But now I realize that you were hiding the body and cleaning up."

Ivy's voice shook almost as badly as her hand, which was trembling pretty hard at that point. "You think you're really clever, don't you?"

"It was mainly the label," I said. "Your stitches are like handwriting." A low, sustained growling sound came from down near my ankles, and I gently bumped Snowdrop with my foot. Then I heard Socrates's tags jangle when he nudged her, too. He must've had greater influence over the feisty poodle than me, because she settled down, so I could ask, "I'm not the only one who figured out your true identity, am I?"

"Bitsy. Bickelheim." Ivy snarled the name. "We spent a lot of time on her ridiculous costumes, our heads bent over my sketch-books. One day, she looked me in the eye, and I knew she'd recognized me." Ivy gave me a sharp look. "How did you know?"

"She slipped and called you by your real last name, Dumphree, at rehearsal one night. I didn't think twice about it — until I saw your picture and your real name in the yearbook tonight."

"Stupid yearbook," Ivy grumbled, under her breath. "I should've killed Ms. Bickel-heim, too." She was speaking more to herself than me. "I counted on her coward-ice to keep her silent, but I didn't factor in how *scatterbrained* she is." Then Ivy met my gaze again and leveled the gun right at my chest. "And I can't have *too many* bodies piling up, can I?"

"Ivy, wait!" I raised my hands, as if I could ward off a bullet, and, desperate for more time, asked, "Why did you leave the play? Why are you even here so early?"

Of all the things I'd said to upset her, my mention of the Sylvan Creek Players' inter-pretation of *A Christmas Carol* seemed to send her over the edge.

"I heard you say, 'I got it!' Which is not something the ghost says!" Ivy complained, practically yelling at me. "I knew you solved murders, and I had to follow you. Plus, I couldn't stand Scrooge's accent *one more second*!"

I was out of time, too. Ivy's hand was shaking like crazy, and she stretched out her arm, her finger twitching on the trigger.

My hands were still raised, and I took a step backward. But there was nowhere to go, and I crashed into one of the half-naked mannequins.

The dummy tumbled sideways — just as Ivy squealed with pain and fell, too, when a posh, but surprisingly tough, poodle who'd darted under the table nipped Ivy's calf, while a low-slung basset hound who knew something about leverage strategically placed himself as a stumbling block.

Ivy seemed to fall in slow motion, her eyes huge with surprise and fear, and, although the small, cramped room had erupted into chaos, I swore there was a terrible moment of silence when Jonathan Black stepped through the back door — and the gun, still clutched in Ivy's hand, went off.

CHAPTER 55

"What took you so long?" I asked Jonathan, when Detective Doebler and the uniformed officers had led Ivy Dunleavy away. I hoped she'd be charged for shooting the poor mannequin I'd knocked over, too. The dummy, which still lay on the floor a few feet from me and Jonathan, had a gaping hole in its chest. Trying not to think about how that could've been me, or one of the dogs, who'd disappeared, I pressed for Jonathan to explain where the heck *he'd* been, after I'd texted to let him know I'd solved the crime. "I sent my message an hour ago!"

Jonathan was clearly torn between frustration, exasperation — and laughter, now that he'd checked me over and found me free of bullet holes. "I was at the high school, watching your play — as I'd promised to do," he informed me. "As per Ms. Bickelheim's instruction, my phone was silenced for the entire . . . let's just say 'interesting' interpretation of a classic tale that I'd never associated with Jamaica, before tonight."

I gasped. "You heard it, too! Asa's accent!"

"It was difficult to miss," Jonathan said dryly. "Although, the real highlight was a silent specter who pointed toward a wall-mounted fire extinguisher, when predicting Scrooge's fate."

"Oh, that is pretty bad," I agreed. "I had no idea where I was pointing. Ms. Bickel-heim and I both have problems with stage right versus stage left."

"You're just lucky you didn't break your neck," Jonathan noted, taking my elbow and gently moving me aside, so one of the uniformed officers could reach past us and bag a pair of scissors. Ivy had refused to identify which one, or ones, were weapons. In fact, she'd pleaded innocence the whole time she was being handcuffed and escorted out of the shop. "I've seen you fall on flat ground."

"The whole thing is Fidelia Tutweiler's fault," I said. "But that's a story for another time."

"I look forward to hearing it," Jonathan assured me, his gaze flicking to the officer, who nodded to indicate that he was done collecting evidence before opening the door and joining everyone else outside. Jonathan met my eyes again. "For now, I need to get back to work — if you're all right?"

"Yes, I'm fine," I promised, adding quickly, "And please don't hold tonight's mishaps against me. I fully expected to solve this crime *with you.*"

"You were actually a few steps behind," he informed me. "Doebler and I had already solved the case. He'd scoured the yearbooks and recognized Ivy Dumphree. We spent the day reconstructing her past and identifying a fingerprint she'd left on Moxie's scissors. I came here because there was a text waiting for me, after the play, that said we had enough evidence to make an arrest."

"Did you see Ivy at the high school?"

Jonathan nodded. "Yes. And if I'd known we were ready to take her in, I would've followed her when she left early. But I had no reason to tail her. In truth, I assumed she just couldn't take the acting anymore, either, and was headed home." He grinned. "No offense."

Jonathan was amused, but I felt strangely crestfallen. "So, you really didn't come here in response to my message?"

"Sorry, Daphne." He squeezed my elbow again, this time to apologize. "I didn't even read my other messages. I just hurried over here to meet Doebler."

"Oh." I shrugged, shaking off my vague sense of disappointment. "Well, it all worked out. And we're still on for dinner, right?"

Jonathan frowned. "About that. Would you take a rain check? I'm afraid I'm going to be busy for the next few days."

I forced a smile. "Yes, of course. Between the holidays and wrapping up this case, I guess you will be preoccupied."

Jonathan smiled, too. "Thanks for understanding."

"No problem," I said, as Detective Doebler opened the door and poked his head inside to let his partner know that people were waiting outside for him, in a blizzard.

Jonathan left without another word, and — still suffering a twinge of disappointment — I went to find the dogs, who'd wandered off when the police had arrived.

I'd thought they wanted to stay out from underfoot, until I found them in front of the window, resting against each other, shoulder to shoulder, quietly watching the snow fall outside.

I didn't have the heart to disturb them, and I gave them another moment while I checked my phone, which had been buzzing the whole time Ivy Dunleavy had been considering shooting me.

Checking my voice mail, I held the phone

to my ear, and I hoped the dogs didn't hear the message that made my heart sink even lower.

"*Daphne Templeton? This is Joyce Jervis, one of the attorneys handling CeeCee French's estate. We're prepared to dispose of the poodle. . . .*"

CHAPTER 56

"So, you have no idea where Snowdrop is?" Piper asked, tearing into silver wrapping paper that covered a small box. My sister, Moxie, Mom, and I were crammed into my living room, gathered around my new, if needle-challenged, tree for our annual girls' gift exchange, on a cold, clear night. Piper and Mom sat on the loveseat, Moxie was on the rocker near the fireplace, and I was moving around the softly lit room, distributing presents while the Bakelite radio played its magical medley of Christmas songs past. Pulling the lid off the box, Piper held up a version of the silk scarf Mom gave us every year, although none of us ever wore scarves.

It seemed that hope sprang eternal for my mother.

Then, since the gift wasn't exactly a surprise, Piper continued the conversation while she tucked the pricey accessory back into the box from whence it came. "How can a poodle just disappear?"

I gave Socrates, who lay by the hearth, a sympathetic glance. Of course, he was being stoic about Snowdrop's absence, but I knew he missed her terribly. Closing his eyes, he pretended to sleep, because he didn't like pity — although he was allowing Tinkleston to curl up with him on his favorite rug.

I firmly believed Tinks understood that Socrates was feeling glum and wanted to be of some comfort. Not that the surly Persian would admit that. When I smiled at him, trying to silently express gratitude, he flattened his ears and twitched his tail with disapproval.

Looking away, so he wouldn't dart off, I returned my attention to the humans in the room.

"The lawyers handling CeeCee's estate won't say anything about Snowdrop's whereabouts," I told everyone, searching around for my scarf. Moxie had already unwrapped hers, so mine had to be lurking under the tree's bristly boughs, which were laden with enough lights and ornaments to hide the many bare spots. I didn't see a silver-wrapped gift for me anywhere under the straggly pine, though. I wasn't sure what to make of that. My mother and I didn't always have the warmest relationship, but she'd never overlooked me at Christmas.

Grabbing a different present marked for me, from Moxie, I looked up at Mom, who'd supposedly enlisted her attorney contacts in the search for Snowdrop, after I'd spent a good half-hour begging for help. I didn't believe my mother was committed to the effort to track down the poodle, but I told my sister, Moxie, and Socrates, "I've been assured by Mom that a *crack legal team* is trying to find some answers."

"I told you, the lawyers I contacted are doing the best they can," Mom said, her chin lifted and one hand fidgeting with a tasteful strand of pearls that glowed against her crimson, holiday-casual cardigan. "You have to understand that they specialize in property law, Daphne!"

"Well, Snowdrop is definitely being treated like property," Moxie noted, watching me closely as I struggled to keep most of the wrapping paper she'd used intact. She was clearly worried about my clumsy fingers and sounded distracted when she muttered, "Poor thing!"

For as long as I could remember, Moxie Bloom had used the same 1940s paper, which featured a repeated pattern of snowmen and snowwomen riding old-fashioned toboggans. Moxie was also the only person

I knew who collected all the paper from the gifts she gave, so she could take it home for use the following year.

I did my best to pull the box from the fragile wrap and, handing the paper to Moxie, lifted the cardboard lid.

"Oh, Moxie!" I cried softly. "Wow!"

"What is it?" Piper sounded skeptical. Maybe even worried. Like my mother, Moxie tended to buy themed gifts, so a version of whatever I'd received was likely to soon be unwrapped by Piper and Mom, too.

I carefully removed the gingerbread version of Flour Power, and a matching replica of my Lucky Paws van, from a nest of cotton and held both things up for inspection. "These are amazing, Moxie!"

"You don't have to be quite so gentle with the cookies," she said, absently petting Sebastian, who'd climbed onto Moxie's lap to rest on her bell-shaped, red-and-black tartan skirt, which she wore with a fitted black sweater. The rat looked fat and happy after snacking on a potato wedge I'd set aside for him. The rest of the russets were paired with a roasted broccoli and cheddar dip that I'd served, along with my mother's favorite merlot, on the steamer trunk coffee table. "I shellacked the pieces of the village I saved when I dismantled it, so you can have your storefronts for years," Moxie informed us, as I handed Mom and Piper their gifts from my best friend, too.

My mother and sister knew the rules about the paper and, although Mom rolled her eyes, both worked carefully. Piper, being a precise surgeon, was first to hold up her miniature animal hospital. "Thanks, Moxie. It's really lovely."

She sounded sincere, while Mom, who'd finally handed over her sheet of wrap and opened her box, peered skeptically inside. "How . . . droll," she noted. "I certainly never expected to see an edible version of my enterprise."

"Oh, gosh, don't eat it!" Moxie warned, while I studied the tiny VW, which featured a dog that was misshapen in exactly the same ways as the one on my actual van. "You'll chip a tooth *and* poison yourself."

"I wasn't about to . . ." Mom started to explain, but I silenced her with a shake of my head. Instead, she smiled benevolently and set aside the box. "Thank you, Moxie, for a *unique* gift."

Checking under the tree one last time, I saw that the only remaining presents were from me, for Socrates and Tinkleston, and I'd hand those out later. I'd already given Moxie an original poster advertising the movie *White Christmas,* signed by Bing Crosby, which had nearly made her cry. Mom had tolerated a turquoise necklace I'd found on a Central American fair-trade site, and practical Piper had appreciated an embroidered lab coat and three months back rent, tucked into a Christmas card. Her gifts to me had been a book and a similar card, with a note saying I was forgiven for two additional months.

Scooching over to the trunk, I dipped a potato into the dip and asked Moxie, "Wasn't it difficult to tear apart something you worked on so hard? You spent hours recreating the town!"

"It was kind of sad — although I had no trouble crushing Ivy Dunleavy's little shop to crumbs," Moxie admitted. "And I felt like the tiny town had served its purpose by helping to solve a murder. I knew that taking all those Polaroids would be worth the effort!"

Mom and Piper exchanged glances that said they would've used their time otherwise, but I grinned at my best friend. "Yes, if you hadn't recaptured every detail, I wouldn't have thought twice about Ivy's comment regarding the lights in her shop. That was definitely one of the clues that helped me put the whole story together."

"I still can't believe you solved *another* crime," Piper said, reaching for the dip, too. The big ring on her finger — which would be joined by a simple gold band in October, according to her latest announcement — glittered in the firelight. "I'm less surprised that you nearly got killed doing it."

Socrates huffed softly, agreeing with my sister, while Mom made a breathy sound that managed to convey her frustration with me, and her relief over not having to plan a funeral during the holidays.

"To be honest, I was convinced that Ms. Bickelheim was the killer when she told me all about how CeeCee had ruined her life. Plus, she practically threatened me, backstage at the play," I told everyone. Then I shrugged. "But it turns out she really was just worried I'd break my neck, up there on the ladder. Apparently, she'd told the school she had private liability insurance for the Players, but the coverage had expired. There could've been a big legal mess if I'd fallen."

Piper groaned and again did her best Charlie Brown impression. "Oh, good grief."

"Insurance is *so* important when renting a space," Mom muttered with quiet disbelief, as if Ms. Bickelheim's lapsed coverage was worse than homicide. "So, *so* important!"

Only Moxie seemed to see the tale of the play in a positive light. "It's a good thing Fidelia Tutweiler auditioned to be the Ghost of Christmas Future, then floated off without a word," she noted, patting Sebastian again. His pink eyes were blinking sleepily. "If you hadn't gotten the part, Daphne, you wouldn't have seen the label in the costume, matched it to the labels in your dress and Snowdrop's outfits, and realized that Ivy *Dumphree* was making designer dog clothes that had been knocked off by CeeCee French!"

"Yes, Ms. Bickelheim's slip, when she used Ivy's real last name, was a big clue, too, as I began to put things together."

"Poor CeeCee and Jeff." Piper shook her head and reached for another potato. "CeeCee shouldn't have bullied Ivy, nor copied her designs. But that certainly doesn't excuse Ivy's behavior."

"Your classmate Jeff Updegrove made mistakes, too," Mom noted, swirling the wine in her glass.

I watched her, wondering if she realized she hadn't gotten me a present. I didn't care about material goods, and I certainly didn't need more scarves I'd never wear, but I had to admit, I was feeling a bit overlooked.

Mom didn't seem to notice. "That young man shouldn't have dumped a dog and a yearbook on Daphne, dragging her deeper into a whole dangerous mess."

I was strangely touched by my mother's defense of me, although I'd come to love Snowdrop. Regardless, the comment partially made up for my lack of an unwanted scarf.

"Jeff Updegrove should've had the courage to tell the police that Ivy Dumphree was in town, masquerading as someone else," Mom continued. "And that she'd likely killed Celeste French, who might've been a bully back in high school, but who — in my humble opinion — had every right to copy those designs." My entrepreneurial and fashionable mother raised an indignant finger. "It's the law of the runway!"

"Well, the law of the . . . law is going to put Ivy away for a long time," I noted. "Ivy's first homicide, at least, was premeditated. And there's probably some sort of penalty for framing people for murder, too."

"Maybe you'll learn more about sentencing in the book I gave you," Piper suggested, gesturing to my new copy of *The Idiot's Guide to Criminology.* She'd admitted that the gift was half a joke, and half concession to the fact that my involvement in murder investigations was starting to seem inevitable. I appreciated the present, but fully intended to hide the book from Jonathan — if I ever saw him again. "There's a subchapter on 'determining punishment.' "

"Now that I've crushed her cookies, I don't really take any joy from whatever will happen to Ivy," Moxie noted, with a sigh. "I'm just glad I'm not headed to jail, and Mike will be okay, too."

It was Piper's and my turn to exchange glances. Uncertain ones. Then Piper dared to venture, "What, if anything, is happening with you and Mike?"

Of course, Mom also knew the whole story, and she asked, bluntly, "Are you a couple, or not? And is he happy with his present living arrangement? Because there's a condo opening up on the golf course that would be perfect for a man interested in doing a little updating."

"You have got to stop pushing that development on single men," I told my mother, forgetting Moxie's relationship — or lack thereof — for a moment. "I really don't think Norm Alcorn is happy there!"

Mom waved dismissively. "He's fine, now that he's admitted to the whole town that he's in financial trouble and hiding a half ton of discount dog food in his garage. His house — which is lovely and gaining value by the second — was *not* Norm's problem."

The day after Ivy's arrest, Sylvan Creek's biggest booster of local businesses had called an emergency chamber meeting, during which he'd first confessed to hiding information about CeeCee's plans for the pet superstore. Then he'd broken down in front of Tessie Flinchbaugh and admitted that he'd stocked up on CeeCee French's cheap kibble, nearly killing Dunston.

Being softhearted, Tessie had gotten emotional and embraced Norm, crushing him against a sweatshirt that featured a picture of a corgi in a yarmulke and the phrase "Yappy Hanukkah." It was quite a touching, redemptive moment, and I was glad I'd bothered to attend. The rest of the chamber members also seemed inclined to forgive Norm.

It didn't hurt that he'd wrapped up the meeting by telling everyone he'd convinced the remaining decision-makers at French's Poodles & More that Sylvan Creek was a terrible place to locate a flagship store. In truth, it sounded as if no one but CeeCee had really liked the idea to begin with. In the end, only my mother, who'd still hoped to score a real estate deal, had been disappointed.

"Well, regardless of his house's monetary value, I don't think Norm loves golf course life," I insisted. "He's very isolated."

Mom had lost interest in Norm Alcorn. Her gaze cut to my woebegone tree. "I don't suppose Brett Pinkney —"

Piper rested a hand gently on our mother's knee. "Maybe you shouldn't keep trying to mine this particular pool of murder suspects for potential clients. I seriously doubt Brett is going to sell a business that's been in his family for generations."

Mom drew back and blinked, as if she didn't understand anything her daughter had just said.

"Brett honestly does seem to love being a tree farmer," I added, looking at Scrappy, too. Needles fell like a light but steady shower from his branches, but he looked right, somehow, in Plum Cottage. "Brett does his best to match people to pines. And I think he's made peace with his life."

At least, that was the sense I'd gotten, trudging back through the snow in silent communion with the former football star. At one point, he'd paused, hoisted his axe to his shoulder, looked up at the stars, and smiled, and I'd felt like he was in the right place.

"Moxie, getting back to Mike . . ." Piper's comment alerted me to the fact that my best friend had been quiet since the original inquiry about her long-ago boyfriend. "What's happening there?"

Moxie chewed her lower lip, while Sebastian, who didn't seem interested in affairs of the heart, yawned. "We're taking things very slowly," Moxie finally said. "We've met twice for coffee, and there's clearly still something between us, but he has a lot of things to work through."

"I think it's time to get over something that happened eons ago," Mom said, frowning ever so slightly. "He's obviously not an abusive person, if he was so upset then and never did anything similar again."

In the wake of Ivy's arrest, Mike — at my urging — had finally told Moxie the truth about the events that ended their relationship. And, in my excitement over solving the murder, I'd also shared the story about Mike's shoving CeeCee with Mom and Piper.

Maybe I needed to share less.

"It *is* a long time to carry guilt about one incident," Piper said quietly. Over by the fire, Socrates raised his head, listening carefully. I knew he was considering my sister's assertion, and likely agreeing that she was right. He probably also believed Mike had been correct to step away from Moxie and do some soul searching. "It's not like he's exhibited a pattern," Piper added. "Although, I respect him for taking a step back from you, if he wasn't sure he could control his temper."

"What happened at the dance definitely drove Mike away," Moxie agreed, cradling Sebastian in her hands. The rat wriggled happily in his sleep. "But a lot of things that trouble him now happened after he joined the service. It's not like that one evening in a high school defined his life. It just sparked a decision to pursue a path that wasn't right for someone who is, ironically, a very gentle soul." She smiled faintly. "Mike Cavanaugh was *not* meant for combat, outside of a football field."

I reached out to squeeze my best friend's knee. "I hope he works through things."

"Thanks, Daph." Moxie's smile grew warmer. "I have to say, I'm hopeful. Detective Black has kind of taken Mike under his wing. He talks with him, and he's helping Mike find some resources."

I felt a surge of warmth toward Jonathan, who quietly reached out to troubled young people, ex-cons, and now a fellow veteran. I also let myself hope that things would work out for Moxie and Mike — and that we'd see more of Tiny Tim. The little trouble-making dog had grown on me.

All at once, I thought of another dog who'd won me over, and who was lost, not outside in the cold, but in a legal system that had swept her away from me — and Socrates.

Everyone seemed to catch the sudden shift in my mood, and, on some wordless cue, we all gathered up our gifts and cleaned up the empty glasses and remaining dip. Within a few minutes, my guests were gone, and I sat down on the loveseat, watching the fire in the quiet company of Socrates and Tinks.

Tinkleston soon fell sound asleep, but Socrates remained awake, obviously feeling contemplative, like me.

"Sorry," I told him softly. "I know you miss . . ."

I was just about to say "Snowdrop" when we both heard a sharp, familiar yip, from just outside the door.

CHAPTER 57

"How did you find her — and get her back?" I marveled, grinning at Jonathan while Snowdrop and Socrates reunited. The poodle wore a fleece jacket and basic leather collar, her diamonds no doubt confiscated and distributed as part of CeeCee's estate, but I could tell that she was fine with her simple outfit. Artie, who danced around the room while Axis looked on patiently, was probably more disappointed with Snowdrop's lack of designer duds than the poodle was. And Socrates was over the moon. I could tell by the way his tail drooped less than usual and occasionally almost wagged. Even Tinks seemed happy — from his safe perch on the mantel, between two candles. I looked up at Jonathan. "How . . . ?"

Jonathan smiled, too, in a self-deprecating way. "I'm afraid I can't take total credit for Snowdrop's return," he admitted.

"Then who . . . ?"

"You *mother*," he informed me, his blue eyes twinkling. "She *harangued* me to use every one of my legal and family connections to get this dog back for you. Snowdrop is meant to be — in her own words — your *Christmas gift.* And I was informed that I *would* deliver a poodle to your doorstep, like Santa Claus. Or else."

That was very threatening, in a way, but I suddenly felt as if I might cry. "My mom did that? For me and Socrates?"

Jonathan nodded. "Yes. Indeed, she did."

"And you made it happen?"

He shrugged. "I was happy to help."

I didn't know what to say for a moment. Thank you seemed inadequate. Plus, I was still close to crying, so we both took a moment to watch the dogs as they all began to run around the small room, threatening to topple the tree. Even Socrates was bounding about, his tail suddenly swinging wide arcs.

Then I finally looked up at Jonathan and quietly confessed, "I don't have anything for you. I kind of thought, when you said 'rain check' you might mean 'good-bye.' Because I keep meddling in murders."

Jonathan broke into a wide grin. The one that transformed his whole face. "Really, Daphne? You think a little thing like my temporary, if admitted, irritation with you for nearly *getting yourself killed again* would make me go back on my word?"

"Maybe?" I confessed, cringing.

Jonathan laughed. "Come on." He inclined his head toward the door. "I don't mind that you don't have anything for me. But I do have a gift for you. Waiting outside. A little something to make up for canceling our dinner plans."

I felt even worse about not having a present for him. But I was also intensely curious, and I hurried to the door, flinging it open.

"Oh, Jonathan," I cried softly, spying a gorgeous black Friesian horse, stamping his feathered feet in the snow as he waited impatiently to draw a gleaming sleigh through the snowy woods. I didn't want to turn away, for fear the scene before me would disappear, and, as I stood there gaping, Jonathan draped my old barn coat around my shoulders.

"Thank you, so much," I told him. "For everything."

The handsome, dark-haired detective who was slowly giving up his secrets smiled down at me. "You're very welcome."

Then he turned and summoned the whole pack. "Come on, everyone," he said, sending the dogs darting past our feet, in a rush for the sleigh. As the classic song, "Sleigh Ride," played on the old, scratchy radio, and a light snow began to fall upon the woods, Jonathan looked down at me again and spoke more seriously. "Ready, Daphne?"

I knew that he was asking about more than the sleigh ride. Jonathan Black was inquiring about . . . us. Giving me one last chance to back out before we changed our relationship forever. But I had no doubts. I slipped my hand into his, smiled up at him, and said, "Let's go."

■ ■ ■ ■

RECIPES

■ ■ ■ ■

PUPPER-MINT CANDY CANE TWISTS

These treats are not only fun for the holidays, but the fresh mint can also freshen up your pup's breath, so he or she is ready to mingle at the season's many social gatherings. **NOTE:** Just be sure to use **fresh mint leaves**. Extracts and oils can be too strong for pets.

3 cups of flour best suited to your dog's diet — whole wheat, barley, rice, sorghum . . . whatever suits your pup best. Feel free to use a mix. I find that actually works best.

1/2 cup nonfat powdered milk

1/2 tsp baking powder

2 large eggs

1 cup chicken broth

4–5 mint leaves

2 tsp pet-friendly food coloring (see below for tips)

1 large egg, for a wash

Preheat your oven to 350 degrees and line a baking sheet with parchment paper.

Whisk together the flour(s), powdered milk, and baking powder. Then whisk the egg into the chicken broth. Add the wet ingredients to the dry ingredients, stir until combined, and knead into a dough. You may want to add extra flour, a teaspoon at a time, if the dough is too sticky. Divide the dough into two parts and let it rest for a moment while you complete the next steps.

Make a paste with the mint by chopping it, adding a bit of water, and muddling it with a mortar and pestle. If you don't have a mortar-pestle set handy, use a small metal bowl and the back of a spoon. The amount is so tiny that it doesn't really make sense to use a food processor. And it doesn't have to be a perfect paste. Even finely chopped mint is just great.

Knead the mint into one of the dough balls.

Add the pet-safe food coloring to the other ball. NOTE: Pet-friendly dyes are readily available online, but you can also use a touch of beet juice. Think about how beets, which are actually good for dogs, stain your hands!

Roll out your two doughs separately, forming rectangles of approximately the same size. Cut both doughs into strips, and roll the strips into "snakes." Form candy canes by twisting two snakes together and shaping into the traditional form. Beat the remaining egg in a bowl and use a pastry brush to apply egg wash to each cookie.

Bake the cookies for about 12 minutes. You'll want to watch them, because cooking time will depend upon thickness. Cool thoroughly before serving to your pet.

SNOWDROP'S FAVORITE SNICKER-POODLES

What's the holiday season without snickerdoodles? The cinnamon-sugary treats are a seasonal staple at Plum Cottage. I'd never thought about adapting a recipe for pets until Snowdrop came to stay with us. Needless to say, the elegant little cookies were a hit with her sophisticated self!

3 cups of flour best suited to your dog's
    diet — whole wheat, barley, rice,
    sorghum . . . whatever suits your pup

best. Feel free to use a mix.

2 tsp ground cinnamon
1/4 cup honey
1 egg
1 tsp vanilla extract
1/2 cup water

Preheat your oven to 375 degrees and line a baking sheet with parchment paper.

In a medium bowl, whisk together the flour(s) and cinnamon. Add the honey, egg, and vanilla extract, and stir everything together. Then, using a fork, begin adding scant amounts of water until the ingredients start to come together as a dough.

Gently knead the dough into a ball and roll it out on a lightly floured work surface until it's about a quarter-inch thick.

This is the fun part. Get your favorite cookie cutters and make shapes, depending upon your mood or the season. (These don't *have* to be holiday cookies!)

Bake until the cookies are golden brown. This usually takes about 10 to 12 minutes, but time will depend upon the shape and thickness of the dough, so keep an eye on them!

Also, make sure they cool before serving. They will harden as they cool down.

MOXIE'S GINGERBREAD DOGHOUSES

These cookies might not be sturdy enough to build an entire miniature replica of your own hometown — and they'd never last long enough, anyhow. The treats, with warming ginger, are a favorite of Tiny Tim, who likes to gobble them up after one of his snowy adventures. They're gone before you can say, "Bah, hum-pug!"

3 cups of flour best suited to your dog's
    diet — whole wheat, barley, rice,
    sorghum . . . whatever suits your pup
    best. Feel free to use a mix.
1 Tbsp freshly ground ginger root
1 tsp ground cinnamon
tiny pinch ground cloves
1/2 cup unsulfured, blackstrap molasses
1/2 cup water
1/4 cup canola oil

Preheat your oven to 325 degrees and line a baking sheet with parchment paper.

Whisk together the flour(s), ginger, cinnamon, and cloves. In a separate bowl, stir together the molasses, water, and oil. Combine the wet and dry ingredients and stir until a dough forms. You may need to use a sturdy spoon. This is a pretty stiff dough!

On a lightly floured surface, roll out the dough to about a 1/2 inch thickness. Use cookie cutters to create shapes. I suggest doghouses and ginger-pups!

Bake for about 20 minutes, watching carefully. The cookies should be getting a tiny bit crunchy on the edges when you take them out. Cool completely before serving.

CRANBERRY-CHICKEN STOCKING STUFFER CAT TREATS

Okay, Santa Claus might still have Tinkleston on his naughty list. But Tinks is trying to behave lately. In order to reward his improving attitude, he'll be getting these tasty treats in his stocking this year. That is, if he stops reaching his stealthy little paw over the side of the mantel and knocking the stocking to the floor.

1 chicken breast, about five ounces
1 cup rolled oats
3 Tbsp dried cranberries (Be sure to buy UNSWEETENED.)
2 Tbsp olive oil
1 Tbsp dried catnip

1 large egg

Preheat your oven to 350 degrees and line a baking sheet with parchment paper.

Boil the chicken until cooked through. Cool and chop into small pieces.

Place the oats in a food processor and grind them up into a flour. Add the dried cranberries and grind again. Add the remaining ingredients — including the chicken — and pulse until well combined. Scrape the mixture into a bowl. If you don't think the mixture will hold together, add a little more olive oil.

Use a 1/4 teaspoon measuring spoon to portion out the treats. Roll them into little balls and press them flat. Cook the snacks for about 15 minutes, until they turn light golden brown. Allow them to cool before serving. Kitty tongues might be rough, but they burn, too!

NUTTY BACON WREATHS

Peanut butter *and* bacon? Talk about a present fit for a dog! These are perfect for Christmas morning, when the rest of the family is snacking while opening gifts. At least, we Templetons tend to snack while exchanging presents!

3 slices of bacon
1/3 cup creamy natural peanut butter (without xylitol)
1 large egg
1 Tbsp honey
3 Tbsp water
1 cup of flour best suited to your dog's diet — whole wheat, barley, rice, sorghum . . . whatever suits your pup best. Feel free to use a mix.
1/2 cup wheat germ

Preheat your oven to 325 degrees and line a baking sheet with parchment paper.

Fry the bacon until crispy and use a slotted spoon to remove it from the pan, saving the grease.

Allow the grease to cool for about five minutes, then add the peanut butter, egg, honey, and water and stir together.

Add the flour(s) and wheat germ, forming a dough.

Roll out the dough on a lightly floured

surface, until it's about a 1/4 inch thick. Using cookie cutters or a knife, cut out wreath shapes. Crumble the bacon and press the pieces into the dough to "decorate" your wreaths.

Bake the cookies for about 10 minutes, watching closely, because the time may vary depending on the thickness of your dough. Remove the cookies when they are lightly browned and cool before serving.

ABOUT THE AUTHOR

Bethany Blake lives in a small, quaint town in Pennsylvania with her husband and three daughters. When she's not writing or riding horses, she's wrangling a menagerie of furry family members that includes a nervous pit bull, a fearsome feline, a blind goldfish, and an attack cardinal named Robert. Visit Bethany at www.bethanyblake author.com.

The employees of Thorndike Press hope you have enjoyed this Large Print book. All our Thorndike, Wheeler, and Kennebec Large Print titles are designed for easy reading, and all our books are made to last. Other Thorndike Press Large Print books are available at your library, through selected bookstores, or directly from us.

For information about titles, please call:
(800) 223-1244

or visit our website at:
gale.com/thorndike

To share your comments, please write:
Publisher
Thorndike Press
10 Water St., Suite 310
Waterville, ME 04901